# THE WHALE WATCHER'S GUIDE

## WHALE–WATCHING TRIPS IN NORTH AMERICA

*To the world's whales,*
*and to those who dare to watch them*

Copyright © 1994 Patricia Corrigan

NorthWord Press, Inc.
P.O. Box 1360
Minocqua, WI 54548

Cover Photograph © Jeff Foott

Designed by Wayne C. Parmley

Icons by Amy Monday

Whale illustrations by David Peters

Printed and bound in U.S.A

**Library of Congress Cataloging-in-Publcation Data**

Corrigan, Patricia.

    The whale watcher's guide : whale-watching trips in North America / by Patricia Corrigan

        p.    cm.

    Includes bibliographical references and index.
    ISBN 1-55971-436-0
    1. Whale watching—Guidebooks. 2. Whales—North America—Identification. 3. North America—Guidebooks. I. Title.
QL737.C4C66  1994
599.5´097—dc20

                                          94-20674
                                            CIP

# THE WHALE WATCHER'S GUIDE

## WHALE–WATCHING TRIPS IN NORTH AMERICA

### PATRICIA CORRIGAN

FOREWORD BY ROGER PAYNE

NorthWord
PRESS, INC

# ILLUSTRATIONS

# TABLE OF CONTENTS

# FOREWORD

I f, after reading this book, you cannot meet the whale of your dreams when and where you wish, it may be time to reprioritize your life.

Every time I approach the guide books in a bookstore and scan the new offerings, I wonder the same thing: Did the person who undertook this daunting task do a thorough job, or did he or she get partway into it and run out of gas?

Pat Corrigan has done her job. She did not run out of anything. The clarity and conciseness with which she writes and the fresh, concise way she sets forth her information means that you and I can find what we're looking for at once. But better: Not only does she think out what you and I want to know more clearly than we do, she presents it straight, succinctly, and without ever saying too much, or being patronizing. What a treat for us to have, when a fine writer and journalist decides to do a book like this!

Pat first tells us the basics about whales and the areas they frequent and then offers us good advice on the nitty-gritty of whale watching: how to choose among the competing tours, what to wear, what to bring along with you, what to eat, how to avoid seasickness, and so on. She garnishes her tips with remarks such as "Inhale deeply of the fresh air and taste the salt on your lips. Memorize the moment with your every pore, and it won't matter whether or not the photographs turn out."

Good advice, that.

That it is possible to get so much solid information about a subject as specialized as whale watching is one of life's little delights. It says that in spite of all the disappointments that sprout like weeds in our society, we still grow some straight-grained hardwood. Pass over the weeds, buy this guide, and then follow its advice. You won't be disappointed, and you will see whales.

ROGER PAYNE, PRESIDENT
*Whale Conservation Institute*
*Lincoln, Massachusetts*
*September 1994*

# ACKNOWLEDGMENTS

I would like to express my heartfelt gratitude and deep affection to the following parties for the reasons noted here.

My son, Joel Krauska, loves learning about and watching whales as much as I do. The wonderful tour operators listed in this book—my new extended family—sent me not only tidily filled-out questionnaires but warm words of encouragement, updates on whale conservation issues, invitations to visit, snapshots of whales, T-shirts, and audio- and videotapes of whale songs and behaviors. And some of them called just to chat or to mention that they remember meeting me or that they grew up in St. Louis, too.

Roger Payne and Stephen Leatherwood spared time for me and my questions, both on and off whale-watch boats. Peter C. Beamish at Ocean Contact Limited, Scott Kraus at the New England Aquarium, and Richard Sears at the Mingan Island Cetacean Study all reviewed the chapter on whale biology. Thanks, too, to the scientists and researchers who contributed to "What You May See At Sea": Peter Beamish, Steven Katona, Scott Kraus, Stephen Leatherwood, Roy Nickerson, Richard Sears, Ted Walker, and Hal Whitehead.

Bob Wilds and the crew of the *Mystery* escorted me on my first whale-watch trip on September 25, 1982. Erich Hoyt directed me to several later whale-watching adventures. Robert Packard wrote the article on whale watching that first captured my imagination.

Thanks also go to my agent, Jeanne Hanson, to Linda Piel Gwyn, Betty Dameris, Joan Bray, and other special friends who provided emotional support, cheerfully attended all my whale parties, and bought me great whale presents. Some of them even went whale watching!

Finally, I would be remiss if I failed to mention the whales themselves, who chose me to write this book so you could go find them.

# WELCOME TO WHALE WATCHING

Whales! The greatest show on earth is in the water, and anyone willing to go where whales are will see it. Whales—swimming, all sea-shiny and slick; diving, flashing enormous fan-shaped tails; spouting, baptizing one and all with a hearty expulsion of air and water; feeding on microscopic shrimp with vast open mouths; hurtling their 50-ton bodies up, up, and completely out of the water, then falling back with a thunderous crash.

Blue whales, fin whales, rare right whales, humpbacks, gray whales, killer whales, minkes, and beluga whales. I've seen them all: in the Atlantic Ocean off Cape Cod, in Hawaiian waters, off Trinity in Newfoundland, in Alaska's Prince William Sound, off the coast of British Columbia, in Canada's St. Lawrence Seaway, near Peninsula Valdes in Argentine waters, in the lagoons off Baja California, off the coast of San Diego, and just yards from the Oregon shore.

I am not a marine biologist, research scientist, conservation specialist, wildlife photographer, or anyone at all with a specialized entree to the world of whales. I do watch whales as often as I can manage, and so can you. Extraordinary experiences are available to anyone willing to go where the whales are.

Humpbacks sometimes smack their fifteen-foot flippers on the water's surface.

The first whale I ever met was a finback, a creature just slightly smaller than the 80-foot, 76-ton boat on which I was a passenger. The whale came toward us, dived, swam under the boat, and was gone before we could comprehend what we had seen. Finback whales are the second largest creatures ever to live on earth, surpassed in size only by the mighty blue whales, and are among the fastest swimmers in the sea, reaching speeds of 20 knots (30 miles) per hour.

That trip was in 1982, out of Barnstable Harbor off Cape Cod. We spent much of the day watching humpback whales feeding, their huge open mouths rising up through the columns of bubbles they blow under water to trap krill and tiny fish. The humpbacks also waved their tails ("threw their flukes") over and over, and two of them swam and dived in unison, as though their dance had been choreographed. It was a magic day.

Once I had seen my first whales, I wanted to see more, to experience again the awe and exhilaration, the sense of deep privilege I felt among them. Seeing whales became a priority, and I began to seek out opportunities to go where they were whenever possible.

In 1984, during a three-day business trip to Maui, I boldly abandoned my traveling companions, headed for Lahaina, and signed on for back-to-back whale-watch trips, a whole day's worth of expeditions. We spotted only a few far-distant flukes on the morning trip, and the afternoon threatened to be even less satisfying. But just as the captain started the boat's engine to return to shore, a humpback whale in the distance breached—hurled itself completely out of the water—seven times.

One look was simply not enough. Two years later I was on a ferryboat trip across Prince William Sound in Alaska when a humpback whale approached the boat and lingered nearby for 45 minutes. Right in front of us, only yards from the boat, the whale breached over and over, slapped its 15-foot flippers on the water, waved its tail with each dive, and smacked its tail repeatedly at the water's surface. Just before the graceful behemoth swam away, it appeared to wave "goodbye" with one long flipper.

The captain said that in his 17 years of crossing the sound, he had never seen such a breathtaking spectacle. The 30 passengers, most of us strangers before boarding the boat, all hugged one another, laughing and crying. The captain joined in the cele-

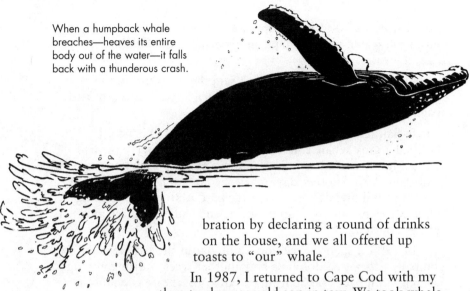

When a humpback whale breaches—heaves its entire body out of the water—it falls back with a thunderous crash.

bration by declaring a round of drinks on the house, and we all offered up toasts to "our" whale.

In 1987, I returned to Cape Cod with my then twelve-year-old son in tow. We took whale-watch trips on four consecutive days and saw whales each time. One afternoon, a humpback that had been lolling around several hundred yards away suddenly surfaced alongside the boat, so we had an unusual up-close look at his impressive 40-foot length. We also saw five fin whales and at least 30 Atlantic white-sided dolphins.

From the back decks of cruise ships, I've seen orcas (killer-whales), gray whales, common dolphins, and blue whales. Surely, sighting blue whales is one of life's rare privileges. In June of 1987, I was on the St. Lawrence River, aboard the S.S. Bermuda Star. The ship's pilot from Quebec had cautioned me that it was too early in the season to see any whales, yet four blue whales showed up on my 39th birthday, and I also observed a dozen or so belugas arching their backs out of the sun-sparkled water at the mouth of the Saguenay River.

Whale watching became up close and personal one day in Trinity Bay, off the north coast of Newfoundland, when a frisky adolescent humpback whale, measuring about 35 feet long and weighing about a ton per foot, draped its 10-foot-wide scalloped tail across the bow of our little rubber boat and gave us a hearty shove.

Late in the summer of 1991, off Bar Harbor, Maine, I saw fish flying above the ocean's surface and then saw the cause of their distress: a 70-foot-long finback whale that lunged halfway out of the water, mouth agape and ventral pleats bulging, enjoying a good meal.

"Hope you got a good look," said the narrator on the boat. "They usually only do that once." Suddenly, the finback hurled itself right out of the water a second time.

In San Ignacio Lagoon, off Baja California, Mexico, I watched a gray whale roll its big blue eye and observe me as I stroked her massive head. The moment was intensely moving, and I started to cry. Another day out in the lagoon that February of 1992, I found myself with a ringside seat at an orgy, watching white water roil up in a flurry of fins and flukes as three gray whales courted.

In 1993, I spent a week on a sailboat in the Bahamas in the company of spotted dolphins and another week cruising among feeding humpbacks on Stellwagen Bank, off the Massachusetts coast.

How did a nice Midwestern woman living on the banks of the Mississippi River become entranced with these magnificent marine mammals?

In July of 1982, I read an article in the New York Times travel section about a whale-watch trip off Cape Cod. A photograph of a whale leaping out of the water accompanied the article. After reading just a few paragraphs, I became obsessed with the idea of encountering a whale. The first opportunity was a week-long business trip to Washington, D.C., that autumn. I made arrangements to add a two-day visit to Cape Cod to the end of the trip. Then I headed for the library for books on whales so that I would recognize what I was looking at in case I saw one.

I did see a whale, and it changed my life. Now I want to change yours.

# HOW TO USE THIS BOOK

This is a book for people who watch whales, people who have been inexplicably moved, often deeply touched, by the sight of these glorious animals in their natural habitat. This is also a book for people who want to watch whales and for those who are about to discover that they too are fascinated with the mighty beasts. What you hold in your hands is a nature guide, a travel planner, an adventure book, and an inspirational text in the broadest sense.

Listed here are more than 200 commercial whale-watch tour operators who are ready and waiting to escort you on more than 250 trips to see whales off the coasts of the United States (including Alaska and Hawaii), Canada, and Mexico. You may use this book to plan a single whale-watching expedition, to devise an entire itinerary devoted to watching whales, or to find information on package tours and research expeditions. You pick a trip, choose a place or time, or select a certain whale species that you want to see, and the book will point the rest of the way.

Guidelines for picking and choosing are in this chapter; the following chapter covers what to expect when you go whale watching (including what to wear). Next you'll read "What You May See at Sea," exciting tales—contemporary legends, actually—told by whale scientists. The following chapter, "Whale Tales," includes information on 16 species of whales and dolphins. The book's final chapter is a calendar that indicates where and when you can find your "whale of choice." You will also find information on more than 30 museums, aquariums, national marine sanctuaries, and parks that have special whale exhibits or programs about marine life; names and addresses to write for tourism information; names and addresses of more than 60 whale conservation and research organizations; information on 13 adopt-a-whale programs; a bibliography; and a list of tour operators who sponsor package whale-watch trips in areas not covered here

The chapters cover the following geographic areas: Northeast U.S. Coast, Pacific Northwest, California, Hawaii, Alaska, Canada, and Mexico. Most of the listings are arranged north to south, and maps are included in each chapter. Each listing includes the tour operator's name, address, and telephone number; what sort of whales you can expect to see; what time of year the trips are available; the type of boat (or boats) used; a daily schedule, if available; the cost; whether reservations are recommended; the point of departure (with simple directions to that point); and a note about whether a naturalist or narrator is on board. Symbols indicate what you may expect in the way of shelter on board, food, drink, binoculars, and hydrophones (to let you hear the whales while you watch them), and whether a brochure is available from the tour operator.

Physically challenged whale watchers are welcome and made comfortable on many boats, including kayaks. On some boats that do not have ramps accessible to wheelchairs, tour operators will carry the passenger and the wheelchair aboard. In general, tour operators do not recommend day-long trips for people in wheelchairs as bathrooms on boats ("heads," as they are called) are uniformly tiny and not at all accessible for wheelchairs. Tour operators also suggest that physically challenged whale watchers go out on calm days, as ocean swells sometimes make boarding dangerous and securing a wheelchair tricky. All that said, most tour operators reported that they regularly take out whale watchers in wheelchairs. When you call for reservations, please mention that you will need help boarding and that you are concerned about finding a safe place for your chair.

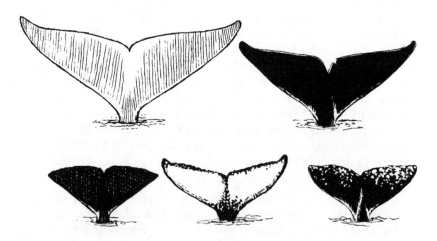

Whale tails, or flukes, come in different sizes and shapes. **Top Row:** Blue whale, right whale. **Bottom row:** sperm whale, Humpback whale, gray whale.

All prices and departure times are subject to change. Since this book went to press, some tour operators may have added to their fleet or replaced less comfortable vessels with sleek new ones designed especially for whale watching. Still others may have merged or gone into another line of work. The moral of this paragraph is this: Call or write to tour operators before you arrive at the pier. If you call or write off-season, you may not get an immediate response. But keep at it. Whale watching is worth it!

## PICK A TRIP

Whale-watch trips may last one hour, two hours, half a day, a full day, two or three days, or up to ten or fourteen days. You may spend as little as $7 per person for an hour-long trip or as much as $3,000 for a two-week expedition with several stops. Vessels listed in this book include large and small excursion boats, fishing boats, small motor craft, sailboats, motorized rafts, and sea kayaks.

Some trips are strictly for pleasure, others are research oriented, and several successfully combine both elements. Although most whale-watch tours listed here are family-run businesses, some are sponsored by scientific institutions and research organizations. Most of the trips are suitable for almost everyone, from the exceptionally sea hardy to those who rely on pills or patches to stave off motion sickness. Whereas trips to the Farallon Islands off San Francisco are particularly rigorous, outings within the confines of Depoe Bay off the coast of Oregon can be remarkably calm. Otherwise, you pay your money and you take your chances, and chances are you'll be just fine.

## PICK A PLACE OR TIME

Most of the trips are listed according to the point of departure. The exceptions are trips in Mexico, all of which are sponsored by tour operators in the United States and Canada. These trips are organized by destination. If you already know where you are going, you can look up that city (or one close by) and see what's available in the way of whale watching. If you don't have a destination in mind, you can check the calendar to see where and when the whales are and make your plans accordingly.

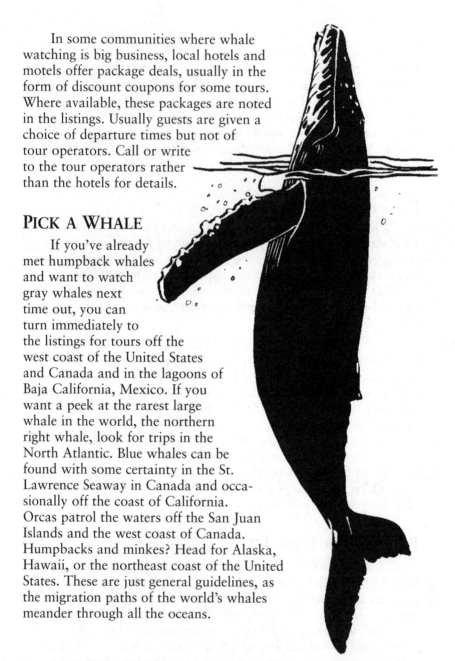

In some communities where whale watching is big business, local hotels and motels offer package deals, usually in the form of discount coupons for some tours. Where available, these packages are noted in the listings. Usually guests are given a choice of departure times but not of tour operators. Call or write to the tour operators rather than the hotels for details.

## PICK A WHALE

If you've already met humpback whales and want to watch gray whales next time out, you can turn immediately to the listings for tours off the west coast of the United States and Canada and in the lagoons of Baja California, Mexico. If you want a peek at the rarest large whale in the world, the northern right whale, look for trips in the North Atlantic. Blue whales can be found with some certainty in the St. Lawrence Seaway in Canada and occasionally off the coast of California. Orcas patrol the waters off the San Juan Islands and the west coast of Canada. Humpbacks and minkes? Head for Alaska, Hawaii, or the northeast coast of the United States. These are just general guidelines, as the migration paths of the world's whales meander through all the oceans.

Sometimes humpbacks (and other whales) stick their heads out of the water, a behavior called "spyhopping."

## About Picking and Choosing

A word is in order about the nature of "naturalists." The term generally refers to the person or persons on board who narrate the whale-watch trips, providing educational information about the whales, their behaviors and habitat, and the other creatures that share the marine environment. Some naturalists are marine biologists or oceanographers; others are affiliated with, and trained by, research organizations and scientific institutions. On some trips, narration is provided by knowledgeable captains who have been going to sea with whales for years and have made a point of educating themselves in order to answer passengers' questions correctly. On some trips where no narration is provided, tour operators show an educational video on whales and hand out written materials provided by whale conservation organizations.

It is probably unwise to judge a trip's worth based solely on whether a naturalist is on board. Once, when I was on a commercial trip off Cape Cod, a "certified" naturalist identified a passing whale as a humpback. My son, then with only one previous whale-watch trip under his belt, took a good look at the animal and insisted it was a finback, based on its color and the shape of its dorsal fin. Off he went to talk to the "expert." Moments later she was back on the public address system, admitting her mistake.

Some tour operators work with scientific research organizations and advertise that affiliation. The tie-in may be full-time and permanent in that each whale-watch trip is a fact-finding research mission; on the other hand, a boat may be chartered from time to time by organizations for its members. Boarding a boat that actively shares in a research effort or donates part of each day's profits to that research doesn't necessarily mean that you'll have a more rewarding trip unless participating in research is exactly what you have in mind.

Keep in mind that booking passage on a whale-watch trip that boasts the presence of a naturalist is no reason not to educate yourself beforehand. Many wonderful books about whales and whale biology are in print, available at libraries and bookstores all over the country. (For more than 70 such titles, see the Bibliography.) Learning about your subject ahead of time makes the experience richer and allows you to ask more specific questions in case there is a naturalist on the trip you take.

## OTHER CONSIDERATIONS

In any given area, all the tour boats go to the same places, sometimes staying in radio contact with one another in case someone sights whales that others have overlooked. For the most part, all whale-watch tour operators are infused with enthusiasm for the sport and are proud to be sharing the experience with their passengers. Cooperation rather than cutthroat competition among tour operators is most often the case. Therefore, if you're not particularly concerned about the size of the boat or the credentials of the naturalist, you might choose a trip that simply departs at a time convenient for you or that charges a fare that suits your budget. If you're a skeptic, seek out those tour operators who "guarantee" that you'll see a whale or they'll give you a free trip—not an uncommon offer in those areas where whales are practically willing to keep appointments with tour operators, year after year. And if you can afford it and you're so inclined, sign up for more than one trip. Because of the nature of the beast, every trip is unique.

Dolphins in all of the world's oceans enjoy bow riding, frolicking in the wake made by boats and ships.

# WHAT TO EXPECT ON
# A WHALE WATCH

Before you can do any whale watching, you will likely have to do some whale waiting. While you're waiting, watch the water's surface for flying fish, other marine mammals, or even shark fins. Confronted with a vast expanse of ocean, many people initially think that "there's nothing out there." But that's just not true. Everything is out there. A whole world is just beneath the water's surface, and if you watch carefully, you will see evidence of that world. Also, look up and meet assorted seabirds that you're not likely to see flying over land-locked cities.

En route to where whales are supposed to be, you can always scan the horizon just in case a whale has meandered into new territory. Whales are blissfully ignorant of our schedules, calendars, and maps, and they often pop up when and where we least expect them. An experienced captain once assured me we were well past the area off British Columbia where orcas are sighted; 30 minutes later, four tall dorsal fins came into view along the shore.

Another orca spent a recent summer off Provincetown, Massachusetts, playing in the surf and delighting tourists and townspeople alike. Government officials actually met several times to determine what to do about the whale, which wasn't where it "should" have been at that time of year. Some gray whales appear to have taken a liking to the coast of Oregon, Washington, and western Canada, where they spend 12 months in residence, rather than joining their species' annual trek between Alaska and Mexico.

Keep your eyes open and watch for that first thrilling sight of a whale spout against the horizon. One naturalist once described it as similar to a car radiator "blowing off steam"; after the steam subsides, look for a glimpse of what appears to be a shiny black stretch limo.

## WHAT NOT TO EXPECT

What you can't expect is to see whales exactly where you want them to be and exactly when you want them to be there. This is nature, real life, not a multimillion-dollar theme park

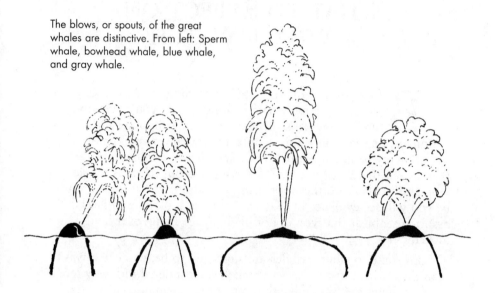

The blows, or spouts, of the great whales are distinctive. From left: Sperm whale, bowhead whale, blue whale, and gray whale.

where every surprise is scheduled. Patience must rule the day. When you do see whales, you will realize they were worth the wait. You will return to shore exhilarated, better educated about a fascinating animal, and more aware of what's at stake if we lose even one species to extinction.

## What You Need to Know Ahead of Time

Sometimes people are disappointed when they first see a whale spout. "That's it?" they say. "That little puff of steam that the wind blew away?" But when you've had a chance to do some more whale watching, you will find out that each of the great whales has a distinctive spout. Literally a large roomful of air and mist is exhaled each time a whale breathes. If you're familiar with the height and shape of the different blows, and if the wind isn't too strong, and if you're facing the whale head on, you can sometimes tell exactly what sort of whale you're seeing even if you don't get a glimpse of the body, the dorsal fin, or other telltale sign. And sometimes, of course, you can't.

If you know that the great whales range in size from 45 to 90 or 100 feet and weigh as much as 1.5 tons per foot, you're less likely to be disappointed at the sight of a spout. If you know that a blue whale can weigh as much as 32 elephants or that a toddler could crawl through the arteries of any full-grown great whale or that a humpback's flipper is more than twice the height of the tallest person you know, then your sense of excitement about even a distant sighting will increase.

Chances are good—guaranteed at some spots during certain times of year—that you will see much more than a spout. Take binoculars, if you have them, to get a closer look at whales in the distance. If you don't have binoculars, don't despair. Most likely you won't need them.

There are laws that restrict how close whale-watch boats may approach the animals. For the most part, these laws are designed to protect the whales from harassment by overeager whale-watch vessels and small pleasure craft. Whales, unaware of our laws and good intentions, often approach idling boats for what appears to be a closer look at whale watchers themselves. In the words of Dr. Peter Beamish, who operates Ocean Contact Limited out of Trinity Bay in Newfoundland, "Whale watching is free in Newfoundland. You can sit on a cliff near Trinity all day and watch whales. We guide people into our spectacular marine environment so that the whales can watch us."

## WHAT TO WEAR

Of course, no matter how close whales come to the boat, you can't watch them comfortably if you're not dressed appropriately. No matter how sunny and warm it is in town or at the dock, once you're out on the water, the temperature may be 10 to 20 degrees cooler. If the wind is blowing, it may be even chillier. Moreover, there is always the possibility that you will get wet, either from occasional spray or the unanticipated rain cloud.

When you pack a backpack or tote for whale watching, put in the obligatory sunscreen, a hat or visor, a sweatshirt or sweater, and a waterproof windbreaker, poncho, or jacket. Earmuffs, mittens, and scarves may come in handy as well. And if you forgo the gloves, remember to smear some sunscreen on your hands, even if they are the only part of you that is exposed. (Don't forget your ears!) Wear sunglasses, long pants or jeans, a comfortable shirt, socks, and rubber-soled shoes. Dresses, pantyhose, sandals or high-heeled shoes, cutoffs, and tank tops are definitely inappropriate attire on a chilly, spray-splashed deck.

As you sail over the bounding main, you may be aware of how wild the ocean seems, how uncontrollable a force it is to reckon with. For most people, that's part of the thrill. If you're not accustomed to being at sea or if you've never managed it comfortably, plant your feet firmly on the deck and keep your knees loose and slightly bent. That way you're not fighting the motion—and it's fun besides!

## WHAT TO BRING

A camera is the obvious answer, and this from a person who has an album full of fuzzy, out-of-focus pictures of whales and where whales just were. Unless you are a professional nature photographer accustomed to shooting from rocking boats, you probably won't get professional-quality nature photos. However, you may get perfectly acceptable snapshots of tail flukes, dorsal fins, a flipper or two, and maybe even a whole whale at midbreach. So bring your camera.

That said, it is also true that documenting whale behavior through a camera lens is not nearly as exciting as taking in the experience with all your senses turned up high. At some point, put

Human beings are only as large as some of the smallest cetaceans. Shown here, from top to bottom, are the blue whale, sperm whale, bottlenose dolphin, humpback whale, and orca.

The humpback whale has a pleated throat that expands when the animal feeds. The whale then filters out the water through its baleen plates.

down the camera and bring your mind's eye into sharp focus. Stare hard at the creature, noting the texture and color of its skin, any scars or scratches, the flash of baleen in its open mouth, the way the water streams down the ventral pleats under the whale's chin, or the places where barnacles are clustered. Listen to that most amazing sound when the whale breathes, the explosion of air and water that may well rain down upon you. Inhale deeply of the fresh air and taste the salt on your lips. Memorize the moment with your every pore, and it won't matter whether or not the photographs turn out.

## WHAT NOT TO BRING

In order for motion sickness pills to be effective, you must take them at least 30 minutes before you board the boat. After you've put out to sea (or worse, started feeling bad), it's too late to take a pill, so be sure to swallow yours in time. Dramamine makes most people sleepy; Bonine makes only some people sleepy. Both are available over the counter. Medicated patches, worn behind the ear, are generally

25

effective if they don't cause a reaction and make the wearer sick. Ginger has a reputation for preventing motion sickness and is available in capsule form at most health food stores. On a positive note, even the queasiest passengers generally feel better when the whales show up.

Of course, many people who take no precautions at all never become seasick. Please don't stay home because you are worried that you might get sick; after all, you might not. If you do start to feel uncomfortable, stay outside in the open air, keep your eyes on the horizon, and breathe deeply. Nibble on plain soda crackers; sip ginger ale. Stave off panic by thinking about anything except being sick. If nothing works, comfort yourself with the thought that everyone, even experienced sailors, gets seasick at least once.

Few children under age five enjoy being confined on a boat for an extended period of time. As for older children, please take into consideration the individual child's behavior in public, level of intellectual curiosity, and need for unrestricted space. If you do decide to bring along a young child, tell him or her what to expect on the expedition and what behavior will be expected.

Most whale-watch boat operators allow passengers to smoke cigarettes in a restricted area out on deck, but they discourage pipe or cigar smoking.

## WHAT YOU WILL SEE FROM SHORE

Sometimes people who have seen whales from shore, either from an official lookout or just meandering along the beach one day, feel that they've had the whole experience and think that they don't need to book passage on a whale-watch boat. Certainly, seeing a whale from shore is a thrill. I actually spotted a gray whale once through a living room window. But it's not the same. Watching whales from shore instead of going out to sea is something like watching a play on television instead of going to the theater and seeing the live performance. Watching from shore is fun, but it's a passive experience, not nearly as exciting as being smack in the middle of the action.

This book is set up to help you get to where the whales are. Make plans to go soon—and let me know what happens.

# WHAT YOU MAY SEE AT SEA

S ay you've been cruising along for longer than you care to recall, with no sea creatures in sight. Suddenly, off the starboard bow, you hear what sounds like an exploding building. You look over just in time to see the wind carrying away the last wafts of a huge column of vapor, and you watch the mottled back of an 86-foot-long blue whale break the water's surface just 30 yards from the boat.

That's exactly what happened one November day off the coast of Big Sur, California, on a trip that was advertised as a good opportunity to sight sea birds and dolphins.

Such are the rewards of putting out to sea for a day of whale watching. Expect the unexpected: Every whale-watch trip, every excursion, is completely different from the last. Scott Kraus, an associate scientist at the New England Aquarium in Boston, puts it this way: "If you watch whales long enough, you're always seeing something new."

Kraus and other "professional" whale watchers, scientists, and naturalists who have spent years observing whales in the wild say they have seen sights and experienced encounters while on the water that they could never have anticipated. Eight of them— Peter Beamish, Steven Katona, Scott Kraus, Stephen Leatherwood, Roy Nickerson, Richard Sears, Ted Walker, and Hal Whitehead— shared some of their stories of amazing moments for this chapter.

This is the stuff of legends.

## CURIOUS CALVES AND PROUD MOTHERS

Stephen Leatherwood says he will never forget the first time that a curious humpback calf left the protection of its mother to swim over to have a look at him.

Leatherwood is chairman of the Cetacean Specialist Group for the World Conservation Union. He also is the coauthor of several books, including *The Sierra Club Handbook of Whales and Dolphins*, *The Sierra Club Handbook of Seals and Sirenians*, and scientific texts on gray whales and bottlenose dolphins.

Back in 1973, Leatherwood was studying humpback whales off Maui. One calm day, a mother and calf swam toward Leatherwood's boat, and he slipped into the water with the animals.

"As I swam toward the mother, she swept the calf under her 15-foot flipper. The calf kept twisting its body and rolling its eye to look at me. At one point the calf peeled out from under Mom's wing and came right for me, staring right at me the whole time," Leatherwood recalls. "At the last minute, it veered off, and I reached out. The whale pressed against my hand, still moving, just like a cat."

That was Leatherwood's first close encounter with a humpback whale. More recently, underwater off the Bahamas in June of 1991, Leatherwood found another mother and calf—this time, a dolphin.

"There was an Atlantic spotted dolphin I was familiar with after visits to the area for three years, but I had never known her to have a calf," Leatherwood said. "One day, I was out on deck when a small group of dolphins came up to the boat. I saw there was a calf among them, so when I got in the water, I just hung there, not moving around. First, the dolphin I knew swam by with the calf on her opposite side. They made another pass by me, this time with the calf between us. Then the mother paused a short distance away. The calf came toward me. When it started to move away, she headed it back toward me.

"I couldn't help but get the impression that she was bringing her calf over to introduce it to me."

## ATTACKS OF CURIOSITY

For years, tales have been told of attacks by orcas, or killer whales, on gray whales as the grays make their annual migration from the Bering and Chukchi seas to Baja California and back again.

Dr. Theodore J. Walker, an authority on gray whales, is convinced that sometimes the orcas are victims of bad press.

"The most dramatic thing I ever saw was a so-called attack on three gray whales by 44 killer whales," Walker said. "It happened in 1969, and the U.S. Navy logged the observation."

Walker, who spent 21 years at Scripps Institution of Oceanography as a research marine biologist, is the founder of the whale observatory at Cabrillo National Monument in San Diego, the first such observatory on the West Coast. He is the author of *Whale Primer*, and he has lectured widely since 1971.

That day in 1969, Walker went up in a small plane to check out the report of the killer whale attack. Flying at an altitude of 500 feet, he saw the 44 orcas traveling north from Ensenada, Mexico. They located three gray whales that were in a circle just below the surface, with their heads together, a formation called a rosette.

"The killer whales made several runs at the gray whales, but nothing ever happened. We did not observe any blood in the water or any signs that the gray whales were impaired," Walker said. "We concluded that the killer whales were not attacking. The three gray whales were courting, and it appeared that the killer whales were having a look."

He added, "I'm of the opinion that unless you can produce the body, it didn't happen."

One day, Walker witnessed a dramatic orca attack, but a gray whale was not the victim. Walker was up in a helicopter, scanning the coast of Southern California for migrating gray whales. He saw an adult male orca swimming alone. The pilot made a few passes high above the animal, and then reported he saw a large shark near the surface of the water not far from the whale.

"I saw it, too, and I photographed it," Walker recalled. "We saw the killer whale attack the shark. And then that whale jumped clear out of the water, up toward the helicopter, with the shark in its mouth, broken in half.

"I have a very bad photograph of that," Walker said, laughing.

## WHALES WATCHING PEOPLE

Richard Sears, director of the Mingan Island Cetacean Study, based in Sept-Iles, Quebec, spends several months each year studying blue whales—the largest animal ever to live on earth—in the Gulf of St. Lawrence and several months in the Sea of Cortez, off Baja California. In his work, Sears also encounters several other species, including some particularly curious humpbacks.

In the Gulf of St. Lawrence, in the fall of 1990, some 25 humpback whales, all known to the researchers, took turns approaching Sears' boat about six at a time and began to spyhop— stick their heads up out of the water very close to the boat.

"Eventually, most of the whales moved off, but two stayed for several hours, continuing to spyhop, looking down into the boat, right at me."

Another day, Sears set out in choppy water and was immediately surrounded by two humpbacks that "followed us all day like dogs."

One of his favorite stories about blue whales is about a calf with a touch of colic.

"In 1989, we were off Baja, observing mother whales with their calves. Flip Nicklin was swimming with one pair, photographing them, when we saw a calf swim up to the water's surface with its mouth open," Sears said. "It was spitting up milk, having a fit of colic."

A year later, Sears was out in the Sea of Cortez, about two miles off Loreto, following a mother and calf. "The whales dived, and the mother's head was within feet of the boat," Sears said. "Then the calf surfaced right off our bow, and suddenly we were framed in blue whales."

Another day in the Sea of Cortez, Sears and company saw what they first thought was a harbor porpoise and then identified as a day-old, nine-foot-long finback calf. A few days later, a pod of 17 orcas, including three calves, swam and played by the research boat for eight full hours.

"That was an amazing sighting," Sears said.

## CAREFUL RESEARCH
## AMONG COURTING WHALES

Scott Kraus, an associate scientist at the New England Aquarium in Boston, has a special fondness for the right whales, which he has studied in the Bay of Fundy since 1980 and off the southeastern U.S. coast since 1984.

Off the Nova Scotia shelf, Kraus and his colleagues are accustomed to seeing right whales in courting groups, which usually consist of one female and as many as 20 males or more.

"The courting groups are oblivious to us," Kraus said. "We like to shut down the engines and observe the whales from a distance, but more than once, a female has tried to use the boat as a barrier, to get away from the males. Once, a large male moved us out of the way to get to a female. That's when you need those engines running because it can be dangerous to be in the way of courting whales."

Kraus said that every year he sees something he never expected to see. "The first time you see a calf nursing, you don't realize what you're looking at. And the behavior of the older calves is always fun to watch," he said. "Once, a right whale calf swam alongside the boat, rubbing its body against a $20,000 piece of scanning equipment that tracks whales underwater. We were afraid we were going to lose the scanning sonar."

Kraus said there are about 300 right whales in the North Atlantic, and each year, 10 or 12 whales swim south to give birth off the southeastern U.S. coast. "We strongly discourage attempts at whale watching there because it is a nursery area. Besides, very few animals are involved, and you never know if you will see them on any given day."

## FOOD FOR THOUGHT

Giant baleen whales troll the oceans in search of the tiny fish and crustaceans that nourish them. Two scientists, Dr. Steven Katona and Dr. Hal Whitehead, have observed how the baleen whales sometimes get a little help from their friends.

Dr. Katona teaches and conducts research in marine biology at the College of the Atlantic in Bar Harbor, Maine. He is the author of *A Field Guide to the Whales, Porpoises, and Seals of the Gulf of Maine and Eastern Canada*. Dr. Whitehead, on the faculty at Dalhousie University in Halifax, Nova Scotia, has studied whales all over the world and is the author of *Voyage to the Whales*, a book about sperm whales in the Indian Ocean.

The two coauthored a paper on the ecological importance of whales, and in that paper they described some communal feeding practices they have observed in Nova Scotian waters. Once, they saw white-sided dolphins herding herring "into balls so dense that we scooped up 30 fish in a single dip of a five-gallon bucket."

"Humpback whales gently maneuvered to eat these schools, after which the dolphins quickly circled the fishes to herd them close together again," Katona and Whitehead reported. "The fish schools appeared to offer a surfeit of food for the dolphins, and we consider it possible that the dolphins were playing and/or herding for the benefit of the whales. We could not identify any immediate mutualistic benefit for the dolphins, although they swam with the whales throughout our observation period."

Katona and Whitehead have also watched communal feasting on the part of whales, herring gulls, and greater black-backed gulls.

While watching a humpback whale in 1987 near Mount Desert Rock, Maine, the scientists saw this feeding pattern repeated for several hours: "The whale exhaled underwater, creating a patch of ascending bubbles. Krill rose to the surface during the next 30 seconds, coloring the surface pink. During the following 30 seconds, herring appeared at the surface jumping so energetically in pursuit of krill that their splashing sounded like a heavy rainstorm.

"Herring gulls and greater black-backed gulls gathered and snatched herring. Apparently, in response to the marauding fishes, the krill pressed together into tight discrete schools up to two meters in diameter. The whale then surfaced, open-mouthed, to engulf krill from these tight schools, which were so thick that our dip net was packed full in one pass."

## CLOSE ENCOUNTERS WITH HUMPBACK WHALES

Dr. Peter Beamish, president of Ocean Contact Limited and director of Ceta-Research based in Trinity, Newfoundland, recalls a breathtaking incident from 1982.

"We arrived at Newman's Cove, a tiny outport in eastern Newfoundland, to find three humpback whales feeding near the community wharf. For one hour, we, in our 15-foot Zodiac, came as close to entering their world as you could imagine, theirs being three dimensional and ours only two."

Beamish said the smallest of the whales (about 35 feet in length) suddenly appeared almost stationary at the surface.

"Then, heading in the same direction as our Zodiac, the whale moved its tail sideways and placed it under the midsection of our vessel. The whale gently lifted the Zodiac approximately two feet into the air and then slowly lowered the boat."

Interspecies communication—not serving as toys for whales—is Beamish's special area of interest. One day in June of 1990, the whales cooperated willingly.

"We were transmitting short underwater sounds exactly every two minutes," Beamish said. "Two humpback whales came near our vessel, and then one animal exhaled exactly as we transmitted a sound."

Beamish issued an opening message of tones underwater, and the animal mimicked the rhythm of the message.

"Then we repeated the experiment using three different sounds, and the whale mimicked the message using three different signals: a tailslap, a full breach, and an exhalation. Message had become independent of signal," Beamish said. "We repeated the experiment, and whales have demonstrated that 'rhythm-based' information can be transmitted independently of signal quality."

Beamish continues, "We must change our emphasis in communication from what animals are doing to when they are doing it."

## MORE HUMPBACK WHALES AND "THE FRIENDLIES"

Roy Nickerson, an eloquent author (*Brother Whale* and *The Friendly Whales*) and naturalist, moved back to Hawaii in 1991 after an absence of 10 years. The whales had a few surprises in store for him.

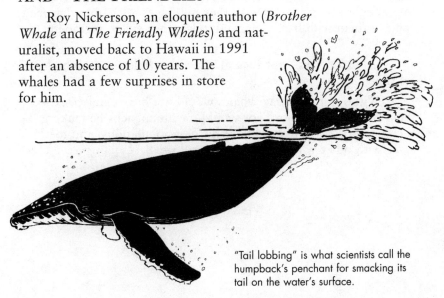

"Tail lobbing" is what scientists call the humpback's penchant for smacking its tail on the water's surface.

"A behavior that was new to me was watching several instances of adult humpback whales breaching in unison, two at a time, only yards apart from each other," Nickerson said. Then, in April of 1992, the humpbacks upped the ante. For the first time, Nickerson observed three humpbacks breaching together in the Auau Channel, the seven miles of water between Maui and Lanai.

"At first, two breached together twice, then they were joined by a third and all three jumped three times in a row together. Then they each jumped three or four more times, but not in unison. It was an astounding display," he said.

"To me, this indicates some intelligent purpose in breaching, and to me, breaching just for the fun of it is an intelligent purpose."

Some of his favorite stories are about the gray whales off Baja California, Mexico, that have come to be called "the Friendlies."

"In San Ignacio Lagoon, I was able to pat baby gray whales on the head, and one mother whale lifted our skiff up out of the water briefly—a very gentle experience that did startle and amaze all six of us in the skiff, as well as those who were watching in nearby boats," Nickerson said.

"These experiences only reaffirm that whales are thinking, reasoning, and intelligent animals; that they have been protected for enough generations now so they no longer remember that men came at them with harpoons, and today, they enjoy interacting with us."

Nickerson sees "our love affair with whales" as a wonderful thing.

"Without it, the gray whales would not have come back to their historic population, nor would the humpbacks be making such good progress toward their historic populations, and the same with other whales, both great and small."

# WHALE TALES

Say "whale" and what comes to most people's minds is an image of a sperm whale. Moby Dick was a sperm whale, and the distinctive shape of Herman Melville's Great White Whale is so familiar that illustrations of that one species are often used to represent all whales. In fact, the mighty sperm whale, with its rectangle-shaped head and its long, narrow lower jaw, is unique among whales.

What the sperm whale has in common with all other whales is that it is a mammal. Aristotle was the first to record the observation that whales were not giant fish and that they did not breathe through gills. Whales are warm-blooded, air-breathing creatures that spend most of their time under water, rising to the surface to exhale and then take in great gasps of fresh air before submerging again.

More than 345 million years ago, an amphibian relative of the land vertebrates climbed out of the water and began to adapt to life on land. One group of mammals eventually returned to the water: those were the early ancestors of today's whales. Over time, the noses of these air-breathing mammals moved from the front to the top of the head. A special valve evolved that allows whales to seal off their air passages when under water. In addition, their external ears disappeared completely. Some whales hear with dense bones located on each side of their heads, where their external ears once were, picking up the smallest of vibrations.

All whales are cetaceans, a word derived from their biological order, Cetacea, from the Greek *ketos* or the Latin *cetus*, which both mean "whale." The order includes at least 77 species of whales, porpoises, and dolphins. One ancient suborder of whales disappeared more than 20 million years ago, but two suborders survive today. The existing suborders are Odontoceti ("toothed whales") and Mysticeti ("mustached whales").

The "mustache" is actually baleen—hard, keratinous fibers that overlap in the whales' mouths and serve as a sieve. When the whales eat, the hundreds of strips of baleen filter water out and leave behind the krill and small fish. Baleen was once known as "whalebone," and whales were butchered so the baleen could be used in corsets, shirt collar stays, brushes, buggy whips, and ribs for umbrellas and lamp shades.

Except for sperm whales, all larger whales are baleen whales. All baleen whales—except for gray whales, right whales, bowhead whales, and pygmy right whales—are rorquals, that is, whales with ventral (underside) pleats that allow their throats to expand while feeding. Baleen whales have two external blowholes. Toothed whales—sperm whales, orcas, narwhals, beluga whales, dolphins, and porpoises—have just one.

Whales are generally believed to be intelligent, curious, and not aggressive toward humans. Most whales travel in "pods," social or family groups. Among behaviors common to some species of the larger whales are spyhopping, where a whale lifts its massive head out of the water and appears to look around, and breaching, where the whale leaps completely out of the water and then falls back with a thunderous crash. Several species raise their broad tails completely out of the water when they "sound," or begin a deep dive. Some whales stick their flippers or tails out of the water or slap them against the water's surface.

Scientists can't explain any particular behavior of whales although they have formulated theories based on years of research. Because whales are difficult to study in their natural habitat, we actually know very little about the live animals.

We know a great deal, however, about dead whales. The United States was once the world's greatest whaling power. By the nineteenth century, Yankee whalers no longer killed whales for meat to survive, but for oil for lamps and machines and for by-products used in candles, crayons, dog food, fertilizer, cosmetics, and perfume. With hand-held harpoons thrown from wooden whaleboats, Yankee whalers had almost depleted the right and bowhead populations; then modern whaling ushered in the

Baleen varies widely in size among whales. Shown here, to scale, are baleen strips from the bowhead whale (top), the blue whale (left), and the gray whale (right).

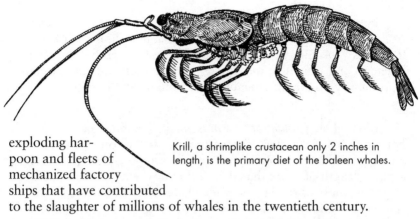

Krill, a shrimplike crustacean only 2 inches in length, is the primary diet of the baleen whales.

exploding harpoon and fleets of mechanized factory ships that have contributed to the slaughter of millions of whales in the twentieth century.

Today there is a relatively inexpensive substitute for every product once sought from whales. Yet 8 of the 20 species of "great whales"—the larger whales—are endangered, close to extinction. And in spite of a moratorium on commercial whaling declared in 1986, Japan, Norway, and Iceland continue to kill whales, claiming "scientific research" as their purpose.

Whales and dolphins also face other threats. Oil spills, such as the 1989 spill from the Exxon *Valdez* in Prince William Sound, kill whales, as do nylon fishing nets (also known as ghost nets) that drift through the open seas, entangling marine mammals and seabirds. Even more insidious are the tens of thousands of man-made toxic substances that we dump into the sea—chemicals that, if we continue dumping, will practically guarantee the eventual extinction of marine mammals and all other life in the ocean. As we sit poised at the top of the food chain, we must ask ourselves, "Will we be next?"

The organizations listed in Appendix 2 believe that it's not too late to save whales and, by extension, ourselves. Write to those that interest you to learn how you can help.

Some of what scientists do know about 16 species of whales and dolphins follows here. This general information relates to the species you are most likely to see on the whale-watch trips in this guidebook. The whales are listed according to size: blues, finbacks, rights, bowheads, sperm whales, humpbacks, gray whales, minkes, orcas, pilot whales, narwhals, belugas, bottlenose dolphins, common dolphins, white-sided dolphins (Atlantic and Pacific), and harbor porpoises. By no means is this information complete. Several fine books on whale biology are listed in the bibliography.

Population estimates, where available, are based on statistics from the International Whaling Commission. Still, many of the figures are speculative, as estimates change frequently. The range in length and weight of the different species is based, unfortunately, primarily on measurements taken from dead whales.

**Blue whale** *(Balaenoptera musculus)*. The blue, or sulphur bottom, whale is the largest creature ever to live on earth. These whales are blue-gray, often with gray mottling. Although they can attain a length of more than 100 feet and weigh between 130 and 150 tons, most of the largest blue whales were killed before the species was granted protected status. Today, most blue whales sighted are between 70 and 90 feet long.

The heart of a blue whale is about the size of a Volkswagen Beetle, and there is room on its tongue for a full-grown elephant. A newborn blue whale measures 20 to 25 feet and weighs about three tons. The calf gains as much as 200 pounds a day while nursing, and an adult blue whale can eat up to two tons of krill a day.

Blue whales are an endangered species. Only 4,000 to 6,000 are left.

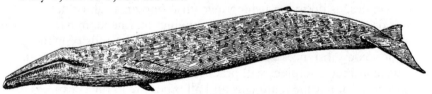

The blue whale is the largest creature ever to live on earth and eats as much as two tons of food a day.

**Fin whale** *(Balaenoptera physalus)*. Although the fin, or finback, whale has to settle for being the second largest animal on earth, it is the fastest of the large whales. The sleek finback can attain a speed of 30 miles an hour, a record only occasionally threatened by the sei whale. Fin whales grow to 80 feet in length and weigh 60 to 70 tons.

Fin whales are dark gray to brownish black with a characteristic white lower right jaw. A narrow ridge on the animal's back extends from the dorsal fin to the tail and gives the whale its nickname of "razorback."

The United States considers fin whales endangered, though they have not been granted that status internationally. An estimated 120,000 live in the seas of the world, down from a pre-exploitation population of 548,000.

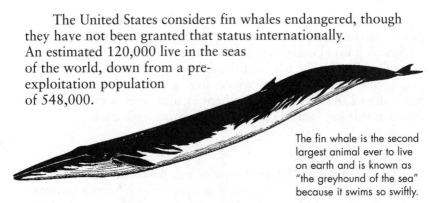

The fin whale is the second largest animal ever to live on earth and is known as "the greyhound of the sea" because it swims so swiftly.

**Right whale** *(Eubalaena glacialis/australis).* Unfortunately, the right whale got its name from nineteenth-century whalers who considered it the "right" whale to kill because it swims slowly, has abundant oil, and its carcass floats after being killed. The arched upper jaw holds baleen that grows to seven feet in length.

Northern and southern right whales, black in color, attain a length of 50 to 60 feet and weigh as much as 45 tons. They have callosities—patches of thickened skin—that grow in the same places that human males have facial hair: mustaches, eyebrows, beard, and sideburns. The callosities are often covered with cyamid crustaceans, or whale lice. The distinctive number, size, shape, and placement of callosities on each right whale make it possible to recognize individuals.

The right whale is the rarest of all the large whales. Both southern and northern right whales are endangered.

The North Atlantic right whale is the rarest of all whales because the whaling industry slaughtered so many of the animals.

When the Pilgrims landed in what is now Massachusetts, the North Atlantic Ocean was home to an estimated 20,000 right whales. A journal entry noted that one could almost walk across Cape Cod Bay on the backs of the animals, so plentiful were they. Today, only about 300 right whales live in the North Atlantic, and fewer than 2,000 live in the Southern Hemisphere. Some scientists fear that it is too late to save the species from extinction.

**Bowhead whale** *(Balaena mysticetus)*. Bowheads take their name from the exaggerated arch of the jaw, which houses baleen that grows up to 14 feet long. These whales are primarily black, with a white band underneath the chin. They grow as large as 65 feet long and weigh as much as 65 tons.

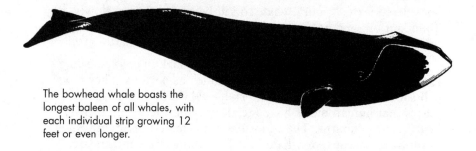

The bowhead whale boasts the longest baleen of all whales, with each individual strip growing 12 feet or even longer.

These mighty giants aren't easy to find, but you may be lucky enough to see one if you travel in the arctic regions. Bowhead whales are endangered, but they are still hunted by Alaskan natives, who are allotted a certain number of "subsistence" kills each year. The Alaskans particularly enjoy muktuk, a delicacy consisting of the outer skin layers of bowhead whales: a tough outer layer, the true skin, and oily blubber. Muktuk may be eaten fresh, frozen, cooked, or pickled. The baleen is used to make intricately woven baskets. As someone once noted, "Nothing is wasted except the whale."

Fewer than 7,000 bowhead whales are believed to exist today, compared with a pre-exploitation population of 30,000.

**Sperm whale** *(Physeter macrocephalus)*. The rectangle-shaped head of the 50- to 60-foot sperm whale accounts for about one third of the animal's length and contains a "case" full of rich oil. Some scientists think that during dives, the waxlike oil solidifies, reducing buoyancy and helping the whale to extend the distance of its dives.

Male sperm whales weigh as much as 59 tons and have the largest brain of any creature on earth. They are dark grayish-brown to brown and have a wrinkled skin behind the head. The animal's lower jaw is long and narrow and contains up to 60 conical teeth, which fit into corresponding sockets in the upper jaw. Sperm whales feed on giant squid; the squid can grow to 55 feet and weigh nearly 4,500 pounds.

One-third of the sperm whale's body is the head, which holds a huge "case" of waxy oil.

Those teeth were once prized by whalers, who carved miniature scenes on them, an art known as scrimshaw. Another once valued product from sperm whales is ambergris, a product from the intestinal bile used by the perfume industry to make permanent blends of various fragrances. The United States considers sperm whales an endangered species; fewer than one million still swim in the world's oceans. The peak of exploitation was reached in the 1960s, when 29,000 sperm whales were killed each year.

**Humpback whale** *(Megaptera novaeangliae)*. The "big-winged New Englander" is perhaps the most gregarious of all the large whales. If you've seen a whale breach, slap the water with its flipper or tail, poke its head up to watch you watching it, and raise its beautiful scalloped tail high out of the water before a long dive, chances are you've seen a humpback whale. The males also sing long, haunting songs.

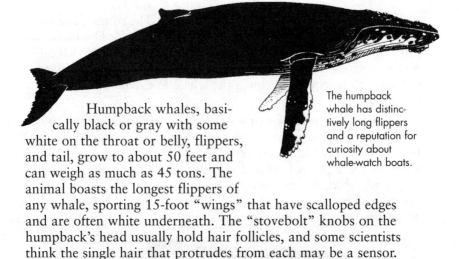

The humpback whale has distinctively long flippers and a reputation for curiosity about whale-watch boats.

Humpback whales, basically black or gray with some white on the throat or belly, flippers, and tail, grow to about 50 feet and can weigh as much as 45 tons. The animal boasts the longest flippers of any whale, sporting 15-foot "wings" that have scalloped edges and are often white underneath. The "stovebolt" knobs on the humpback's head usually hold hair follicles, and some scientists think the single hair that protrudes from each may be a sensor. The pattern on the underside of each humpback's tail is unique, and individual whales are easily recognizable.

Humpback whales are endangered, down to about 10,000 compared to 65,000 estimated to have lived prior to the rise of the whaling industry.

**Gray whale** *(Esrichtius robustus)*. The gray whales are the conservationists' success story. Although the North Atlantic population was brought to extinction in the 1600s, the North Pacific populations have recovered twice from near extinction. In the mid-nineteenth century, so many gray whales were killed that they became classified as "economically extinct," which meant that there were so few left, it wasn't worth the time or trouble to hunt them. The species began to recover, only to be nearly wiped out again in modern times with the advent of mechanized whaling techniques. The government stepped in, and today between 17,000 and 24,000 gray whales migrate each year from the Bering, Chukchi, and western Beaufort Seas to breeding grounds off Baja California, Mexico.

Some scientists believe the gray whales are primitive in many ways and may be direct descendants of the ancient baleen whales. The body, flippers, and flukes (tail) of the stocky animals are mottled with gray and white splotches. The whale's head is bumpy and warty, with bristly facial hairs, and patches of barnacles, algae,

Some scientists believe the gray whale is the most closely
related to the archaic whales.

and whale
lice cover much of the
rest of the body. Gray whales grow to lengths of 45 to 50 feet and
weigh about a ton per foot.

Beauty is only skin deep, of course, and gray whales delight
more than two million whale watchers off the west coast of the
United States and Canada each year. In the quiet lagoons off Baja
California, some gray whales known as "the friendlies" have been
known to approach small boats full of whale watchers and come
in close enough to be petted. And you may recall the international
effort expended off Point Barrow, Alaska, in the fall of 1988 on
behalf of three gray whales trapped in the ice.

In the United States, gray whales are no longer considered
an endangered species. Furthermore, the International Whaling
Commission has reclassified them from "protected stock" to the
status of "sustained management" stock.

**Minke whale** *(Balaenoptera acutorostrata)*. Legend has it that
a Norwegian whaler named Minke mistook this smallest of the
baleen whales for a mighty blue, and his amused peers promptly
named the whale after him to commemorate forever his error.

Minkes are black to dark gray on the back, white on the
belly and across an "armband" on the flipper (in the Northern
Hemisphere). There may
be as many as three
subspecies of

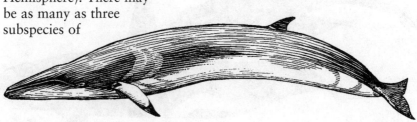

Minke whales are occasionally mistaken for other, larger, baleen whales.

minkes, but generally these streamlined animals grow to about 30 feet and weigh up to seven tons. Some minkes have a reputation for being feisty, swimming close to shore in inlets and bays and popping up right in front of moving boats.

These whales are not considered endangered, and many are killed each year by those nations still active in commercial whaling. Moreover, several minke whales have been held in captivity in Japan, as they are the only member of the genus small enough to be displayed and researched.

**Orca whale** *(Orcinus orca)*. Some orcas, or killer whales, spend their lives in show business at theme parks and oceanariums, and many people have seen the shiny black and white whales up close. Orcas are members of the dolphin family, and like dolphins they are acrobatically inclined. Still, some scientists say that orcas in captivity rarely achieve their full growth potential.

In the wild, male orcas grow to about 30 feet, weigh up to eight tons, and sport striking 6-foot dorsal fins. Females are slightly smaller. The animals have 10 to 13 conical teeth on each side of each jaw, and they prey on fish, squid, birds, seals, turtles, porpoises, and, occasionally, whales.

Research has shown that most orcas kill for food, not for sport, and they do not go after human beings. Legend has it that these whales were originally known as "whale killers" and that over time the name was reversed to the more ominous version. No population estimates are available, and orcas are not considered an endangered species.

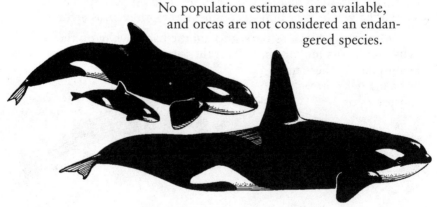

Orcas, commonly called "killer whales," often swim in family groups within the pod.

The long-finned pilot whale is one of the largest animals ever kept in captivity. You may have met one in a marine life park.

**Pilot whale** *(Globicephala melaena* and *G. macrorhynchus).*
At aquariums and theme parks, you can distinguish between long-finned and short-finned pilot whales because there will be large signs identifying them, but at sea even experts find it nearly impossible to tell the two species apart. A good guess is possible, however, because the long-finned pilot whale is generally found in nontropical waters, and the short-finned pilot whale is seen in tropical waters.

Both species have large bulbous foreheads, stocky elongated bodies, and prominent dorsal fins and are slate gray to black in color. The short-finned pilot whales, not surprisingly, have shorter flippers than long-finned pilot whales. Males of both species reach a length of 19 or 20 feet, with females slightly smaller. Both species feed on squid and schooling fish and travel in herds of up to several hundred individuals, often in the company of bottlenose dolphins.

**Narwhal** *(Monodon monocerus).* Male narwhals go through life armed to the teeth, so to speak. The adult male of this unusual species boasts a tooth that grows through the upper lip into an 8-foot-long tusk, which may have inspired the legend of the unicorn. No one is sure of the tooth's function, although males have been seen battling with their built-in swords. Eskimo and Alaskan Indian tribes prized the narwhal's tusk most

The male narwhal has an 8-foot-long tusk, unique among whales, that may have inspired the legend of the unicorn.

45

highly, and such a gift to the chief or the tribal elder was considered a great tribute.

Narwhals are stocky animals, slow swimmers that range in color from dark blue-gray in juveniles to mottled dark brown in adults. Males grow to about 15 feet, excluding the tusk, and weigh about 3,500 pounds. Females are slightly smaller. The whales live in arctic waters, where they feed on squid, fish, shrimp, and crab.

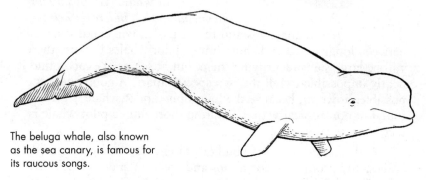

The beluga whale, also known as the sea canary, is famous for its raucous songs.

**Beluga whale** *(Delphinapterus leucas)*. The only true "white" whales are the belugas. These whales are born gray or brown and turn white as they mature.

Belugas, which are not the source of the famous caviar that comes from sturgeons, are also known as "sea canaries" because of their impressive range of vocalizations. They squeal and chirp and are considered among the most vocal of all whales.

The animals are stocky, with a disproportionately small head. Generally they grow to about 16 feet and weigh as much as 2,400 pounds, although there are size differences among different geographical populations. Scientists estimate there are about 50,000 belugas, all living in arctic or subarctic water. The 500 left in the St. Lawrence Seaway are believed to be at the greatest risk because of the toxic pollutants in the river.

**Bottlenose dolphin** *(Tursiops truncatus)*. Remember Flipper? That particular bottlenose dolphin may have been the first, last, and only bottlenose dolphin to star in its own television series,

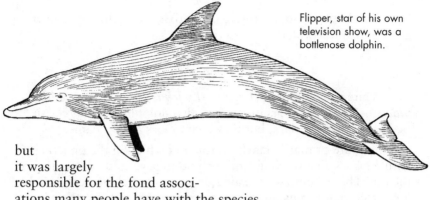

Flipper, star of his own television show, was a bottlenose dolphin.

but
it was largely
responsible for the fond associ-
ations many people have with the species.

Again, the animals vary slightly in different geographical regions of the world, and at least two distinct subspecies may exist. In general, bottlenose dolphins range from dark to lighter gray in color. They grow to about 13 feet and weigh as much as 1,400 pounds. They live in shallow water and are often seen riding the surf.

**Common dolphin** *(Delphinus delphis)*. These are the aerial acrobats that Herman Melville probably had in mind when he wrote, "They always swim in hilarious shoals which upon the sea keep tossing themselves to heaven like caps in a Fourth of July crowd." The pods, or herds, may number as many as 2,000 individuals. In addition to the acrobatics, common dolphins are said to change course for the opportunity to ride the bow wave of a passing ship, or even of a passing larger whale, for that matter.

Common dolphins are often tricolored: black, gray, and cream. They reach a length of seven to eight feet and weigh 200 to 300 pounds. Unlike
the bottlenose
dolphin,

The common dolphin is found in many areas.

47

common dolphins do not thrive in captivity. They live in temperate and tropical waters of all oceans.

**White-sided dolphin** *(Lagen-orhynchus acutus and L. obliquidens)*. Atlantic and Pacific white-sided dolphins are not classified as the same species, but they share more than a name.

Both are primarily black on top and white on the underbelly, with a gray stripe running from behind the eye to the beginning of the tail. The Atlantic white-sided dolphin has a characteristic yellow patch that begins just under the dorsal fin and extends back. Both species have dorsal fins that are tall and quite pointed, and both travel in herds of up to 1,000 animals.

Atlantic white-sided dolphins are the larger of the two, growing to 10 feet and weighing 400 to 550 pounds.

**Top:** The Atlantic white-sided dolphin is often sighted in the North Atlantic Ocean.
**Bottom:** The Pacific white-sided dolphin is a frequent bow-wave rider on whale-watch trips off the California coast.

Pacific white-sided dolphins are seven to eight feet in length and weigh at least 330 pounds. Both species feed on hake, squid, and sardines.

**Harbor porpoise** *(Phocena phocena).* The harbor porpoise is the most commonly seen of all porpoises, and although it does not ride the bow waves of ships, it has been known occasionally to approach small boats. The stocky little animal is usually brown or dark gray, with lighter gray coloring at the flanks.

Harbor porpoises grow to about 6 feet in length and weigh up to 200 pounds. They surface to breathe about every 15 seconds and do not stay submerged longer than three or four minutes. The animals have been described as generally undemonstrative, with a "businesslike" approach to life.

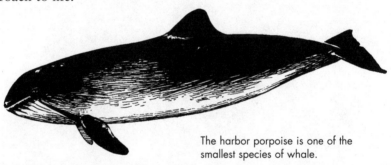

The harbor porpoise is one of the smallest species of whale.

# Tours, Museums, Aquariums, and National Parks

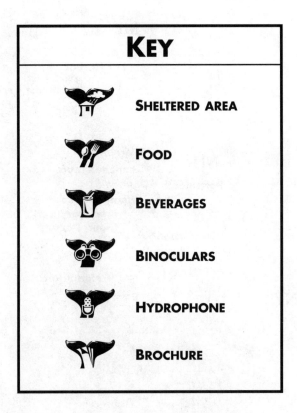

**KEY**

- Sheltered area
- Food
- Beverages
- Binoculars
- Hydrophone
- Brochure

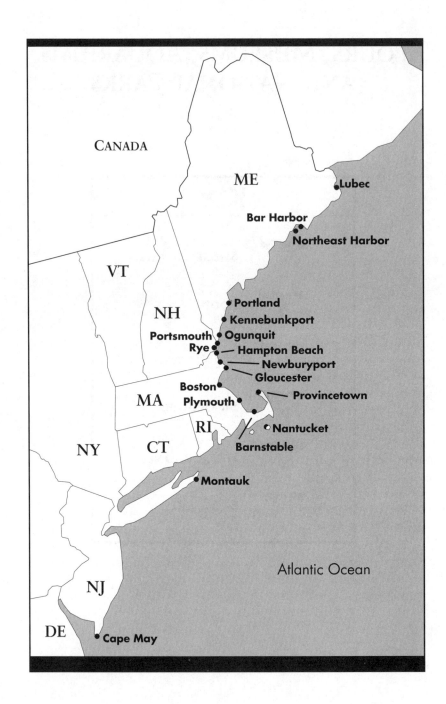

CANADA

ME

Lubec

Bar Harbor

Northeast Harbor

VT

NH

Portland

Kennebunkport

Portsmouth  Ogunquit

Rye  Hampton Beach

Newburyport

Gloucester

Boston

MA  Plymouth  Provincetown

RI  Nantucket

Barnstable

NY  CT

Montauk

Atlantic Ocean

NJ

DE  Cape May

# NORTHEAST U.S. COAST

C ommercial whale-watch tours are said to have originated on the Northeast Coast, and today three New
England states plus New York and New Jersey take
advantage of the whales that come to feed in the Gulf of Maine
from April through October. Whale-watch trips depart from
numerous cities and towns in Maine, Massachusetts, New
Hampshire, New York, and New Jersey, setting out to see humpbacks, finbacks, minkes, the occasional rare right whale, and
assorted dolphins.

Massachusetts leads the way, with nearly 20 whale-watch
tours. Provincetown, on Cape Cod, boasts four! Maine is active in
the industry, with trips originating from six cities along the coast.
Four tours operate out of New Hampshire and one each from
New Jersey and New York. The whale-watch tours on the
Northeast Coast range from trips sponsored by small charter
companies to research-oriented trips run by institutions and organizations. Here, too, are excursion boats built specifically for
whale watching.

# Tourism Information

## MAINE
### Maine Office of Tourism
189 State Street, Augusta, ME 04333
(207) 287-5710

## MASSACHUSETTS
### Cape Cod Chamber of Commerce
Junction Route 6 & 132, Hyannis, MA 02601
(508) 362-3225

### Massachusetts Office of Travel & Tourism
100 Cambridge Street, 13th Floor, Boston, MA 02202
(800) 447-MASS or (617) 632-8038 in Massachusetts

## NEW HAMPSHIRE
### New Hampshire Office of Vacation Travel
P.O. Box 1856, Concord, NH 03302
(603) 271-2666

## NEW JERSEY
### New Jersey Division of Tourism
CN 826, Trenton, NJ 08625
(800) JERSEY 7 or (609) 292-2470

## NEW YORK
### Department of Economic Development
One Commerce Plaza, Albany, NY 12245
(800) CALL NYS

### Long Island Tourism & Convention Commission
Eisenhower Park, 1899 Hempstead Turnpike, East Meadow, NY 11554
(516) 794-4222

# WHALE-WATCHING TRIPS

## MAINE

### BAR HARBOR

### Acadian Whale Watcher

Golden Anchor Pier, 56 West Street, Bar Harbor, ME 04644
(800) 421-3307 or (207) 288-9794 or 9776

| | |
|---|---|
| **Whales:** | Humpback, fin, minke, right, Atlantic white-sided dolphin |
| **Season:** | Mid-May through late October |
| **Boats:** | One boat, the *Acadian Whale Watcher*; 150 passengers |
| **Trips:** | Two 4-hour trips daily in summer at 8 a.m. and 1:30 p.m., and a shorter nature sunset cruise that leaves at 5 p.m. In May and October, the nature cruise runs during the day as well. Midweek is busiest. |
| **Fare:** | Adults, $27; senior citizens, $20; children: ages 9 to 14, $18; ages 6 to 8, $15; 5 and under, free. Fare includes free admission to the Bar Harbor Whale Museum. Group rates and private charter rates. Reservations advised. |
| **Departure:** | Trips leave from the Golden Anchor Pier on West Street in Bar Harbor, at the foot of Rodick Street about half a mile from Route 3. |
| **Naturalist:** | Yes |

"The Acadian is a new vessel that is perfect for the sightseer," says naturalist Robert Wilds, "as we sail around Acadia National Park on our way to the whales' feeding grounds. Also, we whale watch in an area where there are very few vessels." Tapes of the Acadian trips are for sale, available free to groups who charter the boat. Call about trips out of Boothbay Harbor.

**Note:** This same Robert Wilds served as the naturalist on my first whale watch, out of Barnstable Harbor in 1982. The experience can be habit forming!

## Frenchman Bay Company

1 West Street, P.O. Box 153, Bar Harbor, ME 04609
(207) 288-3322

| | |
|---|---|
| **Whales:** | Fin, humpback, right, minke, Atlantic white-sided dolphin |
| **Season:** | Mid-May through mid-October |
| **Boats:** | One boat, the *Whale Watcher*; 300 passengers |
| **Trips:** | One 4- to 5-hour trip daily at noon during off season (late May to late June and early September to mid-October). Two 4-hour trips daily at 9 a.m. and 2 p.m. from late June to early September. Midweek is busiest in the summer. |
| **Fare:** | Adults, $29; senior citizens, $25; children under 15, $18; under 5, free. Private charter rates on smaller vessels available. Reservations advised. |
| **Departure:** | Trips leave from the Frenchman Bay Company pier at the corner of Main and West Streets on the waterfront in Bar Harbor. |
| **Naturalist:** | Yes |

"You'll leave the port of Bar Harbor, past magnificent summer homes and the rocky shores of Acadia National Park. Keep an eye peeled for eagles, ospreys, and seals on the way out," advises a spokesman. "Once at sea, we'll look for shearwaters, petrels, and puffins. About 45 minutes after we leave Frenchman Bay, we'll arrive in the area where whales abound."

# KENNEBUNKPORT

## Indian Whale Watch

P.O. Box 2672, Kennebunkport, ME 04046
(207) 967-5912

| | |
|---|---|
| **Whales:** | Humpback, fin, minke, right, Atlantic white-sided dolphin |
| **Season:** | June through October |
| **Boats:** | One boat, the *Indian*; 72 passengers |

**Trips:**  One 5- to 6-hour trip daily at 10 a.m

**Fare:**  Adults, $25; senior citizens (60 and older), $20; children: 13 to 18, $20; 6 to 12, $15; under 6, free. Group rates and private charters available. Reservations advised.

**Departure:**  Trips leave from Arundel Wharf Restaurant on Ocean Avenue in Kennebunkport.

**Naturalist:**  Yes

"We try to make every trip a good time as well as an educational experience," says owner Karla Kay Brindle. "Each member of my crew is an enthusiastic whale lover, and they have been with us for years. Our naturalist gives a commentary as well as answers questions, and every day we offer a free ticket to anyone who can stump the crew."

Brindle adds, "Our feeling is that everyone should experience whales—these wondrous creatures—and if we didn't have to make a living, I would take everyone out for free." Whale sightings are guaranteed.

## Nautilus Whale Watch

P.O. Box 2777, Route 9, Kennebunkport, ME 04046
(207) 967-0707

**Whales:**  Humpback, fin, minke, Atlantic white-sided dolphin

**Season:**  Mid-May through late September

**Boats:**  One boat; 100 passengers

**Trips:**  One 5- to 6-hour trip daily at 10 a.m.; a second trip four additional days at 3 p.m.

**Fare:**  Adults, $30; senior citizens, $27.50; children under 12, $15. Reservations advised.

**Departure:**  Trips leave from Arundel boatyard, off Route 9.

**Naturalist:**  Captain serves as naturalist.

"All personnel are trained to answer questions about the whales and provide information, but generally, our captain is the official naturalist and handles the microphone," notes Nautilus staffer Diane Emery. Whale sightings are guaranteed.

## LUBEC

### Lubec Marine Services

9 High Street, Lubec, ME 04652
(207) 733-5584

**Whales:** Humpback, finback, right, minke, Atlantic white-sided dolphin

**Season:** June 1 through September 30

**Boats:** One boat; 20-25 passengers

**Trips:** One 3- to 4-hour trip daily at 1 p.m. A second 8- to 9-hour trip to the Bay of Fundy is available on Saturday only from August 1 through September 30, leaving at 8 a.m. On Saturdays the shorter trip is the busier.

**Fare:** Shorter trip: adults, $15; children: 5 to 12, $5; under 5, free. Longer trip: adults, $50; children 5 to 12, $20 (the trip is not recommended for children under 5). Reservations advised.

**Departure:** Trips leave from the Lubec Public Landing. Take Route 1 to Route 189.

**Naturalist:** Yes

Edwin "Butch" Huntley, in business since 1976, says Lubec Marine Services is the only business of its kind in the area.

## NORTHEAST HARBOR

### Maine Whalewatch

P.O. Box 78, Northeast Harbor, ME 04662
(207) 276-5803

**Whales:** Finback, humpback, right, minke, harbor porpoise

**Season:** June 1 through September 30

**Boats:** Two boats; 38 passengers each

| | |
|---|---|
| **Trips:** | One 9-hour trip daily at 8:30 a.m. The busiest day is Friday. |
| **Fare:** | $30 per person: Children under 5, free. Reservations advised. |
| **Departure:** | Trips leave from the Sea Street Pier (the Municipal Wharf) in Northeast Harbor. When entering town, take the only road to the left and head for the water. |
| **Naturalist:** | Naturalists from Allied Whale, the cetacean research group at the College of the Atlantic. |

"Northeast Whalewatch was founded by researchers from Allied Whale. The main motivation behind the trips was, and continues to be, to supply researchers a platform to study whales and to educate students and the general public about marine endangered species," says owner Sam Blanchard.

"We can't guarantee whales, but our sighting average is very high, and passengers feel that even on the possible few days without whales, their time was enjoyably spent." Harbor porpoise and harbor and gray seals are seen on virtually every trip, as are myriad seabirds.

# Richard M. Savage & Sons

P.O. Box 321, Northeast Harbor, ME 04662
(207) 276-3785

| | |
|---|---|
| **Whales:** | Fin, humpback, minke |
| **Season:** | June through September |
| **Boats:** | One boat, the *Poor Richard*; 20 passengers |
| **Trips:** | One full-day trip daily, by charter only. Sunday is the busiest day. |
| **Fare:** | $450 per day. Reservations required. |
| **Departure:** | Trips leave from the town landing at Northeast Harbor. Take Sea Street due east to the water. |
| **Naturalist:** | Captain narrates trips. |

"We're the only vessel that offers private daily charters with a licensed vessel and captain and optional lobster picnics," notes Richard Savage II. Captain Savage, an island native, has been in business since 1970 and has extensive cruising experience on Maine waters.

## OGUNQUIT

### Ugly Anne

P.O. Box 863, 9 King's Lane, Ogunquit, ME 03907
(207) 646-7202

**Whales:** Humpback, fin, minke

**Season:** Mid-June to Labor Day

**Boats:** One boat, the *Ugly Anne*; 35 passengers

**Trips:** Two 4-hour trips daily at 8 a.m. and 1:15 p.m.

**Fare:** $25 per person. Reservations required.

**Departure:** Trips leave from Perkins Cove in Ogunquit. Take Shore Road to Oarweed to the dock.

**Naturalist:** None on board.

Owners Jeanne and Ken Young, Sr., note, "The *Ugly Anne* is primarily a charter fishing boat, but we do see a lot of whales in August and September." Charters are available. And you can buy *Ugly Anne* T-shirts and sweatshirts.

## PORTLAND

### Odyssey Whale Watch

Commercial Street, P.O. Box 1084, Portland, ME 04104
(800) 437-3270 or (207) 775-0727

Winter address: 634 Cape Road, Standish, ME 04084

**Whales:** Finback, humpback, minke, right, Atlantic white-sided dolphin

**Season:** Mid-May through mid-October

**Boats:** One boat, the *Odyssey*; 95 passengers

**Trips:** One 6-hour trip daily at 10 a.m., and a 4-1/2-hour sunset trip at 4:30 p.m. Wednesday through Sunday in season. Weekend day trips are the busiest.

**Fare:** Adults, $30; senior citizens, $25; children: 13 to 17, $25; 12 and under, $20 on the day trips. Sunset cruises cost $25 for adults; $20 for senior citizens; children: 13 to 17, $20; 12 and under, $18. Reservations advised.

**Departure:** Trips leave from Long Wharf on Commercial Street in Portland. From the Maine Turnpike, take Exit 7, then take the exit ramp for Route 295 North. Take Exit 4 off 295 and follow signs for Route 1A, Commercial Street, or the waterfront. Ticket booth is next to Key Bank, just before DiMillo's Restaurant.

**Naturalist:** Yes

"We are the only whale watch in Portland, and we are a small family-run business," notes Daniel Libby. "Our sightings regularly feature seals, dolphins, sharks, and numerous seabirds as well as whales."

The owner and skipper is a marine biology teacher at Bonny Eagle High School in Portland.

# MASSACHUSETTS

## BARNSTABLE

### Hyannis Whale Watcher Cruises at Millway Marina

P.O. Box 254, Barnstable Harbor, Barnstable, MA 02630
(800) 287-0374 or (508) 362-6088; Fax (508) 362-9739

**Whales:** Humpback, finback, minke, right
**Season:** April through October
**Boats:** One boat; 300 passengers
**Trips:** Two 4-1/2-hour trips daily in summer, at 8 a.m. and 12:45 p.m.

Sunset cruises some days. One or two trips daily in the fall.

**Fare:** Rates vary with season and time of day; range is from $10 to $22 per person, with discounts for AAA members, children, senior citizens, and groups. Reservations advised. Discount coupons for trips are available at all lodging facilities on Cape Cod.

**Departure:** Trips leave from Barnstable Harbor, just 3 miles from Hyannis. Take Exit 6 off the mid-Cape highway (Route 6) and make a right turn onto Route 132. At the first traffic light, turn left and follow for 3 miles, straight to the harbor.

**Naturalist:** Yes

"We are the only whale watch located in the mid-Cape area," says Janet Lincoln, director of sales. "Our crew is always friendly and in uniform, and our galley staff offers complete food and beverage service."

# BOSTON

## A. C. Cruise Line

290 Northern Avenue, Boston, MA 02210
(800) 422-8419 or (617) 261-6633; Fax (617) 261-4747

**Whales:** Humpback, finback, Atlantic white-sided dolphin

**Season:** Mid-April through mid-October

**Boats:** Two boats; 146 and 400 passengers

**Trips:** One 7-hour trip at 10:30 a.m. Wednesdays through Sundays. Weekends are busiest.

**Fare:** Adults, $18; children, $12. Reservations advised.

**Departure:** Trips leave from Pier 290 Northern Avenue in the South Station area of Boston. Take the John F. Fitzgerald Expressway to either Northern Avenue or Congress Street.

**Naturalist:** Yes

Captain Alan Circeo cruises among the harbor islands and out to Stellwagen Bank to view the humpbacks and fin whales feeding.

"It's possible to see dolphins, various seabirds, ships, yachts—there's always a surprise every trip," he says. Whale sightings are guaranteed, and the *Cape Ann* and *Virginia C II* are both available for private charters.

## Boston Harbor Cruises

Number One Long Wharf, White Ticket Center, Boston, MA 02110
(617) 227-4321

| | |
|---|---|
| **Whales:** | Humpback, fin, minke, right, pilot, dolphin |
| **Season:** | Mid-May through mid-September |
| **Boats:** | The MV *James J. Doherty*; 300 passengers |
| **Trips:** | One 5-hour trip daily at 9:30 a.m. and one 4-hour trip daily at 5 p.m. |
| **Fare:** | Adults, $16; $13 for children under 12; $10 for senior citizens 65 and over. Reservations required. |
| **Departure:** | Number One Long Wharf in Boston off I-93 Blue Line Aquarium T Station, and steps from Fanueil Hall. |
| **Naturalist:** | Yes |

Boston Harbor Cruises is family owned and operated and has been in business since 1926, says co-owner Julie Doherty. "Whale watching is a favorite among us all, and because of the personal feeling we have for whales and other marine life, we feel that our whale watch is the best in Boston."

## Boston Harbor Whale Watch

60 Rowes Wharf, Boston, MA 02110
(617) 345-9866

| | |
|---|---|
| **Whales:** | Finback, humpback, minke |
| **Season:** | June through early September |

**Boats:**       One boat; 325 passengers

**Trips:**       One 4-1/2-hour trip daily at 10 a.m. on weekdays; two trips on weekends, at 9 a.m. and 2 p.m.

**Fare:**        Adults, $18; senior citizens and children under 12, $15. Reservations advised.

**Departure:**   Trips leave from Rowes Wharf in Boston, directly behind the arch at the Boston Harbor Hotel.

**Naturalist:**  Yes

Owner Jerry Van Dalinda says the Boston Harbor Whale Watch is "the home of fast whales—we'll get you there, fast."

# New England Aquarium

Central Wharf, Boston, MA 02110
(617) 973-5277 for information or (617) 973-5281 for reservations

**Whales:**      Humpback, finback, minke, right, Atlantic white-sided dolphin

**Season:**      April through late October

**Boats:**       One boat, the *Voyager II*; 299 passengers

**Trips:**       Trips last 4-1/2 to 5 hours. April weekends at 10 a.m.; May and June, weekdays at 10 a.m. and weekends at 9:30 a.m. and 3 p.m.; July and August, daily at 11 a.m. and 5 p.m.; September 7 through October 10, weekdays at 2 p.m., weekends at 9:30 a.m. and 3 p.m.; October, weekends at 10 a.m. Holidays are busiest.

**Fare:**        Adults, $24; senior citizens and college students, $19; youths 12 to 18, $17.50; children 3 to 11, $15.50. Group rates available. Reservations advised.

**Departure:**   Trips leave from the New England Aquarium's dock. Boarding begins 30 minutes before departure.

**Naturalist:**  Naturalist from the Aquarium staff on board.

"During the trip, our experienced staff will teach you how to identify the different species of whales and the other marine life that inhabit the area," notes Captain Ken Wright. "On the rare occasion that whales are not seen during your voyage, we will be happy to reschedule you for another trip."

The New England Aquarium is a private, nonprofit organization dedicated to education, conservation, and research; it has sponsored whale-watch trips since 1978.

## Oceanic Society Expeditions

Fort Mason Center, Building E, San Francisco, CA 94123
(800) 326-7491 or (415) 441-1106

Co-Sponsors: Dirigo Cruises, 39 Waterside Lane, Clinton, CT 06413
(203) 669-7068

| | |
|---|---|
| **Whales:** | Humpback, fin |
| **Season:** | August |
| **Boats:** | The 95-foot schooner *Harvey Gamage*; 30 passengers, housed primarily in double cabins |
| **Trips:** | Two 1-week educational whale-watch voyages with stops at Salem, Marblehead, and Gloucester. Participants live aboard. |
| **Fare:** | $795 per person per week. Price does not include airfare to Boston. |
| **Departure:** | Trips leave from Boston. |
| **Naturalist:** | Naturalists from the Oceanic Society Expeditions accompany trips. |

"The marine biologist on board will be familiar with all the marine mammals and birds, and you can expect daily lectures on various aspects of the world of whales and seabirds," said a spokeswoman. We will also have sailing instruction and some great guest lectures. There is also a library of related materials for your use, as well as charts of the area."

## GLOUCESTER

### Cape Ann Whale Watch

P.O. Box 345, Rose's Wharf, Gloucester, MA 01930
(800) 877-5110 or (508) 283-5110

**Whales:** Humpback, finback, minke, right, Atlantic white-sided dolphin

**Season:** Early May through mid-October

**Boats:** Two boats; 140 passengers each

**Trips:** Two 4-hour trips daily in the summer at 8:30 a.m. and 1:30 p.m. Usually one midmorning trip in early spring and late fall. Weekend afternoon trips are the busiest.

**Fare:** Adults, $20; senior citizens over 60, $14; children under 16, $12. Reservations required. Guests at the Twin Light Manor/Best Western Motel receive a discount.

**Departure:** Trips leave from Rose's Wharf, 415 Main Street in historic downtown Gloucester. From Boston, follow Route 128 north to Gloucester. At Exit 10, bear right onto Eastern Avenue, then bear right onto Main Street. Rose's Wharf is about .2 mile on the left, opposite the Old Colony gas station.

**Naturalist:** Naturalists from the Whale Conservation Institute.

Captain Jim Douglass notes, "All trips are research oriented and are led by members of the Whale Conservation Institute, headed by world-renowned Dr. Roger Payne, host of The Discovery Channel's "In The Company of Whales."

"Also, we were the first whale-watching company in the Gloucester area and the second on the East Coast. We've been in this business since 1978."

A percentage of each fare is donated to the Whale Conservation Institute.

### Captain Bill & Sons Whale Watch Cruises

9 Travers Street, Gloucester, MA 01930
(508) 283-6995

**Whales:** Humpback, finback, right, minke

**Season:** May 1 through mid-October

**Boats:**   Five boats; 150, 120, 110, 105, and 70 passengers

**Trips:**   Two 4-hour trips daily at 9 a.m. and 2 p.m. in summer; additional trip on Saturdays according to demand. In spring and fall, one trip daily at 10:30 a.m. on weekdays; trips at 9 a.m. and 2 p.m. on weekends.

**Fare:**   Adults, $20; senior citizens, $14; children under 16, $11. Reservations advised.

**Departure:**   The boats leave from behind Captain Carlo's Seafood Restaurant, 33 Harbor Loop in downtown Gloucester.

**Naturalist:**   Naturalist on board from Cetacean Research Unit.

Captain Bill Cunningham notes, "Captain Bill's boasts a superb sighting record, between 99 and 100 percent each year. Our deep sea fishing boats that leave the dock at 5 a.m. radio back the location of the whales, so we know where to go before we leave the dock." Videotapes of whale behavior are shown throughout the trip on a color television in the spacious main cabin.

# Seven Seas Whale Watch

Seven Seas Wharf, Gloucester, MA 01930
(800) 238-1776

**Whales:**   Humpback, finback, minke, right, pilot

**Season:**   May through mid-October

**Boats:**   Two boats; 100 and 149 passengers

**Trips:**   Two 4-hour trips daily at 9 a.m. and 1:30 p.m. Sunset cruises at 6 p.m. on weekends. The 1:30 p.m. trip on weekends is the busiest.

**Fare:**   Adults, $20; senior citizens, $15; children under 16, $12. Group rates and school rates available. Reservations advised.

**Departure:**   Trips leave from the historic Seven Seas Wharf downtown on Route 127. Take Exit 11 off Route 12 and proceed downtown.

**Naturalist:**   Yes

"Very often we encounter humpback whales which grow to 50 feet in length and weigh up to 50 tons," says a spokesman. "Herman Melville called the humpback 'the most gamesome and lighthearted of all the whales,' and we frequently observe them feeding, flipper-slapping, or breaching clear out of the water."

Seven Seas originated the "guaranteed sightings" policy.

# Yankee Whalewatch

The Yankee Fleet, 75 Essex Avenue, Gloucester, MA 01930
(800) 942-5464 or (508) 283-0313; Fax (508) 283-6089

**Whales:**    Humpback, finback, minke, right, Atlantic white-sided dolphin

**Season:**    May 1 through October 31

**Boats:**    Seven boats; 70, 125, 144, or 150 passengers

**Trips:**    Two or three 4-hour trips daily on weekdays, three to five trips on Saturdays, two to four on Sundays as demand warrants throughout the season. Generally, departure times are 8:30 a.m., 1:30 p.m., 2:30 p.m., and 5:30 p.m. The Saturday 1:30 p.m. trip is the busiest.

**Fare:**    Adults, $21; senior citizens over 65, $15; children under 16, $10. Reservations advised. Package deal available for guests at the Cape Ann Marina Resort.

**Departure:**    Trips leave from Cape Ann Marina complex. From Boston, take I-95 north to Route 128; go north to Exit 14 and head toward Gloucester, about 2-1/2 miles. Look for the Yankee Fleet office on the left.

**Naturalist:**    Naturalists from the Atlantic Cetacean Research Center are aboard to narrate and answer questions.

"The Yankee Fleet has been family-owned and operated since 1944, and we use the newest, fastest vessels for whale watching in the area," says a spokesman. "In 1990, we instituted a general environment awareness program to educate passengers about things everyone can do to make a difference in protecting and cleaning up our environment."

Yankee Fleet has a guaranteed sightings policy with a 100 percent sighting record since 1986. From time to time, the Yankee Fleet offers extended whale-watch trips.

## NANTUCKET

### Nantucket Whale Watch

Straight Wharf, Nantucket, MA 02554
(800) 322-0013 (in the northeast), (508) 283-0313; Fax (508) 283-6089

| | |
|---|---|
| **Whales:** | Humpback, fin, minke |
| **Season:** | Mid-July to mid-September |
| **Boats:** | Two boats, the 70-foot *Yankee Clipper* and the 100-foot *Yankee Spirit* |
| **Trips:** | One 8-hour trip at 9:30 a.m. on Tuesdays, Wednesdays, and Thursdays. |
| **Fare:** | Adults, $65; children, $35. Reservations advised. |
| **Departure:** | Trips leave from the Hy-Line dock on Straight Wharf in downtown Nantucket. |
| **Naturalist:** | Yes |

The Nantucket Whale Watch was started by the Yankee Fleet (out of Gloucester) and Seafarers Expeditions to provide cruises to the Great South Channel near Nantucket Shoals.

"These full-day excursions will allow you to appreciate the grace and beauty of the whales, dolphins, and seabirds of Nantucket's waters on a first-hand basis while contributing to ongoing marine studies," a representative from the Nantucket Whale Watch said.

## NEWBURYPORT

### Newburyport Whale Watch

Hilton's Dock, 54 Merrimac Street, Newburyport, MA 01950
(800) 848-1111 or (508) 465-7165

**Whales:** Humpback, finback, minke, right, harbor porpoise, Atlantic white-sided dolphin

**Season:** April through October

**Boats:** One boat, the 100-foot *Captain Red*; could carry 300, but passengers restricted to 145.

**Trips:** Two daily, at 8:30 a.m. and 1:30 p.m.

**Fare:** Adults, $23; senior citizens, $20; children 16 and under, $16. Group rates. Reservations advised.

**Departure:** Trips leave from the dock at Hilton's Fishing Parties, 54 Merrimac Street in Newburyport, along the Merrimac River half a mile east of U.S. Route 1, next to Captain's Quarters Restaurant.

**Naturalist:** Professional biologists actively involved in marine research serve as naturalists.

Newburyport Whale Watch was one of the very first whale watch businesses in New England. The cruises are research and education oriented, and the researchers on board photographically track and identify individual humpback and right whales, both endangered species.

"We have highly experienced guides with broad experience in the field," says Scott Mercer, founder and owner of New England Whale Watch. Mercer, who is a researcher, author, lecturer, and university professor, is one of those knowledgeable guides.

## PLYMOUTH

### Captain John Boats

117 Standish Avenue, Plymouth, MA 02360
(800) 242-2469 or (508) 746-2643

**Whales:** Humpback, fin, minke, right, Atlantic white-sided dolphin

**Season:** April 1 through October 31

**Boats:** Eight boats, 65 to 250 passengers

**Trips:** Two to five 4-hour trips daily, usually at 9 a.m., 11 a.m., 2 p.m., and 3:30 p.m. Departures vary according to demand. The 2 p.m. trip on weekends is the most popular.

**Fare:** Adults, $21; senior citizens, $18; children under 12, $14. Group and family rates available. Reservations advised.

**Departure:** Trips leave from Plymouth Town Wharf, at the end of Route 44 or via Route 3. (Captain John Boats also has a berth at Provincetown's MacMillan Wharf, where they take interested ferryboat passengers on a whale watch.

**Naturalist:** Yes

Doug Hall, director of sales, notes that Captain John Boats is "the largest fleet of whale-watching and fishing vessels in Massachusetts."

"Since 1977, Captain John Boats has logged sightings of whales and dolphins on more than 99 percent of the excursions."

### Captain Tim Brady & Sons, Inc.

254 Sandwich Street, Plymouth, MA 02360
(508) 746-4809

**Whales:** Humpback, fin, right, minke, orca, Atlantic white-sided dolphin

**Season:** April through November

**Boats:** One boat, the *Mary Elizabeth*; 49 passengers

**Trips:** One 4-1/2-hour trip daily at 2 p.m.; with one additional trip each Saturday and Sunday according to demand. Saturday is busiest.

**Fare:**        Adults, $18; senior citizens, $15; children under12, $12.
Ten percent discounts for families.

**Departure:**    Trips leave from Plymouth's historic Town Wharf, at the end of Route 44 or via Route 3.

**Naturalist:**    Marine biologist serves as naturalist.

Captain Timothy C. Brady says, "We are the only 45-foot-long whale watcher in the area—new, modern, and fast. We usually take only about 35 passengers per trip so no one is crowded. And we can videotape your whale watch."

# Massachusetts Whale Watching Center

Box 1328, Plymouth, MA 02360
(508) 833-0181

**Whales:**    Humpback, right, fin, minke, Atlantic white-sided dolphin

**Season:**    Late April through October 31

**Boats:**    Three boats; 140 or 250 passengers

**Trips:**    Three 4-1/2-hour trips daily on weekdays at 9 a.m., 11 a.m., and 2 p.m. Sunday is busiest.

**Fare:**    Adults, $21; senior citizens 62 and older, $18; children under 12, $14. Special rates for school groups. Reservations required.

**Departure:**    Trips leave from Plymouth's historic Town Wharf, at the end of Route 44 or via Route 3, just 100 yards north of the Mayflower.

**Naturalist:**    Naturalist on board from the Plymouth Marine Mammal Research Center.

"The Massachusetts Whale Watching Center is the only whale-watching operation owned by biologists involved with direct research on local populations of marine mammals," notes director David N. Wiley. "We consider research to be an important component of each whale-watching trip. Our naturalists are specialists in coastal geology, seabird biology, and ecological relationships as well as marine mammals."

## PROVINCETOWN

### Cape Cod Cruises

58 Seven Hills Road, Plymouth, MA 02360
(508) 747-2400

**Whales:** Humpback, finback, minke, right, Atlantic white-sided dolphin

**Season:** May through October

**Boats:** One boat; 250 passengers

**Trips:** One 4-hour trip daily departs at midday from Provincetown. Weekends are busiest.

**Fare:** Adults, $15; senior citizens, $14; children under 12, $13; children under 8, free with parent. Reservations advised.

**Departure:** The cruise originates in Plymouth and the whale watch departs from Fisherman's Wharf in Provincetown, at the foot of Standish Street.

**Naturalist:** Yes

"We are unique in that we pick up passengers from Plymouth as well as Provincetown," notes president Stan Tavares. "We give large groups with variable interests an option when their trip originates in Plymouth. Part of a group can get off in Provincetown to shop or go to the beach, and the remaining passengers may stay aboard for a whale watch."

### Dolphin Fleet of Provincetown

MacMillan Wharf, P.O. Box 243, Provincetown, MA 02657
(800) 826-9300 or (508) 349-1900

**Whales:** Humpback, fin, minke, right, dolphins

**Season:** April 15 through October

**Boats:** Three boats; each holds 300 passengers, but only 147 are allowed on board to ensure comfortable seating

**Trips:** Nine 3-1/2-hour trips daily in peak season, beginning at 8:30 a.m. and scheduled throughout the day until sunset. Tuesday afternoon is busiest.

**Fare:**      Adults, $17; senior citizens and children 12 and under, $15; children under 7, free. Fares are lower in spring and fall. Group rates. Boats available for private charter in spring and fall. Reservations advised.

**Departure:**      Trips leave from MacMillan Wharf, at the foot of Standish Street.

**Naturalist:**      Naturalists from Provincetown's Center for Coastal Studies act as field guides.

Owner and Captain Albert J. Avellar, once referred to as "the patron saint of whale watching," notes, "We are in our third generation in our study of whales; we know the reproductive rate, etc. The scientists from the Center for Coastal Studies make ours educational trips, and we currently have the fastest whale-watch boats in Provincetown."

On some summer weekends, the *Dolphin VII* makes special all-day whale watches. Write for information.

## Portuguese Princess Whale Watch

P.O. Box 1469, MacMillan Wharf, Provincetown, MA 02657
(800) 442-3188 or (508) 487-2651; Fax (508) 487-6458

**Whales:**      Humpback, finback, minke, right, Atlantic white-sided dolphin

**Season:**      April through October

**Boats:**      Two boats; each has room for 270 passengers but carries only 150 to avoid crowding.

**Trips:**      Three to six 3-1/2- or 4-hour trips daily, according to demand. Trips are in the morning, at midday, in the afternoon, and at sunset. In April, May, and early June, weekends are busiest; in summer weekends are not as busy and discounts are available. Tuesdays, Wednesdays, and Thursdays are busiest during the summer.

**Fare:**      Fares range from $12 to $18, depending on the day and time. Reservations required during peak season and suggested in spring and fall.

**Departure:**      Trips leave from MacMillan Wharf, at the foot of Standish Street in Provincetown.

**Naturalist:**      Naturalist/whale experts as field guides on board.

"We serve homemade foods, including Portuguese specialties, and offer folk music on most trips," notes owner Suzanne Carter. "We donate money to many whale conservation organizations, but we don't solicit money from customers during the trips. And we guarantee whale sightings."

The Portuguese Princess also owns and operates the Whale Watchers General Store at 309 Commercial Street in Provincetown.

# Provincetown Whale Watch Inc.

MacMillan Pier, Provincetown, MA 02657
(800) 992-9333 or (508) 487-1582

**Whales:**  Humpback, finback, minke, right

**Season:**  Mid-May through mid-November

**Boats:**  One boat, the *Ranger V;* 415 passengers

**Trips:**  Three 3-1/2-hour trips daily at 9 a.m., 1 p.m., and 5 p.m. The midday trips on Tuesdays, Wednesdays, and Thursdays are the busiest.

**Fare:**  Off-season rates (May through June; September through November): adults, $12; senior citizens, $10; children under 12, $8. In-season rates (July and August): adults, $15; senior citizens, $13; children, $10; children under 7 always ride free. Discounts for AAA members. Guests at the Top Mast Motel in Truro also receive a discount coupon.

**Departure:**  Trips leave from MacMillan Wharf, at the foot of Standish Street in Provincetown.

**Naturalist:**  Yes

Co-owner Helen Costa says, "Your captain, Gerald Costa, brings something to your trip that few others can offer—a lifetime of experience on the sea and a rich family history, dating back to the early days of American whaling."

# NEW HAMPSHIRE

## HAMPTON BEACH

### Al Gauron Deep Sea Fishing

State Pier, Hampton Beach, NH 03842
(603) 926-2469

| | |
|---|---|
| **Whales:** | Humpback, finback, right, minke, Atlantic white-sided dolphin |
| **Season:** | April through October |
| **Boats:** | Four boats; three carry 77 passengers; one, 120 |
| **Trips:** | Three 4- to 5-hour sunset whale-watch cruises each week as weather permits. Daily trips on demand in July and August. Boats available for private charter. |
| **Fare:** | Adults, $17; senior citizens, $16; children, $12. Group rates available. Reservations advised. |
| **Departure:** | Trips leave from Hampton Harbor, by the Hampton River bridge in Hampton Beach. |
| **Naturalist:** | Captain narrates trips. |

"We have four boats in our fleet and have one of the best reputations on the East Coast," says Captain Rocky Gauron. "We are family owned and operated, and all our captains have piloted their boats on at least 100 whale watches. They are able to handle narrations very capably."

## PORTSMOUTH

### Oceanic Whale Watch Expeditions

Isles of Shoals Steamship Company, 315 Market Street, P.O. Box 311,
Portsmouth, NH 03801
(800) 441-4620 or (603) 431-5500

| | |
|---|---|
| **Whales:** | Humpback, fin, minke, right, Atlantic white-sided dolphin |
| **Season:** | Late April through October 31 |
| **Boats:** | Two boats; 149 and 349 passengers |
| **Trips:** | One 6-hour trip daily at 9:30 a.m. (Departure time may vary according to the season.) Saturday is the busiest day. |
| **Fare:** | Adults, $23; senior citizens, $22; children ages 3 to 11, $15. Reservations required on weekends; advised at all times. Guests at the Sheraton Hotel receive a discount on whale watch. |
| **Departure:** | Trips leave from Barker Wharf, 315 Market Street in Portsmouth. Off Interstate 95 (going north or south) take Exit 7 and turn toward downtown Portsmouth. Go about 1 mile. Office is across from the Sheraton Hotel. |
| **Naturalist:** | Yes |

"We are the oldest whale-watch company in northern New England, and our whale watches have consistently been highly rated by the National Marine Fisheries Service, which regulates all whale-watch activity," notes Captain John S. Hunnewell.

"From our location here in Portsmouth, we have access to several whale watch zones. Although we cannot guarantee sightings, we do have a 98 percent success rate. Our naturalist has more than 25 years' experience in this area and is a recognized expert on pelagic birds and will identify and explain all activity."

## Atlantic Fleet

P.O. Box 678, Rye Harbor State Marina, Rye, NH 03870
(603) 964-5220

| | |
|---|---|
| **Whales:** | Humpback, fin, minke, right |
| **Season:** | May 1 through early October |
| **Boats:** | One boat; 149 passengers |
| **Trips:** | One 4-hour trip at 5:30 p.m. on Wednesday and Friday. |
| **Fare:** | Adults, $18; senior citizens, $16; children, $13. Reservations are advised. |
| **Departure:** | Trips leave from Rye Harbor State Marina. |
| **Naturalist:** | Yes |

Owner Brad Cook notes, "Our naturalist provides a precruise discussion and orientation, narration during the trip, and answers questions one-on-one on the return trip. Also, we have fast aluminum vessels, which provide more time on the whale grounds."

## New Hampshire Seacoast Cruises

Rye Harbor State Marina, Box 232, Rye, NH 03870
(800) 872-4753 or (603) 964-5545

| | |
|---|---|
| **Whales:** | Finback, humpback, minke, right, Atlantic white- sided dolphin, harbor porpoise |
| **Season:** | May 1 through mid-October |
| **Boats:** | One boat, the *Granite State*; 150 passengers |
| **Trips:** | One 6-hour trip daily from 8 a.m. to 2 p.m. A second trip is offered on Thursdays and Saturdays during July and August from 5 to 9 p.m. |
| **Fare:** | Adults, $22; children, $15; under 4, free. Discount for senior citizens. Reservations advised. |

**Departure:** Trips leave from Rye Harbor State Marina on Route 1A between Hampton Beach and Portsmouth, next to Saunders' Restaurant. Look for the giant American flag.

**Naturalist:** Yes

"Every whale watch is led by an experienced professional researcher/naturalist, and the cruise is preceded by a lecture with graphics," says owner Leo Axtin. "Also, we are the nearest mainland port to the Isles of Shoals, the southernmost harbor seal nesting area in the western North Atlantic. Almost every whale trip takes us past these islands."

# NEW JERSEY

## CAPE MAY

### Cape May Whale Watch and Research Center

1286 Wilson Drive, Cape May, NJ 08204
(609) 898-0055; Fax (609) 884-8602

| | |
|---|---|
| **Whales:** | Humpback, finback, right, pilot, minke |
| **Season:** | April through December |
| **Boats:** | Two boats; 200 passengers each |
| **Trips:** | Three trips daily; a 2-hour dolphin watch and breakfast cruise at 9 a.m., a 3-hour whale watch at 1 p.m., and a 2-hour sunset cruise and dolphin watch at 6 p.m. |
| **Fare:** | For the three-hour trip, adults, $25; senior citizens, $20; children 7 to 14, $12; children six and under, free. For the two-hour trips, adults, $15; children free (one with each paid adult ticket). Group rates. Reservations advised. |

**Departure:**   Trips leave from the end of Wilson Drive, off Route 109 at the Little Bridge.

**Naturalist:**   Yes

"We offer the opportunity for the entire family and people of all ages to become better educated about environmental issues while enjoying the time spent doing so," says Captain Ron Robbins, who reports sighting as many as 600 whales each season. He's been in business since 1962 and publishes an annual newsletter.

# NEW YORK

## MONTAUK

### Okeanos Whale Watch Cruises

Okeanos Ocean Research Foundation Inc., 278 East Montauk Highway, P.O. Box 776, Hampton Bays, NY 11946
(516) 728-4522

**Whales:**   Fin, minke, humpback, pilot; occasional right, sperm

**Season:**   May through September

**Boats:**   Two boats; 150 and 300 passengers

**Trips:**   One 4- to 7-hour trip daily. Schedule varies according to season and demand.

**Fare:**   Adults, $30; children ages 5 through 13, $12. Senior citizens get a 10 percent discount. Group rates. Trip not recommended for children under five. Reservations advised.

**Departure:**    Trips depart from the Montauk Viking Dock out of Montauk, Long Island, New York. Take the Long Island Expressway to Exit 70 (Manorville); go south on Route 111 to Route 27 (Sunrise Highway). Take Route 27 east all the way to Montauk. Upon entering Montauk business district, turn left at traffic circle with flagpole onto Edgemere Street, which becomes Flamingo Avenue. Continue to Montauk fishing fleet on right side. Look for Viking Fleet dock and OKEANOS WHALE WATCH sign.

**Naturalist:**    Naturalist is either a biologist or an educator.

The Okeanos Ocean Research Foundation is a nonprofit organization primarily interested in research and secondarily in educating the public about marine life. All proceeds from whale watches provide funding for the organization's programs.

"Our on-board team of researchers collect data on a variety of research topics, and we have a large volunteer team on every cruise to assist with everything from data compilation to boat maintenance," notes a spokesman. "It's a unique concept!"

# MUSEUMS, AQUARIUMS, AND SCIENCE CENTERS

## CONNECTICUT

### The Maritime Center at Norwalk

10 North Water Street, Norwalk, CT 06854
(203) 852-0700

In historic South Norwalk, the Maritime Center features 20 marine habitats, a maritime history museum, a wooden boat shop, and an IMAX theater. The Center houses more than 125 different species of marine life, including playful harbor seals, tiny brine shrimp, and 10-foot sharks, all indigenous to Long Island Sound.

Summer hours at the Center (from July 1 through Labor Day) are from 10 a.m. to 6 p.m. In winter, the Center is open from 10 a.m. to 5 p.m. Closed Thanksgiving and Christmas. Admission to Aquarium and the Maritime Hall is $7.50 for adults, $6.50 for children. Admission to the IMAX theater is $6 for adults, $4.50 for children. Combination admission is $11.75 for adults, $9.50 for children.

Each year, the Maritime Center at Norwalk schedules two three-day whale-watch trips off Cape Cod. For information, contact the center.

### Mystic Marinelife Aquarium

55 Coogan Boulevard, Mystic, CT 06355
(203) 572-5955; Fax (203) 572-5969

More than 6,000 sea life specimens, including beluga whales, are displayed in 49 living exhibits in the Mystic Marinelife Aquarium. Seal Island, a 2-1/2-acre outdoor exhibit, shows the natural habitats of seals and sea lions. Whale and dolphin show daily.

From June 30 through Labor Day, the Aquarium is open 9 a.m. to 5:30 p.m.; the rest of the year, 9 a.m. to 4:30 p.m. Closed Thanksgiving, Christmas, New Year's Day, and the last week of January. Admission is $8.25 for adults, $4.75 for children 5 through 12, and $7.25 for senior citizens.

# MAINE

## Bar Harbor Whale Museum

95 West Street, Bar Harbor, ME 04609
(207) 288-2363

In celebration of the marine mammals of the Gulf of Maine—especially the whale—the Bar Harbor Whale Museum offers a variety of exhibits, among them whale skeletons and scale models of whales, dolphins, and porpoises. Computer programs, graphic arts exhibits, an audiocenter, and a 25-seat theater also provide insight into the behavior of whales. Exhibits about seals and seabirds also are on display.

The Museum is open daily from 8:30 a.m. to 9:30 p.m. from May through October. Admission is $5 for adults, $4 for senior citizens, $3.50 for children ages 6 to 12, and free for children 5 or younger.

A ticket on the Acadian Whale Watcher includes free admission to the museum.

## Natural History Museum

College of the Atlantic, 105 Eden Street, Bar Harbor, ME 04609
(207) 288-5015; Fax (207) 288-2328

This small museum is part of the College of the Atlantic and features displays of Mount Desert Island flora and fauna. Daily participatory programs include assembling a 20-foot whale skeleton.

The Natural History Museum is open daily 9 a.m. to 5 p.m., mid-June to Labor Day, and 10 a.m. to 4 p.m. Monday through Friday from Labor Day to June. Admission is $2 for adults, $.75 for children.

The Northeast Whalewatch, out of Northeast Harbor, is sponsored by Allied Whale, an affiliate of the College of the Atlantic. See the listing under Northeast Harbor for details.

# MARYLAND

## National Aquarium in Baltimore

Pier 3, 501 East Pratt Street, Baltimore, MD 21202
(301) 576-3800

The main building of the National Aquarium is a seven-level building where more than 5,000 salt- and freshwater species are on display. Special exhibits include a South American tropical rain forest, an outdoor 70,000-gallon rock pool, and a 220,000-gallon ocean tank that houses sharks, rays, and large fish. The Marine Mammal Pavilion, which opened in December, 1990, is primarily dedicated to dolphins but includes a life-size model of Scylla, a known humpback that lives in the Atlantic Ocean.

From May 15 to September 15, the Aquarium is open from 9 a.m. to 5 p.m. Monday through Thursday and from 9 a.m. to 8 p.m. Friday through Sunday. From September 16 through May 14, hours are 10 a.m. to 5 p.m. Saturday through Thursday and 10 a.m. to 8 p.m. on Friday. Admission is $11.50 for adults; $9.50 for students and senior citizens; $7.50 for children ages 3 to 11. Children under three are free.

## MASSACHUSETTS

### New Bedford Whaling Museum

18 Johnny Cake Hill, New Bedford, MA 02740
(508) 997-0046; Fax (508) 997-0018

This is the largest museum in the United States devoted to whaling in the age of sail. Exhibits include a humpback whale skeleton, a 98-foot mural of sperm whales painted by Richard Ellis, and galleries devoted to scrimshaw, whale boats, and whaling equipment. There also is an extensive collection of art related to whaling.

The focal point of the exhibits is a half-scale model of the whaling bark Lagoda, which visitors may board. A 22-minute segment of a silent film showing the chase and capture of a whale is shown daily at 10:30 a.m. and 1:30 p.m. in July and August and at 2 p.m. on Saturday and Sunday the other months of the year.

The Whaling Museum is open 9 a.m. to 5 p.m. Monday through Saturday and 1 to 5 p.m. on Sunday. In July and August Sunday hours are 11 a.m. to 5 p.m. Closed Thanksgiving, Christmas, and New Year's Day. Admission is $4.50 for adults; $3.50 for senior citizens; $3 for children 6 through 14.

### New England Aquarium

Central Wharf, Boston, MA 02119
(617) 973-5200

More than 70 exhibits, with new displays each year, continue to delight visitors to the New England Aquarium on Boston's historic waterfront. The 187,000-gallon Giant Ocean Tank extends from floor to ceiling, and huge sea turtles, sharks, and moray eels swim alongside as you descend the spiral ramp around the tank. California sea lions perform daily aboard Discovery, a floating marine mammal pavilion.

From July 1 through Labor Day, the Aquarium is open 9 a.m. to 6 p.m. on Monday, Tuesday, and Friday; 9 a.m. to 8 p.m. on Wednesday and Thursday; 9 a.m. to 7 p.m. on Saturday, Sunday, and holidays. From Labor Day to June 30, open 9 a.m. to 5 p.m. on Monday, Tuesday, Wednesday, and Friday; 9 a.m. to 8 p.m. on Thursday; and 9 a.m. to 6 p.m. on Saturday, Sunday, and holidays. Closed Thanksgiving and Christmas; open at noon on New Year's Day.

Admission is $8.50 for adults; $4.50 for children 3 to 11; and $7.50 for senior citizens.

The New England Aquarium operates whale watches on its own boat. See listing under Boston, Massachusetts.

## Peabody Essex Museum of Salem

East India Square, Salem, MA 01970
(508) 745-1876; Fax (508) 744-6776

Among the many treasures at the Peabody Essex Museum are exhibits on the natural resources, environment, and marine ecology of Essex County. Exhibits include birds, reptiles, fish, plants, mammals, and pond life. "Maritime New England," a permanent exhibit, includes paintings and artifacts documenting the history of maritime fishing and whaling industries. Special programs for children include classes on whale biology and Yankee whaling.

The Peabody Essex Museum is open 10 a.m. to 5 p.m. Monday through Saturday; until 8 p.m. Thursday, and noon to 5 p.m. Sunday. Admission is $6 for adults; $5 for senior citizens and students; $3.50 for children 6 to 18.

# NEW YORK

## American Museum of Natural History

Central Park West at 79th Street, New York, NY 10024
(212) 769-5100

Said to be the largest museum of its kind, the American Museum of Natural History offers 40 exhibit halls and numerous special display areas, with more than 30 million artifacts and specimens. The Hall of Ocean Life includes a 94-foot model of a diving whale.

The American Museum of Natural History is open 10 a.m. to 5:45 p.m. Monday, Tuesday, Wednesday, Thursday, and Sunday and 10 a.m. to 8:45 p.m. Friday and Saturday. Closed Thanksgiving and Christmas. Suggested admission is $5 for adults, $2.50 for children.

The Museum schedules an annual three-day whale watch off Cape Cod in May. The chartered trip includes a visit to the Mystic Aquarium. For more information, contact the museum's Department of Education.

# MARINE SANCTUARIES

## Stellwagen Bank National Marine Sanctuary

14 Union Street, Plymouth, MA 02360
(508) 747-1691

Just 25 nautical miles east of Boston lies Stellwagen Bank, a submerged sand bank in waters that support large populations of marine mammals and fish. Three species of endangered whales (humpback, fin, and right) use the area as a nursery and feeding ground. Other cetaceans often spotted are Atlantic white-sided dolphins, harbor porpoise, orcas, pilot whales, and minke whales. Write for a free brochure.

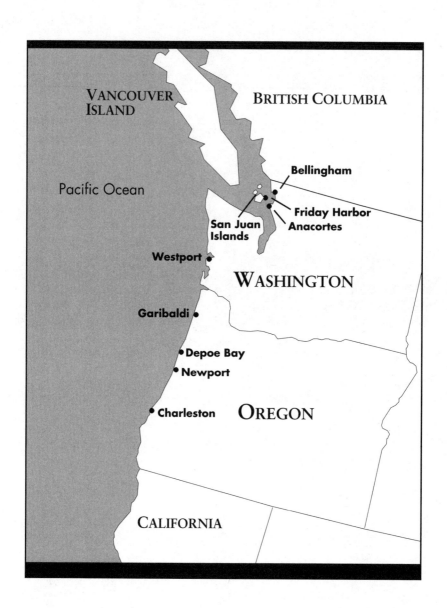

# THE PACIFIC NORTHWEST

Whale watchers in Washington enjoy two seasons, in two different areas. Westport, on the Pacific Coast, boasts several tour operators who take whale watchers to see the annual migration of the gray whales. April and May are considered the best months; the weather has calmed sufficiently, and the whales swim more slowly as they head north to the Bering and Chukchi Seas. The summer months, especially June and July, find whale watchers in search of three large populations of orcas and an abundance of minkes off the San Juan Islands.

Trips in the San Juan Islands, which depart from several cities, are available for one, two, three, or four days on excursion boats, sailboats, and sea kayaks. Beginners are welcome on the kayak trips, which include instructions on maneuvering the craft. One tour operator notes, "Kayaking among whales is quite a thrill."

Oregon celebrates the annual migration of the gray whales and also welcomes those sperm whales, orcas, and humpbacks that are occasionally seen in the area. Like their colleagues on the Washington coast, whale-watch tour operators in Oregon are at the mercy of the weather. Depoe Bay has the only "inside" whale watching, within the protection of the bay. Because of this geographical advantage, Depoe Bay bills itself as "The Whale-Watching Capital of the Oregon Coast." Trips are also available in other cities.

Gray whales traveling south reach Oregon early in December and are gone by mid-February. Whale watching peaks early in January. Heading north on the return trip, adult males and some females pass by Oregon from early March through mid-April; females with calves can be seen from early May through mid-June.

Even when the cold, rainy weather keeps the boats in their harbors, the state of Oregon has whale watchers in mind.

Volunteers trained at the Extension Service at Oregon State University stand at lookout points at numerous locations along the Oregon coast. On duty from 10 a.m. to 1 p.m., December 26 through January 1 and again during the third week of March, the volunteers point out the passing whales and answer questions about the migration.

The lookout points, marked with signs that read "WHALE WATCHING SPOKEN HERE," include North Head, Fort Stevens State Park, Ecola State Park, Neahkahnie Mountain, Cape Meares State Park, Cape Lookout State Park, "D" River State Wayside, Boller Bay Wayside, Depoe Bay seawall, Rocky Creek Wayside, Cape Foulweather, Cape Perpetua overlook, Sea Lion Caves turnout, Umpqua Lighthouse State Park, Shore Acres State Park, and Harris Beach State Park.

# TOURISM INFORMATION

## OREGON

### Economic Development Department
### Tourism Division

595 Cottage Street N.E., Salem, OR 97310

(800) 547-7842 (outside Oregon)

### Oregon Coast Association

P.O. Box 670, Newport, OR 97365

(800) 858-8598

## WASHINGTON

### Department of Trade and Economic Development
### Tourism Development Division

101 General Administration Building, P.O. Box 42500,
Olympia, WA 98504

(800) 544-1800

### Westport-Grayland Chamber of Commerce

2985 South Montesano Street, P.O. Box 306,
Westport, WA 98595

(800) 345-6223

# WHALE-WATCHING TRIPS

## OREGON

### CHARLESTON

## Betty Kay Charters

P.O. Box 5020, Charleston, OR 97420
(800) 752-6303

| | |
|---|---|
| **Whales:** | Gray |
| **Season:** | January, March, April |
| **Boats:** | Two boats; 30 and 10 passengers, respectively |
| **Trips:** | Trips are offered according to demand and the tide. Weekends are the busiest. |
| **Fare:** | $20 per person for a 3-hour trip. Minimum of four people. Reservations required. |
| **Departure:** | Trips leave from the Charleston boat basin. Cross the Charleston Bridge, turn right toward the small boat basin, and follow the signs. |
| **Naturalist:** | None on board. |

Bill Whitmer, skipper and owner of Betty Kay Charters, has been going to sea since the early 1970s.

## Bob's Sportfishing

P.O. Box 5018, 7788 Albacore Avenue, Charleston, OR 97420
(503) 888-4241

**Whales:** Gray

**Season:** December through March

**Boats:** One boat, the *Miss Carol*; 13 passengers

**Trips:** Trips are scheduled according to demand and tide. Fare: $20 per person for a 3-hour trip. Reservations required.

**Departure:** Trips leave from Charleston small boat basin. Follow signs from Coos Bay/North Bend to Charleston; park at the small boat basin near Coast Guard station.

**Naturalist:** None on board.

"The crew is very helpful and friendly," note owners Dick and Donna Harrington. "Our 36-foot charter boat is only used for up to thirteen passengers, which gives everyone plenty of room."

## DEPOE BAY

## Dockside Charters

P.O. Box 1308, 270 Southeast Coast Guard Place, Depoe Bay, OR 97341
(800) 733-8915 or (503) 765-2545

**Whales:** Gray

**Season:** Year-round

**Boats:** Two boats; 30 passengers each

**Trips:** Trips scheduled every hour from 10 a.m. until dark. Saturday is the busiest day.

**Fare:** Adults, $10 an hour; children 12 and younger, $7 an hour. Reservations advised during holidays.

**Departure:** Trips leave from the town harbor. Off Highway 101, turn east at Bay Street (the only stoplight in town) and follow the road past the Coast Guard station. Dock is 100 feet inside the parking lot.

**Naturalist:** None on board.

Owner James M. Tate says that Depoe Bay is the "whale-watching capital of Oregon" because the whales come closer to the coast than anywhere else and because some whales spend all spring, summer, and fall in the area. "That provides us with great whale-watching cruises year-round," Tate says. "Overall, we want people to feel safe, good, and happy. That's what we're about." The fewest sightings come in the months of February, May, and November.

# Enterprise

P.O. Box 575, Depoe Bay, OR 97341
(503) 765-2245

**Whales:** Gray

**Season:** December through April

**Boats:** One boat; 30 passengers

**Trips:** Trips regularly scheduled from 9 a.m. until dark, according to demand and the tide. Weekends are the busiest days.

**Fare:** Adults, $8 per hour; children: ages 7 to 12, $5 per hour; 7 and younger, free. Reservations advised.

**Departure:** Trips leave from the town harbor. Off Highway 101, turn east at Bay Street (the only stoplight in town) and follow the road past the Coast Guard station. Dock is 100 feet from the parking lot.

**Naturalist:** None on board.

"Depoe Bay is the world's smallest harbor, and whales come in close to shore," says Mary de Belloy, who with her husband, Dave, owns the Enterprise. "We have seen whales feeding, mating, breaching, spyhopping, and cows with their calves. The north migration, in the spring, is the best time because the whales are slower."

## Tradewinds Charters

P.O. Box 123, Depoe Bay, OR 97341
(800) 445-8730 or (503) 765-2345

| | |
|---|---|
| **Whales:** | Gray |
| **Season:** | All year |
| **Boats:** | Twelve boats; 180 passengers altogether |
| **Trips:** | Nine trips daily; some 1-hour and some 2-hour. Hourly trips leave from 9 a.m. until dark. The 2-hour trips leave at 11 a.m. and 1 p.m. Hourly trips on weekends are the most crowded. |
| **Fare:** | Adults, $9 an hour; children: ages 5 to 12, $6 an hour; 4 and younger, free. Group rates available. Reservations advised. Custom packages are available through several local motels; write for information. |
| **Departure:** | Trips leave from Tradewinds office on Highway 101 in downtown Depoe Bay at the north end of the bridge. Check-in is 30 minutes before departure. |
| **Naturalist:** | Sometimes. |

"Our crews are extremely friendly and make each trip a fun experience," owner Rich Allyn notes. "We have clean, modern vessels, and if a naturalist is not aboard, each of our crew is extremely knowledgeable and provides a very good talk about the whales."

## GARIBALDI

## Troller Deep Sea Fishing Charters

P.O. Box 605, 604 Mooring Basin Road, Garibaldi, OR 97118
(800) 546-3666 or (503) 322-3666

| | |
|---|---|
| **Whales:** | Gray |
| **Season:** | February through April |
| **Boats:** | Eight boats; 140 passengers altogether |

| | |
|---|---|
| **Trips:** | Two 2-hour trips on weekdays and three on weekends, scheduled whenever the ocean permits. Saturday is the busiest day. |
| **Fare:** | $15 per person. Reservations required. |
| **Departure:** | Trips leave from the Garibaldi boat basin, just off Highway 101. |
| **Naturalist:** | None on board. |

Captain Jim Violette, the owner of Troller Deep Sea Fishing Charters, says his pelagic bird trips are as popular as his whale-watch trips.

## NEWPORT

# Adventure Travel Service

P.O. Box 159, Newport, OR 97365
(503) 336-1332

| | |
|---|---|
| **Whales:** | Gray |
| **Season:** | Early spring and late fall |
| **Boats:** | Two boats; 20 and 6 passengers |
| **Trips:** | Two-hour trips scheduled according to demand |
| **Fare:** | Adults, $16; children under 3, free. Group rates available. Reservations advised. |
| **Departure:** | Trips leave from Dock 3 on Bay Boulevard. |
| **Naturalist:** | None on board. |

"We do excursions and fishing trips year-round, but the best time to treat the whole family to the majesty of the gray whale is early spring and late fall," says a spokeswoman.

## Newport Sportfishing

1000 S.E. Bay Boulevard, Newport, OR 97365
(800) 828-8777 or (503) 265-7558

| | |
|---|---|
| **Whales:** | Gray |
| **Season:** | December 1 through May 1 |
| **Boats:** | Seven boats; 30 passengers each |
| **Trips:** | One 2-hour trip daily at 1 p.m. |
| **Fare:** | Adults, $15; children under 12, $7.50. Reservations required. |
| **Departure:** | Trips leave from the Embarcadero Marina, on Bay Boulevard. |
| **Naturalist:** | Yes |

"Location and friendly people" are what make Newport Sportfishing special, according to owners John and Roz Vostinak.

## South Beach Charters

P.O. Box 1446, Newport, OR 97365
(503) 867-7200

| | |
|---|---|
| **Whales:** | Gray |
| **Season:** | November through June |
| **Boats:** | Four boats; 6 to 28 passengers each |
| **Trips:** | One 2-hour trip daily at 1:30 p.m. (A second trip may be added, according to demand.) Saturday is the busiest day. |
| **Fare:** | $16 per person. Reservations required. |
| **Departure:** | Trips leave from the South Beach Marina, on the south side of Yaquina Bay in Newport. |
| **Naturalist:** | None on board. |

Owners Russell and Marilyn Sisley work with the Hatfield Marine Science Center.

# WASHINGTON

## ANACORTES

### Discovery Charters

P.O. Box 636, Anacortes, WA 98221
(206) 293-4248

| | |
|---|---|
| **Whales:** | Orca, minke |
| **Season:** | May through September |
| **Boats:** | One boat; 46 passengers |
| **Trips:** | One 7- to 8-hour trip daily; usually departs at 9 a.m. Weekends are the most crowded. Occasional two-day trips are available and include a night in Friday Harbor. |
| **Fare:** | Individual fares: adults, $40; children under 12, $25. Group tours: $25 per person per day. Motel fee extra for two-day trips. Prices include lunch. Reservations required. |
| **Departure:** | Trips leave from Cap Sante marina in Anacortes. From Commercial Avenue (the main street), turn right on Eleventh Street. Cross the railroad tracks and go into the Cap Sante marina parking lot. |
| **Naturalist:** | Knowledgeable skipper serves as narrator. |

"All our trips are nature tours. We regularly see tufted puffins, bald eagles, harbor seals, seabirds, California sea lions, river otters, and porpoises as well as whales," tour operator Jess Starnes says. "And lunch is always rated as outstanding!"

On the two-day trips, participants stay overnight in Friday Harbor on San Juan Island and tour the Whale Museum there.

## Elakah! Kayak Tours

P.O. Box 4092, Bellingham, WA 98227
(206) 734-7270

| | |
|---|---|
| **Whales:** | Orca, porpoise |
| **Season:** | July through September |
| **Boats:** | Six kayaks; 2 passengers each |
| **Trips:** | Trips lasting from one to four days, kayaking and camping in the San Juan Islands. |
| **Fare:** | Extended trips range from $69 to $395. Fare includes kayak instruction, guides, gear, and meals on overnight trips. Reservations required. Custom trips for one to ten days are available for groups of four or more. Call for dates and prices. |
| **Departure:** | Kayaks leave from Lopez Island, a 45-minute ferry ride from Anacortes. |
| **Naturalist:** | Guides knowledgeable about the natural and cultural history of the area accompany each trip. |

"Elakah! Kayak Tours has the capability of bringing nature and people together and producing a very special form of magic," says owner Jennifer Hahn. "The non-motorized aspect of Elakah! is enchanting in itself; what better way to see, feel, and enjoy nature than in a small, quiet boat not much above sea level!"

## Seattle Aquarium

Pier 59, Waterfront Park, Seattle, WA 98101
(206) 386-4329

| | |
|---|---|
| **Whales:** | Orca |
| **Season:** | June through August |
| **Boats:** | One boat; 40 passengers |
| **Trips:** | Eighteen 8-hour trips from mid-July through the end of August. Trips are scheduled for Saturdays or Sundays at 9:30 a.m. |
| **Fare:** | Adults, $65; children, $60. Reservations required. Cost includes pretrip lecture scheduled for a day or two before each cruise. |

**Departure:**    Trips leave from Cap Sante marina in Anacortes. From Commercial Avenue (the main street), turn right on Eleventh Street. Cross the railroad tracks and go into the Cap Sante marina parking lot.

**Naturalist:**    Yes

"The Seattle Aquarium offers boat trips for the general public to observe whales during two seasons of the year," says Leo J. Shaw, marine education specialist at the Aquarium. "During March and April, the Aquarium offers gray whale-watching trips from Westport, Washington, on weekends. During the months of June, July, and August, we offer cruises in the San Juan Islands of Washington state to search for the local killer whales."

## BELLINGHAM

# Island Mariner Cruises

#5 Harbor Esplanade, Bellingham, WA 98225
(206) 734-8866

**Whales:**    Orca, minke

**Season:**    Late May through mid-September

**Boats:**    One boat; 149 passengers

**Trips:**    One 8-hour trip every Saturday from late May through mid-September; also one 8-hour trip every Monday and Wednesday in July and August.

**Fare:**    This 90-mile cruise through the San Juan Islands costs $45 for adults, $40 for senior citizens, and $35 for children 15 and under. Reservations advised.

**Departure:**    Trips leave from Squalicum Harbor in Bellingham. From Interstate 5, take the Meridian Street exit (Exit 256) and drive south for 0.5 miles. Turn right on Squalicum Way and drive 1.8 miles. Turn right on Coho Way and drive 2 blocks to the Esplanade Building. The office is at the far east end.

**Naturalist:** Yes

"We are the only company offering whale-watching cruises in the San Juan Islands that has a departure point on the mainland," owner Terry Buzzard writes. "Our company has provided cruises for the National Audubon Society, National Wildlife Federation, Pacific Science Center, and Greenpeace Northwest."

## SAN JUAN ISLANDS

### Blue Moon Explorations

P.O. Box 2568WW, Bellingham, WA 98227
(206) 966-8805

| | |
|---|---|
| **Whales:** | Orca |
| **Season:** | May through September |
| **Boats:** | Eight 2-person kayaks |
| **Trips:** | Nine 3-, 4- and 5-day trips in the San Juan Islands and Johnstone Strait, which include whale watching, bird watching, hiking, and kayaking. Participants camp. Some trips are for women only. |
| **Fare:** | Fares range from $80 to $100 a day, which includes kayaks, camping accommodations and meals, safety equipment, instruction, and guides. Reservations required. |
| **Departure:** | Trips begin on San Juan Island or at Alert Bay, B.C. |
| **Naturalist:** | Yes |

Owner Kathleen Grimbly says, "Blue Moon Explorations are designed to expand our awareness of the many intricate relationships in the web of life. Traveling by kayak, we experience the whales and the web of life that supports them more intimately and less intrusively. Our trips are designed for people of all ages and abilities."

## Bon Accord Charters

P.O. Box 472, Friday Harbor, WA 98250
(206) 378-5921

| | |
|---|---|
| **Whales:** | Orca, minke |
| **Season:** | May through October |
| **Boats:** | One boat, the 30-foot *Bon Accord*; 6 passengers |
| **Trips:** | One 5-hour trip daily at noon. Other trips available on request. |
| **Fare:** | $55 per person. Reservations advised. |
| **Departure:** | Trips leave from Slip M-8 at the main dock at the foot of town in Friday Harbor. |
| **Naturalist:** | The captain is a naturalist, trained by Earth Trust. |

"We are the only operator that takes small groups for a custom, personalized tour," says Captain Richard Karon. "Our boat is a custom-built wood trawler with all comforts. In addition to whales, we see harbor seals, Dall's porpoise, elephant seals, bald eagles, and numerous seabirds."

## Northwest Outdoor Center

2100 Westlake Avenue North, Seattle, WA 98109
(206) 281-9694

| | |
|---|---|
| **Whales:** | Orca |
| **Season:** | June through August |
| **Boats:** | Kayaks |
| **Trips:** | Three-day trips in the San Juan Islands. Participants camp overnight. |
| **Fare:** | Adults, $195. Reservations required. |
| **Departure:** | Trips leave from Smallpox Bay, west of Friday Harbor on San Juan Island. |
| **Naturalist:** | Yes |

The Northwest Outdoor Center was founded by five "paddling enthusiasts/mani-acs" in 1980. Co-founder Bill Stewart notes, "Seeing a pod of killer whales up close from a kayak is a very moving experience." Classes, longer trips, and Christmas caroling by kayak are also available.

## Resource Institute

2319 North 45th Street, #139, Seattle, WA 98103
(206) 784-6762

| | |
|---|---|
| **Whales:** | Orca, minke, humpback, sometimes gray |
| **Season:** | May through October |
| **Boats:** | 65- to 72-foot classic wooden boats; 8 to 10 passengers |
| **Trips:** | Numerous trips, lasting from three to ten days, including several to southeast Alaska. The San Juan Island trips go in search of orcas and minkes in May and October; humpbacks are seen in Alaska June through September. Participants live on board. |
| **Fare:** | Trips cost about $150 to $200 per day. Reservations required. |
| **Departure:** | Trips depart from Friday Harbor in Washington and also from Sitka, Petersburg, Juneau, and Ketchikan in Alaska. |
| **Naturalist:** | Yes |

Seminars along the way (from the San Juan Islands to Alaska) may include natural history, marine biology, wood-carving, photography, psychology, poetry, anthropology, and conservation.

"Groups live on board as we travel and study," says Paige Tyley. The Resource Institute is a nonprofit educational organization.

## San Juan Boat Rentals

P.O. Box 2281, Friday Harbor, WA 98250
(206) 378-3499

| | |
|---|---|
| **Whales:** | Orca, minke |
| **Season:** | May through September |
| **Boats:** | One 30-foot tour boat; 12 passengers |
| **Trips:** | One 3- to 4-hour trip daily, usually at 1:30 p.m. Morning and evening trips during the summer months as needed. |
| **Fare:** | $40 per person. Reservations advised. |
| **Departure:** | Trips leave from Slip M-4 in the Port of Friday Harbor, one block north of the ferry landing. |
| **Naturalist:** | Yes |

Owner and skipper Darrell Roberts says the San Juan Islands are one of the best places in the world to see whales. "Our 30-foot, high-speed tour boat means you spend less time getting to the whales and more time watching them."

## San Juan Kayak Expeditions Inc.

P.O. Box 2041, Friday Harbor, WA 98250
(206) 378-4436

| | |
|---|---|
| **Whales:** | Orca, minke, harbor porpoise |
| **Season:** | Late May through September 30 |
| **Boats:** | Kayaks that hold two people each |
| **Trips:** | Three-, four- and five-day trips available. Participants camp overnight. Weekends are busiest. |
| **Fare:** | Prices range from $220 for the three-day trip to $345 for the five-day trip. Reservations required. |
| **Departure:** | Trips leave from Friday Harbor, with transportation to the launch point. |
| **Naturalist:** | Yes |

Guide and founder Tim Thomsen notes, "Kayaking among whales is quite a thrill."

## Sea Quest Expeditions/Zoetic Research

P.O. Box 2424R, Friday Harbor, WA 98250
(206) 378-5767

| | |
|---|---|
| **Whales:** | Orca, minke, Dall's porpoise, harbor porpoise |
| **Season:** | May through October |
| **Boats:** | Sea kayaks |
| **Trips:** | One-, two-, three-, and five-day kayak trips in the San Juan Islands. Participants camp overnight at locations accessible only by boat. |
| **Fare:** | Depending on the length of the trip, fares range from $49 to $399 per person, including meals. Reservations required. |
| **Departure:** | Trips leave from the ferry terminal in Friday Harbor. Transportation is provided to the launch site, which varies according to the tides. |
| **Naturalist:** | A professional field biologist/educator serves as naturalist. |

Mark Lewis, executive director, notes, "On numerous occasions, we have found our flotilla of kayaks completely infiltrated by orcas! We have never felt threatened during these exciting encounters. In fact, the whales are very careful about their movements when close to kayaks. We have even had participants be able to reach out and touch a wild orca that spyhopped next to the kayak!"

Lewis says that beginners are welcome—90 percent of the participants have never been in a kayak before. He adds that no other kayak outfitter in the area operates trips designed specifically to see whales 100 percent of the time or uses biologists as naturalists.

Sea Quest Expeditions also offers research trips and will design custom trips. College credit is available for all programs.

## Shearwater Adventures

P.O. Box 787, Eastsound, WA 98245
(206) 376-4699

| | |
|---|---|
| **Whales:** | Orca, minke, harbor porpoise |
| **Season:** | April through October |
| **Boats:** | Sea kayaks |
| **Trips:** | One 6-hour trip daily at 10 a.m. |
| **Fare:** | $49 per person. A portion of the fare goes to the Whale Museum's research program. Reservations required. |
| **Departure:** | Trips leave from the Whale Museum in Friday Harbor. Transportation to launch site provided. |
| **Naturalist:** | Yes |

"We use sea kayaks, so we have less impact on the whales, plus we are in a craft that is less separate from the water environment than a motorboat," says Tom Carter at Shearwater Adventures. "Because we do not always see orcas, we integrate the natural history of Puget Sound as a whole, including marine mammals, birds, flora, and fauna. But it sure is a special and unique occasion to be in the presence of whales."

Carter says that many people ask if the orcas hit the kayaks, but after more than 14 years paddling with whales, he says it has never happened.

## Western Prince Cruises

P.O. Box 418, Port of Friday Harbor, Friday Harbor, WA 98250
(206) 378-5315 or (800) 757-ORCA (in service January 1995)

| | |
|---|---|
| **Whales:** | Orca, minke, Dall's porpoise |
| **Season:** | May through early October |
| **Boats:** | Two boats; 33 and 6 passengers respectively |
| **Trips:** | One 4-hour trip daily (except Tuesday) at 1 p.m. plus morning trips on some Wednesdays and Saturdays |
| **Fare:** | Adults, $40; children: 12 through 17, $29. Private charter rates available. |

**Departure:**    Trips leave from the Port of Friday Harbor, 80 miles northwest of Seattle on I-5 and via the San Juan ferry from Anacortes.

**Naturalist:**    Naturalist narrates each trip.

"Our departure point is less than one hour from prime whale territory," says owner Jean Van Leuven. "We've operated whale search/wildlife tours for nine years, and besides whales, we regularly see harbor seals, bald eagles, and Dall's porpoises. Calm waters are the norm since we operate on a protected inland sea."

## WESTPORT

### Cachalot Whale Watch

2511 Westhaven Drive, , P.O. Box 348, Westport, WA 98595
(206) 268-0323

**Whales:**        Gray

**Season:**        March through May

**Boats:**         One boat; 30 passengers

**Trips:**         One 2-1/2-hour trip daily at noon on weekdays; two trips daily at 11 a.m. and 2 p.m. on weekends

**Fare:**          Adults, $19.95; children 12 and under, $11.50 Reservations advised.

**Departure:**     Boat leaves from Float 12 in the Westport Marina.

**Naturalist:**    Captain narrates.

Owners Darlene and David Camp are carrying on the family whale-watching business.

## Deep Sea Charters/Whale Watching Headquarters

Across from Float 6, Box 1115, Westport, WA 98595
(206) 268-9300

**Whales:**      Gray

**Season:**      March through May

**Boats:**       Nine boats; 6 to 20 passengers

**Trips:**       Several 2-1/2-hour trips scheduled daily.

**Fare:**        $25 per person. Family and school rates available. Reservations required. Deep Sea Charters and several local motels offer a $39.50 package deal that includes a night's lodging and a whale watch.

**Departure:**   Trips leave from Float 6 off Westhaven Drive, northeast of the Westport Maritime Museum.

**Naturalist:**  None on board.

Owner Larry Giese notes, "Before we leave the dock, we have an educational discussion about the gray whale and what you can expect. Gray whales are sighted 98 percent of the time." Free illustrated informational brochures are also available.

## Seattle Aquarium

Pier 59, Waterfront Park, Seattle, WA 98101
(206) 386-4329

**Whales:**      Gray

**Season:**      Mid-March through the end of April

**Boats:**       Several small fishing boats; maximum of 100 passengers altogether

**Trips:**       Three-hour trips are offered on Saturdays or Sundays.

**Fare:**        Adults, $28; children, $19.50. Reservations required. Fee includes pretrip educational program scheduled a few days in advance and on day of trip.

**Departure:**   Trips leave from Westport dock at the foot of Dock Street at Westhaven Drive.

**Naturalist:**    Naturalist on board from the Aquarium staff.

The Seattle Aquarium offers boat trips for the general public to observe whales during two seasons of the year: from Westport during March and April, to observe gray whales, and from Anacortes in June, July, and August, to search for orcas in the San Juan Islands.

"The Seattle Aquarium does not display whales, dolphins, or porpoises," notes Leo J. Shaw, marine education specialist. "Our marine mammals on display are harbor seals, northern fur seals, and sea otters."

# Westport Whale Watch/Ocean Charters Inc.

2315 W. Westhaven Drive, P.O. Box 548, Westport, WA 98595
(206) 268-9144

| | |
|---|---|
| **Whales:** | Gray, sometimes orca |
| **Season:** | March 1 through mid-May |
| **Boats:** | Six boats, all 50 feet or longer; from 6 to 25 passengers |
| **Trips:** | One 2-hour trip daily at 10 a.m. on weekdays; two trips at 10 a.m. and 2 p.m. on Saturdays and Sundays. (Times may vary with the tides.) Saturday is the busiest day. |
| **Fare:** | Adults, $24.50; children 12 and under, $13.50. Group rates and special youth group fares available. Reservations required. |
| **Departure:** | Trips leave from Float 6 at the Westport Marina. In the dock area, turn left at the blinking light. Look for the only two-story building on the block. |
| **Naturalist:** | Sometimes. |

"Westport Whale Watch/Ocean Charters was the pioneer in establishing whale-watch tours out of Westport in 1979," notes the owner. "Our tour includes a seminar, presented by knowledgeable narrators to familiarize you with the history, migration, and social habits of the gray whales."

## Whales Ahoy/Salmon Charters Inc.

P.O. Box 545, 2329 Westhaven Drive, Westport, WA 98595
(206) 268-9150

**Whales:**      Gray, occasional orca

**Season:**      March through May

**Boats:**      Five boats; 24 passengers each

**Trips:**      One 2-1/2-hour trip daily at 9:30 a.m. on weekdays; two on weekends, at 9:30 a.m. and 1 or 1:30 p.m., depending on the tide. Saturday is the busiest day.

**Fare:**      Adults, $23; senior citizens over 60, $21; children 12 and under, $13. Group rates available. Reservations advised.

**Departure:**      Trips leave from Float 8 at the Westport Marina. All roads in Westport lead to the water. When you reach the sea, turn left and go about one block to Whales Ahoy/Salmon Charters office.

**Naturalist:**      All trips narrated.

"As a retired marine biologist and president of our company, I try to provide maximum educational delivery to the whale-watching public," says Dr. John Smith. "I personally provide a lecture on whales every Saturday and Sunday at the Westport Museum."

# MUSEUMS, AQUARIUMS, AND SCIENCE CENTERS

## OREGON

### Oregon Coast Aquarium

2820 S.E. Ferry Slip Road, Newport, OR 97365
(503) 867-3474; Fax (503) 867-6846

Opened in May of 1992, the Oregon Coast Aquarium sits on 32 bayfront acres. Indoors, three galleries focus on plant and animal communities living near shore and marine environments along the Oregon coast. A large changing exhibit area houses exciting new displays each year. A theater presents one program on the gray whale migration and another on sharks. The outdoor exhibits include a walk-through seabird aviary, an undersea coastal cave, and landscaped habitats where sea otters, seals, and sea lions are on display.

In summer, the Aquarium is open daily from 9 a.m. to 6 p.m. Winter hours are 10 a.m. to 4:30 p.m. daily. Adults, $7.75; senior citizens and students, $5.50; children ages 4 to 12, $3.30.

### Oregon State University

Mark O. Hatfield Marine Science Center, 2030 South Marine Science Drive, Newport, OR 97365
(503) 867-0100; Fax (503) 867-0105

Aquarium tanks and interpretive exhibits draw nearly half a million people each year to the Science Center, where visitors may observe and touch sea creatures. Special exhibits include sculptures of thirteen different whales, with accompanying text in Braille, and the skeletons of a minke whale and a harbor porpoise. Special school programs are also available. The public area is open daily, 10 a.m. to 4 p.m.; summer hours are 10 a.m. to 6 p.m. Admission is free.

The Extension Service of Oregon State University also trains volunteers who are posted along the Oregon coast from December 26 through January 1 and again during the third week in March, at sites from Astoria to Brookings. Signs at the staffed lookouts read "WHALE WATCHING SPOKEN HERE," and volunteers are available from 10 a.m. to 1 p.m., rain or shine. They hand out educational materials and answer questions for the more than 20,000 people who visit the lookouts each year. Indoor programs are also available. A free talk and film are presented daily at 2 p.m. during whale-watch season.

## WASHINGTON

## Seattle Aquarium

Pier 59, Waterfront Park, Seattle, WA 98101
(206) 386-4320; Fax (206) 386-4328

The Seattle Aquarium features exhibits on sea life, a tide pool, a discovery lab, a salt marsh, and the Underwater Dome, where visitors may see salmon, sharks, octopus, and numerous other marine marvels that live in Puget Sound. In addition to permanent and special exhibits, the Aquarium also offers tours, classes, and a lecture series.

The Aquarium is open from 10 a.m. to 6 p.m. daily. Admission is $6.75 for adults; $5.25 for senior citizens over 65; $4.25 for children 6 to 18; and $1.75 for children age 3 to 5. Under 3, free.

## The Whale Museum

62 First Street North, Friday Harbor, WA 98250
(206) 378-4710

A research and development institution as well as a museum, the Whale Museum collects and disseminates information on the marine environment, with special emphasis on whales, dolphins, and porpoises. Programs include exhibits, workshops, field courses in whale biology, a teaching curriculum, lab work, and educational programs as well as whale-watch trips.

The Whale Museum is open seven days a week, 10 a.m. to 5 p.m. Memorial Day weekend through September and 11 a.m. to 4 p.m. October through May. Admission is $3 for adults, $2.50 for senior citizens and students; children under 12, $1.50; under 5, free. Group rates are available.

## Westport Maritime Museum

2201 Westhaven Drive, P.O. Box 1074, Westport, WA 98595
(206) 268-0078

Housed in a former Coast Guard station, the Westport Maritime Museum reflects Westport's ties to the bounty of the sea, forests, and Gray Harbor. Adjacent to the station sits a Whale House, which contains marine mammal skeletons, including complete gray and minke whales.

Hours are noon to 4 p.m. on weekends in April and May, noon to 4 p.m. Wednesday through Sunday from June through September, and tours by request from noon to 4 p.m. in the winter months. Admission is free, with donations to the Westport-South Beach Historical Society heartily welcomed.

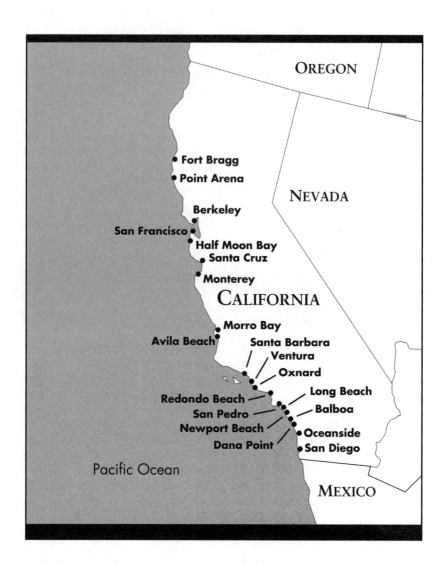

# CALIFORNIA

You may choose from nearly 50 whale-watch trip operators off the coast of California. In southern California, competition is lively in areas where several trip operators in the same area vie for passengers.

In northern California, where the tides and weather are less consistent than in southern California, whale watching is less popular but entirely possible.

If you plan to be in California sometime during the annual gray whale migration (between late December and April), you will have no trouble booking a whale-watch trip in most coastal towns. Yet surprisingly few companies offer trips from June to October, when blue whales, orcas, and humpbacks are in the area. If you plan to be in California then, call or write to ask about "off-season" whale-watch trips or private charters.

Many trip operators on the California coast are primarily sportfishing charter companies that turn their attention to whale watching during the early months of the year. Their commitment to customer service has kept them in business for 15 or 20 years or more, and most of them strive to provide enjoyable, educational whale-watch trips.

Because it's so unusual not to see gray whales during the annual migration, many trip operators guarantee sightings and offer a "whale check" for a free trip in the unlikely event that whales are nowhere to be found.

# TOURISM INFORMATION

**CALIFORNIA**
### California Division of Tourism
801 K Street, Suite 1600, Sacramento, CA 95814

(800) TO-CALIF

# WHALE-WATCHING TRIPS

## CALIFORNIA

### AVILA BEACH

#### Paradise Sportfishing

P.O. Box 356, Pier 3, Avila Beach, CA 93424
(805) 595-7200

| | |
|---|---|
| **Whales:** | Gray, humpback |
| **Season:** | January 1 through April 1 |
| **Boats:** | Four boats; 58, 48, 48, 41 passengers |
| **Trips:** | Two 2-hour trips daily at 10 a.m. and 1 p.m. Saturday is the busiest day. |
| **Fare:** | Adults, $15; children 12 and under, $10. Reservations advised. |
| **Departure:** | Trips leave from Pier 3 on Avila Beach, just 3 miles off Highway 101. |
| **Naturalist:** | None on board. |

Owner John Howell is eager to take whale watchers out to sea during the gray whale migration.

## BALBOA

### American Cetacean Society

Orange County Whalewatch, 400 Main Street, Balboa, CA 92661
(714) 675-9881

| | |
|---|---|
| **Whales:** | Gray, minke, blue, orca, sperm, Pacific white-sided dolphin |
| **Season:** | December 26 through late March |
| **Boats:** | Three boats; 120, 147, and 350 passengers |
| **Trips:** | Weekdays, two trips at 10 a.m. and 1 p.m.; Saturdays and Sundays, three trips at 9 a.m., noon, and 2:30 p.m. All trips last 2 hours. Weekend noon trips are the busiest. |
| **Fare:** | Adults, $12; children 12 and younger, $9; seniors, $9. Groups of 20 or more on weekdays, $9 each. Reservations advised. |
| **Departure:** | Trips leave from Balboa Pavilion, on the Pacific Coast Highway and Balboa Boulevard. Take the 55 Freeway south to Newport Boulevard; follow to Main Street and turn left. |
| **Naturalist:** | Naturalist from the American Cetacean Society/Orange County Chapter. |

The American Cetacean Society promotes education, conservation, and research related to marine mammals and their habitat. According to whale-watch coordinator Melissa Groswald, the Orange County chapter supports those activities and makes the public aware of them through special programs. A percentage of each ticket price goes to the American Cetacean Society.

### Catalina Passenger Service

Balboa Pavilion, 400 Main Street, Balboa, CA 92661
(714) 673-5245; Fax (714) 673-8340

| | |
|---|---|
| **Whales:** | Gray, occasional minke, blue, and dolphins |
| **Season:** | January through mid-March |
| **Boats:** | One luxury catamaran; 400 passengers |
| **Trips:** | One 2- to 3-hour trip at 10 a.m. on Tuesdays and Wednesdays. |

**Fare:** Adults, $12; children 12 and under, $6. Group rates and senior citizen rates available. Reservations required.

**Departure:** Trips leave from Balboa Pavilion. Take the 55 Freeway south to Newport Boulevard; follow to Main Street and turn left.

**Naturalist:** Naturalist from the American Cetacean Society.

Betsy Sturgeon from Catalina Passenger Service notes that passengers ride on a luxury catamaran with three decks, inside and outside seating, a bar, and a snack bar.

# Davey's Locker Sportfishing

400 Main Street, Balboa, CA 92661
(714) 673-1434

**Whales:** Gray, Pacific white-sided dolphin, common dolphin

**Season:** December 26 through April 1

**Boats:** Five boats; up to 148 passengers each

**Trips:** Weekdays, two trips at 10 a.m. and 1 p.m. Saturdays and Sundays, three trips at 9 a.m., noon, and 2:30 p.m. All trips are 2 hours long. Weekends are the busiest times.

**Fare:** Adults, $12, children, $6. Special school rates available. Reservations required.

**Departure:** Trips leave from Balboa Pavilion. Take the 55 Freeway south to Newport Boulevard; follow to Main Street and turn left.

**Naturalist:** Naturalist from the American Cetacean Society.

## BERKELEY

### Dolphin Charters

1007 Leneve Place, El Cerrito, CA 94530
(800) 548-7555 or (415) 527-9622; Fax (707) 839-4656

| | |
|---|---|
| **Whales:** | Gray in winter; humpback and blue in spring and fall |
| **Season:** | October through May |
| **Boats:** | One boat, the 50-foot *Delphinus*; 44 passengers |
| **Trips:** | Selected day-long trips on weekends, some overnight and weeklong trips in summer to various destinations, including Point Reyes, San Francisco Bay, and the Farallon Islands. Saturday is the busiest day. |
| **Fare:** | Trips range from $49 to $69. Reservations advised. |
| **Departure:** | Trips leave from the Berkeley marina, at the foot of University Avenue, just off I-80. |
| **Naturalist:** | Yes |

Dolphin Charters and its sister company, Biological Journeys, specialize in whale-watch trips worldwide. "We have had nearly 100 percent success in seeing gray whales on trips to Point Reyes in January and March," says owner and marine biologist Ronn Storro-Patterson.

The Farallon Islands cruises provide an opportunity to see a variety of whale species, including blue and humpback, as well as sharks, pinnipeds (seals, sea lions, walruses, etc.), and other sea life.

## DANA POINT

### Dana Wharf Sportfishing

34675 Golden Lantern, Dana Point, CA 92629
(714) 496-5794

| | |
|---|---|
| **Whales:** | Gray |

**Season:**     December 26 through March 31

**Boats:**      Ten boats; 6 to 99 passengers each

**Trips:**      Weekdays, three trips at 10 a.m., noon, and 2 p.m.; Saturdays and Sundays, five trips at 8 a.m., 10 a.m., noon, 2 and 4 p.m. Nine trips daily during the annual Dana Point Festival of Whales, which includes educational programs and cultural events as well as whale-watch trips. All trips last 2 hours. Early morning trips on Saturdays are the busiest.

**Fare:**       Adults, $12; senior citizens, $7; children 12 and under, $7 on weekdays. Reservations required. Discounts on whale-watch trips are available for guests at Dana Point Resort, the Ritz-Carlton, Dana Point Inn, and Best Western Marina Inn.

**Departure:**  Trips leave from the Dana Wharf Docks in Dana Point Harbor. From the Pacific Coast Highway, follow Golden Lantern down to the water.

**Naturalist:** Yes

The Dana Point Festival of Whales is held each year in February and March to celebrate the arrival of the gray whales. Mike Hansen, general manager of Dana Wharf Sportfishing, notes, "Emphasis is placed on the local marine environment, but the whales are the center of attention."

# FORT BRAGG

## Captain Jack

P.O. Box 1002, Fort Bragg, CA 95437
(707) 964-4550

**Whales:**     Gray

**Season:**     January 1 through April 15

**Boats:**      One boat, the *Trek II*

**Trips:**      Afternoon trips on some weekdays, according to demand. One trip on Saturdays and one on Sundays, at 1 p.m. Up to 4 whale-watch trips a day during the Mendocino-Fort Bragg Whale Festival in March. All trips are 1 to 2 hours long. Generally, Saturday is the busiest day.

| **Fare:** | Adults, $20; children, $15; senior citizens over 65, $17.50. Reservations required. Guests at the Trade Winds Motel receive discount coupons for Captain Jack whale watches. |
| --- | --- |
| **Departure:** | Trips leave from Sportsman's Dock on the Noyo River. The dock is at the end of North Harbor Drive on the north side of the river under the green bridge. |
| **Naturalist:** | None on board. |

Captain Jack notes, "The *Trek II* is high in the bow, so you can look right down on the whales. Great for photographers! Not only will you have a perfect view of the whales but also a fantastic panorama of the rugged Mendocino coastline."

# Lady Irma II

P.O. Box 103, Fort Bragg, CA 95437
(707) 964-3854

| **Whales:** | Gray, occasional orca, humpback, finback |
| --- | --- |
| **Season:** | January 1 through April 15 |
| **Boats:** | One boat; 22 passengers |
| **Trips:** | One 2-hour trip daily at 1 p.m. |
| **Fare:** | Adults and children, $20. Reservations advised. |
| **Departure:** | Trips leave from the Wharf Restaurant on the Noyo River. As you travel north on Highway 2, make the first right after the Noyo River Bridge. |
| **Naturalist:** | None on board. |

"There is a whale festival in this area that starts in Mendocino the second weekend in March and ends in Fort Bragg the following weekend. On those weekends, we run four whale-watch trips a day. A wine tasting, whale run, and arts and crafts shows are all part of the festival," says owner Rick Thornton.

## Misty II Charters

P.O. Box 223, Fort Bragg, CA 95437
(707) 961-7161

| | |
|---|---|
| **Whales:** | Gray |
| **Season:** | February through April |
| **Boats:** | One boat; 26 passengers |
| **Trips:** | Two to three trips daily, by reservation. Departure times vary, but all trips are two hours long. |
| **Fare:** | $20 per person. Reservations required. Discounts for groups of 10 or more. |
| **Departure:** | Trips leave from Noyo Fishing Center on the Noyo River, at the foot of the hill on North Harbor Drive. |
| **Naturalist:** | None on board. |

Charlie and Peggy Johnson specialize in personal attention. "We're family owned and operated. During the whale festivals in Mendocino and Fort Bragg, a whale-watching trip is a must!"

# HALF MOON BAY

## Huck Finn Sportfishing

P.O. Box 1432, El Granada, CA 94018
(800) 572-2934 or (415) 726-7133

| | |
|---|---|
| **Whales:** | Gray |
| **Season:** | Mid-December through April |
| **Boats:** | Four boats: the *Quite A Lady*, 22 passengers; the *Hull Cat* and the *Captain Pete*, 38 passengers each; the *Queen of Hearts*, 46 passengers |

**Trips:** Trips by request only on weekdays; 2 or 3 on Saturdays and Sundays at 10 a.m. and 1:30 p.m. All trips are 2-3 hours long. Saturday afternoon trips are the most popular.

**Fare:** $18 for adults, $15 for children ages 5 to 12. No children under five, please. Reservations advised.

**Departure:** Trips leave from Pillar Point Harbor at Half Moon Bay, 25 miles south of San Francisco on Highway 1 (4 miles north of Half Moon Bay on Highway 1).

**Naturalist:** None on board.

"Our primary income is from fishing, but whale watching is something that is a thrill for both my husband, Bill, and me. If the whales were here all the time, we could easily do it every day," says co-owner Peggy Beckett.

"We provide written information on the whales for passengers to take home, books to look at on board, a running commentary on what we are looking for and seeing, and whale certificates for those days we are successful."

## Oceanic Society Expeditions

Fort Mason Center, Building E, San Francisco, CA 94123
(800) 326-7491 or (415) 474-3385

**Whales:** Gray

**Season:** December 26 through April

**Boats:** One boat, the 56-foot *Salty Lady*; 48 passengers

**Trips:** Every Saturday and Sunday and selected Fridays at 10 a.m. and 1:30 p.m. Trips are 3 hours long.

**Fare:** On Fridays, adults, $29; children 5 through 15 and senior citizens over 60, $27. On weekends, adults, $32; children 5 through 15 and senior citizens over 60, $30. No one under 5 permitted on the boat. Group rates available. Reservations required.

**Departure:** Trips leave from Pillar Point Harbor in Half Moon Bay.

**Naturalist:** Naturalists on board from Oceanic Society Expeditions.

Oceanic Society Expeditions was founded in 1972 to create educational world-wide nature programs. The organization's whale-watch program strives to increase public awareness of the importance of protecting our fragile marine environment.

## LONG BEACH

### Belmont Pier Sportfishing

Ocean Avenue and 39th Place, Long Beach, CA 90803
(310) 434-6781

| | |
|---|---|
| **Whales:** | Gray |
| **Season:** | December through April |
| **Boats:** | Two boats; 104 and 149 passengers |
| **Trips:** | One 3-hour trip daily at 10 a.m.; also at 1 p.m. on Saturdays and Sundays. Weekends are busiest. |
| **Fare:** | Weekdays: adults, $8; children 12 and under, $6.50. Weekends: adults, $10; children, $7.50. Group rates are available. Reservations required. |
| **Departure:** | Trips leave from Belmont Pier at Ocean Boulevard and Termino. |
| **Naturalist:** | Skipper narrates each trip. |

Whale-watch coordinator June Ithurralde notes, "Friendly crew and staff coordinator are on hand at all times to ensure your trip is a success." The narrator talks about the migration of the gray whales and their behavior and hands out whale-watch certificates to passengers at the end of each trip.

## Catalina Cruises

320 Golden Shore Boulevard, Long Beach, CA 90802
(800) 888-5939 or (310) 436-5006

| | |
|---|---|
| **Whales:** | Gray |
| **Season:** | December 26 through early April |
| **Boats:** | Five boats; 700-passenger capacity each, but whale-watch cruises are limited to 450 passengers |
| **Trips:** | One 3-hour trip at 10 a.m. most weekdays; two 3-hour trips on Saturdays and Sundays at 10 a.m. and 1:30 p.m. Saturday morning trips are the most popular. |
| **Fare:** | Adults, $14; senior citizens 55 and older, $12; children: ages 3 through 11, $10; under 3, $3. Group rates available. Reservations are required. |
| **Departure:** | Trips leave from the Catalina Landing, 320 Golden Shore Boulevard in downtown Long Beach, at the south end of the Long Beach Freeway 710. |
| **Naturalist:** | Naturalist from Cabrillo Aquarium/American Cetacean Society. |

Manager Paul Sokolowski says, "We have the largest whale-watching vessels on the West Coast, and the most comfortable, too, with three levels of outside viewing and two spacious interior cabins with large windows."

## Long Beach Sportfishing

555 Pico Avenue, Long Beach, CA 90802
(310) 432-8993

| | |
|---|---|
| **Whales:** | Gray, pilot, occasional orca |
| **Season:** | December 26 through early April |
| **Boats:** | Five boats; 497 passengers total |
| **Trips:** | Two 2-hour trips daily at 10 a.m. and 1 p.m. The morning trip is the most popular. |
| **Fare:** | Adults, $12; children ages 2 to 15 and senior citizens, $9. Group rates. Reservations required. |

**Departure:**     Trips leave from Berth 55 at the Long Beach marina. Take the 710 Freeway south to the off-ramp at 7th Avenue and Pico. The marina is across from the ramp.

**Naturalist:**     Captains serve as naturalists.

Between them, owners Veronica Wegner and Don Ashley have two decades in the sportfishing business. "All our captains have been running whale watches for years and have extensive knowledge of gray whales' physical and biological features and their migration and feeding habits," Wegner says.

# Shoreline Village Cruises

429 Shoreline Village Drive, Suite N, Long Beach, CA 90802
(213) 495-5884

**Whales:**     Gray

**Season:**     December 26 through mid-April

**Boats:**     Four boats: a 50-foot cruiser, a 90-foot sailing ship, a 65-foot motor yacht, and a 90-foot motor yacht; 49, 103, 125, and 150 passengers respectively

**Trips:**     Weekdays, one trip at 11 a.m.; two trips on Saturdays and Sundays at 11 a.m. and 1:30 p.m. Trips are about 2 hours long. The Sunday afternoon trip is the busiest.

**Fare:**     Adults, $15; children ages 2 to 12, $8. Twenty percent discount on weekday trips. Reservations required.

**Departure:**     Trips leave from Long Beach and San Pedro, depending on which trip you book. Call for details and directions.

**Naturalist:**     Captain serves as naturalist.

Staff member Kristin Wilson notes, "We guarantee a whale sighting. And we use charter boats with seating for everyone, not old fishing boats."

## Star Party Cruises

140 Marina Drive, Long Beach, CA 90803
(310) 431-6833

| | |
|---|---|
| **Whales:** | Gray |
| **Season:** | January through mid-April |
| **Boats:** | One 65-foot boat; 109 passengers |
| **Trips:** | Two 2-hour trips daily at 10 a.m. and 1 p.m. Weekends are the busiest. |
| **Fare:** | Adults, $13; senior citizens, $12; children, $10. Reservations required. |
| **Departure:** | Trips leave from Seaport Village in Long Beach. |
| **Naturalist:** | Naturalist on board from the Cabrillo Aquarium/American Cetacean Society. |

## MONTEREY

## Chris' Fishing Trips

48 Fisherman's Wharf, Monterey, CA 93940
(408) 375-5951

| | |
|---|---|
| **Whales:** | Gray in winter; blue, minke, and orca in summer and fall |
| **Season:** | December 25 through late March |
| **Boats:** | Four boats; 49 to 75 passengers each |
| **Trips:** | Weekday trips at 10 a.m., noon, and 2 p.m., according to demand. Four 2-hour trips on weekends at 9 a.m., 11 a.m., 1 p.m., and 3 p.m. Saturday is busiest day. |
| **Fare:** | Adults, $12; children, $6. Reservations advised. |
| **Departure:** | Trips leave from Fisherman's Wharf in Monterey, just off the Pacific Grove/Del Monte exit off Highway 1, going south. |

**Naturalist:**    Skipper narrates trips.

Todd Arcoleo, an office staff member, says, "Enjoy an outing with family and friends on Monterey Bay with the gray whales."

# Monterey Sport Fishing
# and Princess Monterey Cruises

96 Old Fisherman's Wharf #1; Monterey, CA 9394
(800) 200-2203 or (408) 372-2203; Fax (408) 375-0391

| | |
|---|---|
| **Whales:** | Gray, humpback, blue, orca, and dolphins |
| **Season:** | Mid-December through March for gray whales; August through October for humpback and blue |
| **Boats:** | Two boats; 80 and 100 passengers |
| **Trips:** | Hourly trips daily starting at 9 a.m. for a minimum of 10 passengers. Trips are 2-3 hours long. Early trips on weekends are the busiest. |
| **Fare:** | Fares vary: $12 to $15 for adults; $8 to $14 for children under 12, depending on length of trip. Group rates available. Reservations required. Discount coupons for whale watches given to guests at Doubletree Hotel, Gosby House Inn, Hyatt Regency, Monterey Plaza, the Sheraton Monterey, and local inns. |
| **Departure:** | Trips leave from Monterey's Fisherman's Wharf, just off the Pacific Grove/Del Monte exit off Highway 1, going south. |
| **Naturalist:** | Naturalist from the American Cetacean Society. |

"Our boats provide excellent opportunities for close-up viewing of one of the world's largest animals in a special and diverse habitat," says a spokesman.

## Oceanic Society Expeditions

Fort Mason Center, Building E, San Francisco, CA 94123
(800) 326-7491 or (415) 441-1106

| | |
|---|---|
| **Whales:** | Humpback, blue |
| **Season:** | August, September, October |
| **Boats:** | One boat, the 55-foot *Point Sur Clipper*. Participants sleep in comfortable lodges. |
| **Trips:** | Six 7-day research expeditions in Monterey Bay and adjacent areas, with 5 days spent on the water observing and photo-identifying Pacific white-sided dolphins, humpbacks, and possibly blue whales and other cetaceans. |
| **Fare:** | $1,190 per person, which includes accommodations, most meals, boat charter, and leadership. Does not include airfare or transfers. |
| **Departure:** | Trips begin and end in Monterey, California. |
| **Naturalist:** | Oceanic Society Expeditions researchers. |

"Monterey Submarine Canyon and adjacent waters support one of the highest diversities of marine mammals in the world: 26 different species have been observed here," says a spokeswoman. "This expedition offers a special opportunity to observe a variety of dolphins and whales, and to contribute to a scientific project."

## Randy's Fishing Trips

66 Fisherman's Wharf #1, Monterey, CA 93940
(408) 372-7440; Fax (408) 372-7445

| | |
|---|---|
| **Whales:** | Gray; occasionally orca, blue |
| **Season:** | January through March |
| **Boats:** | Three boats; 48, 48, and 68 passengers |
| **Trips:** | Three trips each weekday, at 10:30 a.m., 12:30 p.m., and 2:30 p.m. 4 trips on Saturday and Sunday, beginning at 8:30 a.m. All trips last about 2 hours. The busiest day is Saturday. |
| **Fare:** | Adults, $12; children 12 and younger, $8. |

**Departure:**  Trips leave from Fisherman's Wharf, off the Pacific Grove/Del Monte exit off Highway 1, going south.

**Naturalist:**  Crew members narrate trips on weekdays; a marine biologist is on board every weekend.

Owner Peter Bruno, in recognition of the "immeasurable assistance the Society for the Protection of Cruelty to Animals offers our sea life," donates 50 cents to that organization for each passenger.

## Shearwater Journeys

P.O. Box 1445, Soquel, CA 95073
(408) 688-1990

**Whales:**  Gray, blue, fin, humpback, orca, minke

**Season:**  Whale watches all year

**Boats:**  Four boats; 50 to 60 passengers each

**Trips:**  Gray whale trips in January (selected dates). Trips to see blue whales are scheduled from August to October. Weekends are the busiest time.

**Fare:**  Half-day and full-day whale watches in January range from $28 to $55 per person. 1- and 2-day trips from August through October range from $65 to $165. Group rates available. Reservations required.

**Departure:**  Most trips leave from Fisherman's Wharf in Monterey, just off the Pacific Grove/Del Monte exit off Highway 1, going south. Some leave from San Diego or Bodega Bay.

**Naturalist:**  One naturalist from the American Cetacean Society is on board for every 10 passengers.

Owner Debra Love Shearwater notes, "We specialize in seabird trips. The best time of the year is August through October, which is also the best time for seeing blues and humpbacks. One year, on every trip from August through October, we saw blue whales and as many as five species of dolphins in one day." She has made more than 900 boat trips in Monterey Bay.

## MORRO BAY

### Virg's Sportfishing & Whale Watching

1215 Embarcadero, Morro Bay, CA 93422
(800) 932-3473 or (805) 772-1222; Fax (805) 772-2921

| | |
|---|---|
| **Whales:** | Gray |
| **Season:** | Mid-December through March 31 |
| **Boats:** | Six boats; 35 to 75 passengers each |
| **Trips:** | One or two trips, according to demand, on weekdays. Three trips on Saturday and Sunday at 8:30 a.m., 11:30 a.m., and 2:30 p.m. Trips are 2 hours long. The busiest day is Saturday. |
| **Fare:** | Adults, $15; children under 12, $10; children under 5, $5. Discounts for groups. Reservations required. |
| **Departure:** | Trips leave from the dock across from Pacific Gas and Electric. |
| **Naturalist:** | Naturalist on some trips. |

"Sail alongside the gray whale on its way to its winter quarters, and learn about the whales from the experts," says a spokesman from Virg's Sportfishing. "Our knowledgeable sea captains narrate each cruise. Bring your camera!"

## NEWPORT BEACH

### Burns Charters

919 Bayside Drive, #F-2, Newport Beach, CA 92660
(714) 760-1436

| | |
|---|---|
| **Whales:** | Gray, pilot, Pacific white-sided dolphin |
| **Season:** | December 26 through mid-April |
| **Boats:** | One 40-foot sailing yacht, the *Candace Star*; 6 passengers |
| **Trips:** | Half-day or full-day trips by reservation only |

**Fare:** A 3-hour trip costs $249; a full-day charter costs $349. Reservations required.

**Departure:** The *Candace Star* leaves from several convenient marinas; call for information.

**Naturalist:** Captain serves as narrator.

"We offer personalized adventure for individuals, families, and groups who want to charter a fully equipped sailing yacht," says Captain Robert Burns. "The charterer can sail the boat or learn about sailing from us as we cruise toward the migrating whales." Burns has a master's degree in science and extensive teaching experience, and says he is an expert at finding the whales.

# Newport Landing Sportfishing

309 Palm, Suite F, Balboa, CA 92661
(714) 675-0550

**Whales:** Gray, minke, several species of dolphin

**Season:** December 26 through early April

**Boats:** Four boats; 116, 88, 48, and 45 passengers

**Trips:** Two trips each weekday at 10 a.m. and 1 p.m.; three trips on Saturdays and Sundays at 9 a.m., noon, and 2:30 p.m. All trips last 2 to 2-1/2 hours.

**Fare:** Adults, $12; senior citizens, $6; children 12 and younger, $6, on weekdays. Group rates for schools, churches, and community groups. Reservations advised. Newport Beach Meridian Hotel guests receive discounts on Newport Landing Sportfishing whale watches.

**Departure:** Trips leave from Newport Landing Sportfishing dock between Adams and Palm Street, just off Balboa Boulevard.

**Naturalist:** Skipper serves as naturalist.

"Since the gray whale can be readily found within a few miles of the coast, a simple cruise of a few hours lets thousands of people view not only the whales in their natural habitat, but also many species of resident marine animals, such as the common dolphin, bottlenose dolphin, sea lions, birds, and occasionally killer whales and sharks," says staff member George Eddy.

## OCEANSIDE

### Helgren's Oceanside Sportfishing

315 Harbor Drive South, Oceanside, CA 92054
(619) 722-2133; Fax (619) 433-4804

**Whales:** Gray

**Season:** December 26 through March 31

**Boats:** Two boats; 125 and 135 passengers

**Trips:** Weekdays, two trips at 10 a.m. and 1 p.m.; Saturdays and Sundays, two trips at 11:30 a.m. and 2 p.m. All trips are 2 hours long. Saturday midday trip is the busiest.

**Fare:** Adults, $12; senior citizens, $10; children, $9. Group rates available. Reservations required.

**Departure:** Trips leave from Oceanside Harbor. Take Harbor Drive exit off I-5; follow to the boat harbor.

**Naturalist:** Captain narrates trips.

Helgren's has been a family-owned business since 1979. All information provided during the captain's narration is from Dr. Raymond Gilmore at the American Cetacean Society.

## OXNARD

### Channel Islands Sportfishing Center

4151 South Victoria Avenue, Oxnard, CA 93035
(805) 985-8511; Fax (805) 984-6714

**Whales:** Gray

**Season:** January 1 through April 1

**Boats:** One boat, the *Speedtwin*, 100 passengers

**Trips:** Two 3-hour trips daily at 9 a.m. and 1 p.m. Fridays and weekends are the busiest.

| **Fare:** | Adults, $20; senior citizens and children under 11, $15. Reservations advised. |
| **Departure:** | Trips leave from Channel Islands Sportfishing Center at Oxnard. From the 101 Freeway, take Victoria Avenue exit. Follow the sign for Channel Islands Harbor, about 7 miles south on the right. Watch for the big white anchor on the corner. |
| **Naturalist:** | None on board. |

## POINT ARENA

### North Coast Adventures

P.O. Box 84, Point Arena, CA 95468
(707) 882-1626

| **Whales:** | Gray |
| **Season:** | December through April |
| **Boats:** | One boat, a Boston whaler outrage; 6 passengers |
| **Trips:** | Several 2-hour trips daily; call for departure times |
| **Fare:** | $25 per person. Reservations are required. |
| **Departure:** | Trips leave from Arena Cove Pier |
| **Naturalist:** | None on board. |

"Watching whales from a small boat such as mine is a unique experience," says Captain Brian Robbers. "Because Point Arena sticks so far out into the ocean, the whales appear to be 'funnelled' in close to shore. It is not uncommon to sight two or three dozen whales in one trip."

## REDONDO BEACH

### Redondo Sport Fishing

223 North Harbor Drive, Redondo Beach, CA 90277
(310) 372-2111 or (213) 772-2064; Fax (310) 376-4764

**Whales:**       Gray, orca, blue, pilot

**Season:**       December 26 through April 1

**Boats:**        One boat, the *Voyager*; 125 passengers

**Trips:**        Two 3-hour trips daily: 10 a.m. and 1:30 p.m. on weekdays, 9:30 a.m. and 1:30 p.m. on Saturdays and Sundays. Saturday is the busiest day.

**Fare:**         Adults, $12; children under 12, $8. Group rates available, and ride two-for-one on weekday afternoons.

**Departure:**    Trips leave from the Redondo Sport Fishing Pier. From the 405 Freeway, go west on 190th Street to Harbor Drive and then turn south. Pier is across from the Holiday Inn.

**Naturalist:**   Naturalist from the Cabrillo Aquarium/American Cetacean Society aboard each trip.

Owner Terry Turk says, "The *Voyager* is a double-deck excursion boat designed specifically for whale watching, with ample seating for all passengers. This is not a fishing boat, which often has limited seating. Also, we are just minutes from the open ocean, which increases our whale-watching time. We guarantee whales!"

## SAN DIEGO

### Classic Sailing Adventures

2051 Shelter Island Drive, San Diego, CA 92106
(619) 542-0646

**Whales:** Gray

**Season:** December 15 through March 15

**Boats:** One boat, the 35-foot cutter *Mariposa*; 6 passengers

**Trips:** Two trips daily, 8:30 a.m. to 12:30 p.m. and 1 to 5 p.m. Weekend afternoon trips are the most popular.

**Fare:** $40 per person. Price includes beverages and snacks. Lunch is also available. Reservations required.

**Departure:** Trips leave from Shelter Island Marina Inn.

**Naturalist:** None on board.

Captain Roger Anderson says, "As we take only six passengers on each excursion, there is a more personalized experience for everyone on board. If wind permits, we sail as much as possible. Passengers may participate in the sailing or just go along for the spectacular view."

### H&M Landing

2803 Emerson Street, San Diego, CA 92106
(619) 222-1144

**Whales:** Gray

**Season:** December 15 through March 15

**Boats:** Twenty boats; 6 to 100 passengers; limited passenger loads on whale watches

**Trips:** Two 3-hour trips daily at 10 a.m. and 1:30 p.m.; 5-hour trips Thursday through Sunday at 10 a.m. The busiest day is Saturday.

**Fare:**  Adults, $12 for 3 hours and $25 for 5 hours; senior citizens, $10 and $20; children 17 and under, $10 and $15. Overnight cruises also available. Reservations required.

**Departure:**  Trips leave from San Diego Bay, on Emerson, which is off Rosecrans, just before Shelter Island Drive.

**Naturalist:**  Narrative provided by staff.

"We guarantee whale sightings or you get a free reride," notes Katrina Coleman, manager. "We run every day, weather permitting."

# Harbor Sailboats

2040 Harbor Island Drive, Suite 118, San Diego, CA 92101
(800) 854-6625

**Whales:**  Gray

**Season:**  December 15 through March 15

**Boats:**  Thirty sailboats; 6 passengers each

**Trips:**  Two 4-hour trips daily at 9 a.m. and 1 p.m. Weekends are the busiest time.

**Fare:**  Weekdays, $180 for up to 6 passengers; weekends, $230 for up to 6 passengers. Price includes luxury yacht and certified skipper. Reservations required.

**Departure:**  Trips leave from Harbor Island West Marina, 2040 Harbor Island Drive, overlooking San Diego Bay.

**Naturalist:**  Captain serves as narrator.

Owner Tom Hirsh, in business for 25 years, says "We have been able to customize trips exactly to suit the desires of the clients. Since sailing is a quiet way to view the whales, we can get a little closer without as much risk of disturbing them."

## Hornblower/Invader Cruises Inc.

1066 North Harbor Drive, San Diego, CA 92101
(619) 686-8700; Fax (619) 686-8733

| | |
|---|---|
| **Whales:** | Gray |
| **Season:** | Mid-December to mid-March |
| **Boats:** | One boat, the 151-foot luxury yacht *Lord Hornblower*; 500 passengers |
| **Trips:** | Two 3-hour trips daily at 9:30 a.m. and 1:30 p.m. The busiest day is Saturday. |
| **Fare:** | Adults, $15; children ages 3 through 12 and senior citizens over 55, $7.50. Reservations advised. |
| **Departure:** | Trips leave from 1066 North Harbor Drive, on the Embarcadero, next to the cruise ship terminal. |
| **Naturalist:** | All trips narrated. |

Built in 1984 and patterned after the classic steamers of the early 1900s, *Lord Hornblower* has three decks, two dining salons, two parquet dance floors, four bars, and an expansive sundeck for viewing whales. Reservations manager Kevin M. Taylor guarantees whale sightings.

## Islandia Sportfishing

1551 West Mission Bay Drive, San Diego, CA 92109
(619) 222-1164

| | |
|---|---|
| **Whales:** | Gray, finback, Pacific white-sided dolphin |
| **Season:** | Mid-December through late March |
| **Boats:** | One boat, the 85-foot *Dolphin*; 147 passengers |
| **Trips:** | Two trips daily at 10 a.m. and 1 p.m. Trips last 2-3 hours. Saturday midday trips are the busiest. |
| **Fare:** | Adults, $12; senior citizens and children; $8. Guaranteed sighting or ride again free. Group rates are available. Reservations advised. |

**Departure:**   Trips leave from the dock by the Islandia Hyatt Hotel, off West Mission Bay Drive.

**Naturalist:**   Yes

Captain Tim J. Voaklander notes that he and his co-captains have a total of three decades of experience running whale-watch trips. "Symbolically, whales represent great spiritual truths. No wonder whale watching brings peace and tranquillity."

## Orion Charters Inc.

3842 Liggett Drive, San Diego, CA 92106
(619) 574-7504

**Whales:**   Gray, finback, Pacific white-sided dolphin

**Season:**   December 15 through March 31

**Boats:**   Two boats; the 64-foot sailing yacht *Orion* that carries up to 20 passengers and the 34-foot *Catalina* that holds up to 6 passengers

**Trips:**   Two trips daily on weekdays; two on Saturdays and Sundays. Weekend days are the busiest.

**Fare:**   Adults, $39; children, $19.50 for 3-hour personalized sailing and whale-watching trip. Reservations suggested.

**Departure:**   Trips leave from Slip C at the Sheraton Harbor Island East Hotel marina, just across the street from the San Diego International Airport.

**Naturalist:**   The owner holds a degree in marine biology with a special emphasis on oceanography and serves as naturalist.

"Whale watching is a special experience aboard a sailing vessel—quiet, smooth," notes Captain Keith Korporaal. "We quite literally sail alongside the wonderful animals, and we'd love to have you come with us."

## Point Loma Sportfishing

1403 Scott Street, San Diego, CA 92106
(619) 223-1627

| | |
|---|---|
| **Whales:** | Gray |
| **Season:** | December 26 through March 31 |
| **Boats:** | One boat; 107 passengers |
| **Trips:** | One 3-1/2-hour trip daily on weekdays, at 1 p.m.; two 3-1/2-hour trips on weekends, at 9 a.m. and 1 p.m. The afternoon trip on the weekends is the most popular. |
| **Fare:** | Adults, $14; children under 15, $10. Reservations required. |
| **Departure:** | Trips leave from the office, on San Diego Bay, just two miles west of the airport. |
| **Naturalist:** | None on board. |

Owner Ross Hecht has been taking people out to sea since 1947.

## San Diego Harbor Excursion

570 North Harbor Drive, San Diego, CA 92101
(619) 234-4111

| | |
|---|---|
| **Whales:** | Gray; occasional fin, orca, pilot, blue |
| **Season:** | December 26 through the end of March |
| **Boats:** | One boat, the 65-foot *Morning Star*; 103 passengers |
| **Trips:** | Two 3-hour trips daily at 10 a.m. and 1:30 p.m. The most popular day is Saturday. |
| **Fare:** | Adults, $15; senior citizens 55 and older, $13; children 12 and under, $7.50. Reservations required only for large groups. |
| **Departure:** | Trips leave from San Diego Harbor Excursions, at the foot of Broadway on the waterfront. |
| **Naturalist:** | Captain serves as naturalist. |

Ben Griffith, owner and captain of the *Morning Star*, has been in the sportfishing business since 1960. "We completely narrate the whale-watch trips, including information on the harbor and the history of San Diego. We also show a gray whale video on return trip," he said. "I personally try to see that one and all enjoy themselves. We're run more like a family operation than a large company operation."

An open-ended rain check is issued if no whales are sighted.

## San Diego Natural History Museum

Balboa Park, P.O. Box 1390, San Diego, CA 92112
(619) 232-3821; Fax (619) 232-0248

| | |
|---|---|
| **Whales:** | Gray; occasionally fin, blue, orca, humpback |
| **Season:** | December through mid-March |
| **Boats:** | One boat, the *Pacific Queen*; 60 passengers |
| **Trips:** | Occasional 2- to 3-hour trips off San Diego and day trips to circle the Coronados Islands. |
| **Fare:** | The shorter trips cost $15; the day trip costs $62. Call for schedule. Reservations required. |
| **Departure:** | Trips leave from Fisherman's Landing in San Diego Bay. Call for directions. |
| **Naturalist:** | Naturalist from the San Diego Natural History Museum. |

"Dr. Raymond Gilmore, a former museum staff member, was instrumental in starting whale-watching programs in southern California and Baja California," notes Sandy Kuntz, the museum's program coordinator. The museum also offers a nine-day whale-watch trip to Baja California and shorter "drive-down" trips. Write for more information.

## Seaforth Sportfishing Corp.

1717 Quivira Road, San Diego, CA 92109
(619) 224-3383

| | |
|---|---|
| **Whales:** | Gray |
| **Season:** | December through mid-March |
| **Boats:** | Three boats; 105, 118, and 149 passengers |
| **Trips:** | Two 2-1/2-hour trips on weekdays at 10 a.m. and 1 p.m. Three trips on Saturdays, Sundays, and holidays at 9 a.m., 11:30 a.m., and 2 p.m. Weekends are the busiest days. |
| **Fare:** | Adults, $12; children, senior citizens, and military, $8. Group rates available. Reservations advised. |
| **Departure:** | Trips leave from Seaforth Landing at 1717 Quivira Road in Mission Bay. From the east and south, take I-8 west to the Sports Arena Boulevard turnoff. Exit right and follow the "TO WEST MISSION BAY" signs to the cloverleaf. Exit on West Mission Bay Drive, turn left at Quivira Road. From the north, take I-5 to Sea World Drive exit. Pass Sea World and follow the "TO WEST MISSION BAY" signs to the cloverleaf. Then repeat as above. |
| **Naturalist:** | Yes |

"We invite you to journey with us and experience these magnificent creatures in their natural habitats," notes an employee at Seaforth Sportfishing. "Guaranteed whale sighting, or ride again free!"

## SAN FRANCISCO

## Oceanic Society Expeditions

Fort Mason Center, Building E, San Francisco, CA 94123
(800) 326-7491 or (415) 474-3385

| | |
|---|---|
| **Whales:** | Gray |
| **Season:** | December 26 through April |

| **Boats:** | One boat, the 85-foot *Ranger*; 78 passengers |
|---|---|
| **Trips:** | Every Saturday and Sunday and selected Fridays at 9:30 a.m. Trips are 7 hours long. |
| **Fare:** | On weekends, adults, $48; children 10 through 15 and senior citizens 60 or older, $46. On Fridays, adults, $45; children 10 through 15 and senior citizens 60 or older, $44. No one under 10 permitted on the boat. Group rates available. Reservations required. |
| **Departure:** | Trips leave from San Francisco Yacht Harbor/Marina Green. |
| **Naturalist:** | Naturalist on board from Oceanic Society Expeditions. |

Oceanic Society Expeditions also sponsors eight-hour trips to the Farallon Islands on selected dates from June through mid-November. Blue and humpback whales are sometimes spotted on these trips, which cost $58 per person. Write for more information.

# SAN FRANCISCO, SAUSALITO, MONTEREY BAY, AND BODEGA BAY

## Footloose Forays/Michael Ellis

P.O. Box 1175, Sebastopol, CA 95473
(713) 829-1844

| **Whales:** | Gray in winter and spring; blue and humpback in summer and fall |
|---|---|
| **Season:** | Year-round |
| **Boats:** | Two boats, about 50 passengers each; one whale–watch conducted from shore |
| **Trips:** | Trips scheduled at various times in winter and spring to see gray whales and in summer and fall to see blue whales and humpbacks. Summer trips to the Farallon Islands are the most popular. Land-based trips also available. |
| **Fare:** | Range is from $23 to $55 per person, depending on length of trip. Reservations required. |

**Departure:**    Depending on destination, trips leave from San Francisco, Sausalito, Monterey Bay, and Bodega Bay.

**Naturalist:**    Yes

Owner Michael Ellis, a well-versed naturalist, accompanies every trip. Ellis also writes a syndicated nature column for several northern California newspapers and is a commentator on KQED-FM in San Francisco.

## SAN PEDRO

### L.A. Harbor Sportfishing

1150 Nagoya Way, Berth 79, San Pedro, CA 90731
(213) 547-9916

**Whales:**    Gray, orca, dolphins

**Season:**    December 26 through March 31

**Boats:**    A new 93-foot boat with an upper sundeck; 150 passengers

**Trips:**    Two trips on weekdays at 11:30 a.m. and 2 p.m.; three trips on Saturdays and Sundays at 9 and 11:30 a.m. and 2 p.m. Trips last about 2 hours. The morning trip on Saturdays is the most popular.

**Fare:**    Adults, $11; children 12 and under, $9. Group rates available for 25 or more. Reservations are not required but are advised.

**Departure:**    Trips leave from L.A. Harbor Sportfishing, located at Berth 79 in the Ports O'Call Village at San Pedro.

**Naturalist:**    The captain serves as naturalist.

"We use a spotter plane to further our success rate," says a spokeswoman. "The plane locates marine life, and we are able to go directly there, giving the passengers more viewing time than ever."

## Skipper's 22nd Street Landing

141 West 22nd Street, San Pedro, CA 9073
(310) 832-8304

**Whales:** Gray

**Season:** January through March

**Boats:** Two boats; 96 and 122 passengers

**Trips:** Two trips on weekdays at 10 a.m. and 1 p.m.; 3 trips every Saturday and Sunday at 9 and 11:30 and 2 p.m. Trips last 2 to 2-1/2 hours. Saturday morning is the busiest time.

**Fare:** Weekdays: adults, $11; children 12 and under and seniors 62 and over, $8. Weekends: adults, $12; children 12 and under and seniors 62 and over, $9. Reservations required.

**Departure:** Trips leave from Cabrillo Marina. Take the Harbor Freeway south to the end. Turn left onto Gaffey Street; go to 22nd Street and turn left. Drive 4 blocks. The landing is on the right; free all-day parking on the left.

**Naturalist:** Naturalist on board from Cabrillo Aquarium/American Cetacean Society.

"Join us and observe the greatest creatures on earth as they make their way to the breeding grounds off Mexico's coast," says manager Dian Peterson.

## Spirit Cruises and Whale Watch

Ports O'Call, Berth 77, San Pedro, CA 90731
(310) 548-8080

**Whales:** Gray

**Season:** December 26 through mid-April

**Boats:** Four boats; 49, 100, 125, and 150 passengers

**Trips:** One trip on weekdays at 11 a.m.; two trips on Saturday and Sunday at 11 a.m. and 1:30 p.m. Trips last 2 to 3 hours. The Sunday afternoon trip is the most popular.

**Fare:** Adults, $15; children ages 2 through 12, $8. Reservations required. With advance reservations, you get a discount on weekday trips.

**Departure:**   Trips leave from Ports O'Call in San Pedro and Shoreline
Village in Long Beach; call for directions.

**Naturalist:**   Yes

Owner Jayme S. Wilson says, "We use sailing ships and motor yachts that are
the nicest boats in southern California. Guaranteed whale sightings or you get a
free pass for another trip!" Wilson adds that a new, 600-passenger boat will be
added to the fleet in 1995.

## SANTA BARBARA

### Capt. Don's Coastal Cruises

P.O. Box 1134, Summerland, CA 93067
(805) 969-5217

**Whales:**   Gray, common dolphin

**Season:**   Mid-February to mid-April

**Boats:**   Two boats; 49 passengers each

**Trips:**   Three 2-hour trips daily at 9 a.m., noon, and 3 p.m. Weekends
are busiest.

**Fare:**   Adults, $20; senior citizens, $16; children 12 and under, $12.
Reservations required.

**Departure:**   Trips leave from Stearn's Wharf, at the base of State Street in
Santa Barbara.

**Naturalist:**   Captain serves as naturalist.

Captain Donald L. Hedden notes, "Over 22,000 gray whales migrate through
the Santa Barbara Channel during our season, within five miles of shore."

## SEA Landing Sportfishing

1321 Los Alamos Place, Santa Barbara, CA 93109
(805) 963-3564; Fax (805) 965-0942

| | |
|---|---|
| **Whales:** | Gray, common dolphin, Pacific white-sided dolphin |
| **Season:** | February 15 through April 30 |
| **Boats:** | One boat, the 88-foot *Condor*; 125 passengers |
| **Trips:** | Three 2-hour trips daily (except Wednesday) at 9 a.m., noon, and 3 p.m. The most popular trip is on Saturday morning. |
| **Fare:** | Adults, $22; children 12 and younger, $12. Group rates available for schools on weekdays. Reservations required. The Santa Barbara Radisson Hotel offers guests discount coupons for trips on the *Condor*. |
| **Departure:** | Trips leave from SEA Landing in the Santa Barbara Harbor. |
| **Naturalist:** | Yes |

Captain Fred Benko has been providing whale-watching trips since 1973. From July through December, he also runs one- and two-day trips on the *Condor* in search of humpbacks, orcas, minkes, and blue whales. Call or write for schedule and costs.

## Santa Barbara Museum of Natural History/Sea Center

211 Stearns Wharf, Santa Barbara, CA 93101
(805) 962-0885

| | |
|---|---|
| **Whales:** | Gray, occasionally humpback, blue, minke, orca |
| **Season:** | March |
| **Boats:** | One boat, the 88-foot *Condor*; 125 passengers |
| **Trips:** | One narrated 2-hour trip at 9 a.m. on 3 weekends in March. |
| **Fare:** | Adults, $20; children, $10. Non-members add $2. Written reservations required. |
| **Departure:** | Trips leave from Santa Barbara Harbor. From Stearns Wharf, go west along Cabrillo Boulevard. Turn in at the harbor entrance, park and walk to SEA Landing boats. |
| **Naturalist:** | Museum naturalists and docents are on board. |

Gary Robinson, a spokesman for the museum, says their whale-watch trips have become a tradition. "All trip participants have the opportunity to hold a gray whale vertebra, look at baleen, examine a killer whale rib, and touch a sea otter's pelt." The Sea Center sometimes schedules full-day whale-watch trips.

## SANTA CRUZ

### Pacific Yachting and Sailing

Santa Cruz Yacht Harbor, 333 Lake Avenue, Santa Cruz, CA 95062
(800) 374-2626 or (408) 476-2370

| | |
|---|---|
| **Whales:** | Gray |
| **Season:** | Mid-December through mid-February |
| **Boats:** | Seventeen luxury sailing yachts; 6 passengers each |
| **Trips:** | All yachts available for skippered whale-watch charters or "bareboat" (unskippered) sailing seven days a week. Weekends are busiest. |
| **Fare:** | A 4-hour skippered charter costs $295 for 6 people. Reservations required. |
| **Departure:** | Trips leave from the Santa Cruz Harbor, near the Crow's Nest Restaurant. |
| **Naturalist:** | None on board. |

"We have a fleet of ten luxury sailing yachts, with auxiliary diesel engines, sleeping quarters for six, as well as all cooking appliances and bathing conveniences, " says owner Marc Kraft.

## Stagnaro Original Fishing Trips

Box 1340, Santa Cruz, CA 95061
(408) 423-2010

| | |
|---|---|
| **Whales:** | Gray |
| **Season:** | December through April |
| **Boats:** | Two boats; 49 and 60 passengers |
| **Trips:** | Trips on request by private charter on weekdays; two 3-hour trips on Saturdays and Sundays at 11 a.m. and 2 p.m. Please call to confirm times. |
| **Fare:** | Adults, $16; children under 12, $12. Reservations advised, but not required. |
| **Departure:** | Trips leave from Santa Cruz Wharf, at the foot of Washington Street on Beach Street. |
| **Naturalist:** | None on board. |

"Set off with us for a morning or afternoon trip on the waters of Monterey Bay to enjoy sightings of one of the greatest wonders of our coast, the gray whale," says the Stagnaro family.

## VENTURA

## Island Packers

1867 Spinnaker Drive, Ventura, CA 93001
(805) 642-1393

| | |
|---|---|
| **Whales:** | Gray, minke |
| **Season:** | December 26 through March 31 |
| **Boats:** | Four boats; 25, 48, 48, and 80 passengers |
| **Trips:** | One or two trips on weekdays; 2 on Saturdays and 2 on Sundays. According to demand, trips are offered at 9:30 and 11 a.m. or 1:30 p.m. Saturday is the busiest day. |

**Fare:** Half-day excursions: adults, $21; children, $14. Anacapa Island whale-watch trips: adults, $39; children, $22. Whale-watch trips to Santa Cruz Island: adults, $50; children, $40. Reservations required. The Doubletree Hotel in Ventura offers guests discount coupons for Island Packers whale watches.

**Departure:** Trips leave from Ventura Harbor. Take the Seaward off-ramp south on Harbor Boulevard and turn right on Spinnaker Drive in the Ventura Harbor.

**Naturalist:** Crew members, most of whom have degrees in environmental science or biology, serve as naturalists.

"Island Packers is a family-owned and operated business," notes owner William Mark Connally, son of the founder. "We are the concessionaire to the Channel Islands National Park and provide transportation to the park and interpretive services for the National Park Service."

# MUSEUMS, AQUARIUMS, AND SCIENCE CENTERS

## CALIFORNIA

### Cabrillo Marine Aquarium

3720 Stephen White Drive, San Pedro, CA 90731
(213) 548-7562

The Cabrillo Marine Aquarium has more than thirty aquariums and exhibits that provide a close-up look at a wide variety of sea creatures of the southern California area. Among the exhibits is one on the migration of the gray whales. Recreational and educational programs are available, including whale-watch trips from January through April.

Open noon to 5 p.m. Tuesday through Friday; 10 a.m. to 5 p.m. Saturday and Sunday. Closed on Mondays. Admission is free, but beach parking is $6.60 per car, with reduced rates from December through February.

### California Academy of Sciences

Golden Gate Park, San Francisco, CA 94118
(415) 221-5100; Fax (415) 750-7346

The Academy is a natural history museum, aquarium, and planetarium all rolled into one. Classes on marine mammals, including whales, are held periodically for adults and children. For information on adult education classes, call (415) 750-7100.

Open daily 10 a.m. to 5 p.m.; extended hours in the summer. Adults, $7; senior citizens and students 12 to 17, $4; children ages 6 through 11, $1.50. Admission is free on first Wednesday of each month.

### Long Marine Laboratory

100 Shaffer Road, Santa Cruz, CA 95060
(408) 459-4308; Fax (408) 459-3383

Long Marine Laboratory serves as the marine research and instructional facility of the University of California at Santa Cruz. Exhibits include an 85-foot skeleton of a blue whale, tidepool animals in touch tanks, an aquarium, and displays related to current research.

Open 1 to 4 p.m. Tuesday through Sunday; closed on Mondays and holidays. Group tours available at expanded hours by appointment.

# Monterey Bay Aquarium

886 Cannery Row, Monterey, CA 93940
(408) 648-4800

More than 120,000 specimens representing 525 species are housed in the aquarium. Special features are several undersea habitats, including a three-story kelp forest and a 90-foot-long exhibit of Monterey Bay habitats. From the public entrance, a parade of life-sized marine mammals, including a 43-foot gray whale and her 22-foot calf, wends its way overhead into the Marine Mammals gallery.

Open daily from 10 a.m. to 6 p.m. Adults, $11.25; students and senior citizens, $8.25; children, $5.

# San Diego Natural History Museum

P.O. Box 1390, Balboa Park, San Diego, CA 91112
(619) 232-3821

Exhibits on marine life, shells, desert ecology, and the Foucault pendulum are on display. Open 9 a.m. to 4 p.m. seven days a week. Adults, $6; seniors, $5; children 6 through 17, $2; children 5 and younger, free. Free admission once a month. For dates call (619) 239-0512.

The museum sponsors whale watches out of San Diego.

# Santa Barbara Museum of Natural History

2559 Puesta del Sol Road, Santa Barbara, CA 93105
(805) 682-4711

Marine life exhibits include a 72-foot skeleton of a blue whale and several marine life and habitat displays in Marine Hall. A research laboratory, library, observatory, and planetarium are on the Museum grounds.

Open 9 a.m. to 5 p.m. weekdays; 10 a.m. to 5 p.m. Sunday and holidays. Closed Thanksgiving, Christmas, and New Year's. Admission $4 for adults; $3 for youths and seniors; $1 for children under 12.

A lifesized model of a gray whale is on display at the Sea Center, #211 Stearns Wharf, which is a branch of the Museum. The Sea Center has a touch tank and other marine displays and is open every day from 10 a.m. to 5 p.m. Adults, $2; children 17 and under, $1.

## Stephen Birch Aquarium

Scripps Institution of Oceanography, 2300 Expedition Way, LaJolla, CA 92093
(619) 534-3474; Fax (619) 534-7114

In addition to displays of oceanic wonders, the Stephen Birch Aquarium sponsors occasional whale-watch cruises, snorkel and scuba expeditions, tidepooling trips, and classes for children and adults. Write for a brochure and calendar of events.

Open daily 9 a.m. to 5 p.m. Closed on Thanksgiving and Christmas. Admission is $6.50 for adults, $5.50 for seniors, $4.50 for students, $3.50 for children ages 4 to 12, and free for children under 4.

# NATIONAL PARKS AND MARINE SANCTUARIES

## CALIFORNIA

### Channel Islands National Park

1901 Spinnaker Drive, Ventura, CA 93001
(805) 658-5700

### Channel Islands National Marine Sanctuary

735 State Street, Santa Barbara, CA 93101
(805) 966-7107

Five of the eight Channel Islands make up Channel Islands National Park. They are Anacapa, Santa Cruz, Santa Rosa, San Miguel, and Santa Barbara, plus 125,000 acres of submerged lands. The Marine Sanctuary encompasses 1,252 square nautical miles of nearshore and offshore waters. Boat trips, diving, fishing, visits to the Sea Center, and wildlife watching are all available. Write for a free map and brochures about island life, ecology, and activities.

### Gulf of the Farallones National Marine Sanctuary

National Oceanic and Atmospheric Administration, GGNRA
Fort Mason, Building 201, San Francisco, CA 94123
(415) 556-3509

The Gulf of the Farallones National Marine Sanctuary encompasses 948 square nautical miles of water off the California coastline north of San Francisco. Designated in 1981, the sanctuary consists of an offshore marine region of the Gulf of the Farallones and the nearshore waters of Bodega Bay, Tomales Bay, Drakes Bay, Bolinas Bay, Estero San Antonio, Estero de Americano, Duxbury Reef, and Bolinas Lagoon. Write for a free brochure and map of the area.

### Monterey Bay National Marine Sanctuary

299 Foam Street, Suite D, Monterey, CA 93940
(408) 647-4201

The Monterey Bay National Marine Sanctuary which covers 4,024 square nautical miles is a haven for sea otters, seals, shorebirds, squid, sardines, and thousands of other species, including many that are threatened or endangered. The sanctuary was so designated in 1992. Write for a free brochure.

## Point Reyes National Seashore

Point Reyes, CA 94956
(415) 663-1092

The Point Reyes National Seashore, about 50 miles north of San Francisco, has a rich cultural and natural heritage to explore. Visitor's centers, hiking trails, exhibits, and stationary whale watching from several points are all available in the 73,000-acre recreational area. From December 30 through February, free shuttle bus service for whale watchers is available. Ask at the Bear Valley Visitor Center for the pick-up point. Rangers are always on hand to answer questions. Write for a free brochure, map, and calendar of events.

# MONUMENTS

## CALIFORNIA

### Cabrillo National Monument

P.O. Box 6670, San Diego, CA 92106
(619) 557-5450

Cabrillo National Monument is located at the southern end of Point Loma, within the city limits of San Diego. Whale Watch Weekend, held annually in January, includes informal lectures, presentations, and displays as well as opportunities to sight the migrating gray whales from a sheltered overlook. Educational materials about whales are available all year. Open every day, 9 a.m. to 5:15 p.m.; extended hours in summer. Admission is $4 per vehicle.

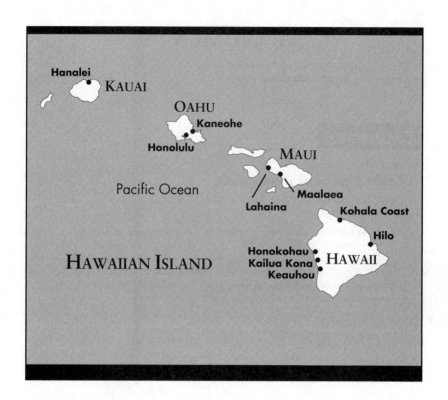

Hanalei

KAUAI

OAHU

Kaneohe

Honolulu

Pacific Ocean

MAUI

Maalaea

Lahaina

Kohala Coast

Hilo

HAWAIIAN ISLAND

Honokohau
Kailua Kona
Keauhou

HAWAII

# HAWAII

Lahaina, on the island of Maui, was once the capital of the American Pacific whaling fleet. Today whale-watch tour boats stand in the harbor, waiting to carry passengers to see the whales that swim in Hawaiian waters each year from December to April.

Just a few years ago, the only whale-watch tours in the Hawaiian Islands operated out of Lahaina, although some sport and fishing boats based on other islands were available for private charter. Today, wherever you succumb to the seductive languor of Hawaii, you can book passage on a whale-watch trip. Excursion boats, sailboats, and inflatable rafts are all available, with departure points from Kauai, Maui, Oahu, and the "Big Island," Hawaii. (Can Lanai be far behind?)

The attraction is primarily humpback whales, which come to Hawaii each year to mate and give birth. Some areas are so replete with mothers and calves that they have been dubbed "nurseries" and declared sanctuaries. In addition to the frolicsome humpbacks, other smaller cetaceans such as pilot whales and bottlenose dolphins are frequently seen in Hawaiian waters.

If you miss the boat, so to speak, and happen to be lying on a beach on the northwestern coast of Maui at the right time of year, you may think that you see whales breaching along the shore of Lanai.

That's probably more than just a Mai Tai-induced illusion.

# TOURISM INFORMATION

## HAWAII

### Hawaii Visitors Bureau

2270 Kalakaua Avenue, Suite 801, Honolulu, Oahu, HI 96813

(808) 924-0266

# WHALE-WATCHING TRIPS

## HAWAII

### HILO

## Blue Moon Explorations

P.O. Box 2568WW, Bellingham, WA 98227
(206) 966-8805

| | |
|---|---|
| **Whales:** | Humpback |
| **Season:** | February and March |
| **Boats:** | Eight 2-person kayaks |
| **Trips:** | Several 10-day trips to the Big Island, including whale watching, snorkeling, kayaking, and hiking. Accommodations include a retreat center and camping. Some trips are for women only. |
| **Fare:** | Fares range between $855 and $945, which includes kayaks, camping accommodations, most meals in Hawaii, accessories, group camping equipment, a VHF radio, safety equipment, guides and instruction. Reservations required. |
| **Departure:** | Trips begin in Hilo. |
| **Naturalist:** | Yes |

Owner Kathleen Grimbly says, "Blue Moon Explorations are designed to expand our awareness of the many intricate relationships in the web of life. Traveling by kayak, we experience the whales and the web of life that supports them more intimately and less intrusively. Our trips are designed for people of all ages and abilities."

## HONOKOHAU, KAILUA, AND KEAUHOU

### Captain Zodiac Raft Expeditions

P.O. Box 5612, Kailua-Kona, HI 96745
(808) 329-3199; Fax (808) 329-7590

| | |
|---|---|
| **Whales:** | Humpback |
| **Season:** | January to mid-April |
| **Boats:** | Rigid-hull inflatable rafts; 16 passengers each |
| **Trips:** | Two 4-hour trips daily at 8 a.m. and 1 p.m. Trips may involve exploring the coast and snorkeling as well as whale watching. Wednesday is the busiest day. |
| **Fare:** | Adults, $62; children ages 2 to 11, $52. Beverage, brunch or lunch, and snorkel gear provided. Reservations advised. |
| **Departure:** | Boats leave from Honokohau Harbor, Kailua Pier, and Keauhou Pier. |
| **Naturalist:** | None on board. |

"We use 23-foot Zodiac rafts popularized by Jacques Cousteau," says general manager Steve Lambert. "We are the pioneer rafting company in Hawaii, having started the rafting tour business here in 1978. We have three locations in Hawaii (Kauai, Maui, and the Big Island), and we are the largest rafting company in the islands."

### Dan McSweeney's Whale Watching Adventures

P.O. Box 139, Holualoa, Hawaii, HI 96725
(808) 322-0028; Fax (808) 329-2094

| | |
|---|---|
| **Whales:** | Humpback, pilot, sperm, dolphins |
| **Season:** | All year, except May and June |
| **Boats:** | One boat, the 38-foot *Lady Ann*; 42 passengers |
| **Trips:** | One 3-1/2-hour trip at 9 a.m. Monday through Friday from July 1 to December 19; Two 3-hour trips daily at 9 a.m. and 1 p.m. from December 20 to April 30. |

**Fare:**    Adults, $39.50 plus tax; children 12 and under, $29.50 plus tax; infants under 1, free. Reservations recommended.

**Departure:**    Trips leave from Honokohau Harbor in Kailua-Kona. Please call for directions to the boat.

**Naturalist:**    Narration by Captain Dan McSweeney, a whale scientist.

"You can see whales here any day, any season," says Dan McSweeney. "I guarantee a whale sighting, and also that participants' experience will be valuable as they see, learn about, and appreciate these intriguing animals." McSweeney has studied Hawaii's whales since 1974 and logged 25,000 hours of whale watching.

## Kamanu Charters

P.O. Box 2201, Kailua-Kona, Hawaii, HI 96740
(808) 329-2021

**Whales:**    Humpback, pilot whales

**Season:**    January 15 through March 31

**Boats:**    One boat, the *Kamanu*, a sailing catamaran; 24 passengers

**Trips:**    One 2-hour sail daily at 2 p.m.

**Fare:**    Adults, $25; children, $15. Juice, fruit, cheese, and snacks provided. Reservations advised.

**Departure:**    Boat leaves from Honokohau Harbor off Highway 19.

**Naturalist:**    Knowledgeable crew on board.

"Enjoy an afternoon sail on our catamaran looking for humpbacks, pilot whales, false killer whales, dolphins, and turtles," says Captain Jay Lambert.

## Kona Whale Watching

P.O. Box 1622, Kailua-Kona, HI 96745
(808) 325-5556

| | |
|---|---|
| **Whales:** | Humpback, pilot, dolphins |
| **Season:** | Mid-December through mid-April |
| **Boats:** | One 28-foot boat; 6 passengers |
| **Trips:** | Two 3-hour trips daily at 8:30 a.m. and 12:30 p.m. |
| **Fare:** | $45 per person |
| **Departure:** | Trips leave from Honokohau Harbor |
| **Naturalist:** | Skipper narrates all trips. |

"We provide a personal and uncrowded experience with humpback whales," says owner and skipper Thomas Bottrell, who has degrees in oceanography and ecology, and experience on Kona waters since 1975. Kona Whale Watching also provides marine eco-touring year-round.

## KOHALA COAST

## Ocean Sports Waikoloa

69-275 Waikoloa Beach Drive, Kohala Coast, HI 96743
(808) 885-5555; Fax (808) 885-5863

| | |
|---|---|
| **Whales:** | Humpback |
| **Season:** | December 15 to April 15 |
| **Boats:** | Five boats; 6, 18, 25, 36 and 49 passengers |
| **Trips:** | Four trips daily. Three-hour snorkel and whale watch at 8:30 a.m.; a 1/2-hour motor/sail cruise at 12:30 p.m. and 2 p.m.; a 1/2-hour sunset sail at 4:30 p.m. Saturday is the busiest day. |
| **Fare:** | Early trip: adults, $45; children under 12, $29. Midday trip: adults, $35; children, $19. Sunset trip: adults, $39. Reservations advised. |

**Departure:**    Boat leaves from Anaehoomalu Bay Beach, in front of the Royal Waikoloan Hotel.

**Naturalist:**    Naturalist on most trips.

"Ocean Sports' approach to whale watching is unique in that the captains and crews are as excited and enthusiastic about seeing these gentle creatures as are our guests, and all have a genuinely good time," says Rick Conners.

"Some groups are treated to an unofficial initiation as honorary crew members as they learn our whaling song."

## KONA

## Hawaii Sailing Company

P.O. Box 1813, Honokaa, HI 96727
(808) 326-1986

**Whales**:    Humpback

**Season:**    November to May

**Boats:**    One 38-foot sailing yacht; 6 passengers

**Trips:**    Two- to 6-day sailing trips around the "Big Island" of Hawaii. Participants live on board.

**Fare:**    $160 per person per day includes meals, whale watching, snorkeling, body surfing, and cruising. Reservations required.

**Departure:**    Boat leaves from Kona, Hawaii

**Naturalist:**    None on board.

"Up until April, the humpback whales will be arriving in Hawaii for the mating season. Sailing is the perfect way to enjoy this yearly migration," notes Captain Bill Chambers.

"The anchorages range from the peaceful out-of-the-way harbors to active resort areas. The beaches are some of the finest in the world, the waters clear and warm for snorkeling and body surfing, and the scenery pure Hawaii."

# KAUAI

## HANALEI

### Captain Zodiac Raft Expeditions

P.O. Box 456, Hanalei, Kauai, HI 96714
(800) 422-7824 or (808) 826-9371

| | |
|---|---|
| **Whales:** | Humpback |
| **Season:** | January to mid-April |
| **Boats:** | Inflatable rafts; 16 passengers each |
| **Trips:** | Trips range from 3 to 5 hours, depending on demand. Trips include snorkeling off coral reefs, weather permitting. Wednesday is the busiest day. |
| **Fare:** | Adults, $55 to $105. Beverages, brunch or lunch provided. Reservations advised. |
| **Departure:** | Boats leave from Hanalei Harbor. Check in at the Captain Zodiac office on Highway 56, just before the Ching Young Shopping Village. |
| **Naturalist:** | None on board. |

"We use 23-foot Zodiac rafts popularized by Jacques Cousteau," says manager Clarence H. Greff, Jr. "We are the pioneer rafting company in Hawaii, having started the rafting tour business here in 1976. We have two locations in Hawaii—Kauai and the Big Island—and we are the largest rafting company in the islands."

# Hanalei Sea Tours

P.O. Box 1437, Hanalei, Kauai, HI 96714
(800) 733-7997 or (808) 826-7254; Fax (808) 826-7747

| | |
|---|---|
| **Whales:** | Humpback |
| **Season:** | December to April |
| **Boats:** | Eight boats; rigid-hull inflatable rafts, 15 passengers; power-driven catamarans, 16 passengers |
| **Trips:** | Trips for 2-1/2, 4, and 5 hours daily, with morning and afternoon departures. |
| **Fare:** | For adults, $55; $35 for children 12 and under for 2-1/2-hour trip; $75 for adults and $55 for children 12 and under for 4-hour trip (includes snorkeling and snacks); $100 for adults and $80 for children for 5-hour trip (includes hike, beach picnic, snorkeling, and beverages). Group rates available. Reservations required. |
| **Departure:** | Boats leave from Hanalei Bay. Meet at Hanalei Sea Tours office, the second building on the left after the first one-lane bridge in Hanalei. |
| **Naturalist:** | Captain serves as naturalist. |

"Hanalei Sea Tours operates year-round, offering scenic cruises of the beautiful NaPali coastline," says Ronnie Grover, general manager. "During these adventures, we enjoy viewing marine life, including dolphins, sea turtles, and the humpback whales in season."

A portion of all fares is donated to save the whales.

"NaPali is our objective—to get our passengers out to explore the majestic cliffs that are so rich in Hawaiian history, cruise through sea caves and lava tubes, and experience seeing marine life in their natural habitat."

# MAUI

## LAHAINA

### Hawaiian Rafting Adventures

1223 Front Street, Lahaina, Maui, HI 96761
(808) 661-7333; Fax (808) 667-4348 or 667-5862

| | |
|---|---|
| **Whales:** | Humpback |
| **Season:** | December to late April |
| **Boats:** | Rigid-hull inflatable rafts; 15 passengers each |
| **Trips:** | Four 2-hour trips daily at 7:30 a.m., 10 a.m., 12:30 p.m., and 3 p.m. Two 3-hour snorkel/whale watch trips at 9 a.m. and 12:30 p.m. |
| **Fare:** | For 2-hour trips, $45; $59 for 3-hour trips. Cold juices, snacks, and snorkel gear provided. Reservations advised. |
| **Departure:** | Boats leave from Mala Wharf in Lahaina. Check in at the Front Street office first. |
| **Naturalist:** | Experienced captains or marine biologist narrates. |

"A marine biologist and the former captain for the Cousteau expedition on Maui have teamed up to offer you an unforgettable and educational adventure," says office manager Angela Parsons.

### Island Marine Activity

505 Front Street, #225, Lahaina, Maui, HI 96761
(800) 833-5800 (from mainland), (800) 533-6899 (from Oahu), or (808) 661-8397

| | |
|---|---|
| **Whales:** | Humpback |
| **Season:** | Mid-December to May |

| **Boats:** | Two vessels, the *Maui Princess* and the *Lahaina Princess*; 298 passengers total |
| **Trips:** | Three 2-1/4-hour trips daily at 8:30 a.m., 11:30 a.m., and 2:30 p.m. |
| **Fare:** | Adults, $31; children ages 3 to 12, $17.50; infants, free. Portion of fare goes to Maui Whale Aid, a private foundation established to fund whale research and education in Hawaii. Reservations advised. |
| **Departure:** | Boats leave from Slip 3 in Lahaina Harbor, just across the street from the banyan tree and the Pioneer Inn. |
| **Naturalist:** | Naturalist accompanies some trips; experienced captain and crew narrate the other trips. |

"Every year between Christmas and Easter, the waters surrounding Maui, Molokai, and Lanai become the vacation playground for thousands of tourists and about 400 North Pacific humpback whales," says Robin Miller of Island Marine Activity. "During this four-month period, the habits, antics, and awesomeness of these creatures fascinate researchers and delight the casual whale watcher."

Sightings are guaranteed, with a free cruise offered if no whales show up.

# Maui Rafting Expeditions

P.O. Box 1773, Lahaina, Maui, HI 96767
(808) 667-5678

| **Whales:** | Humpback |
| **Season:** | December through April |
| **Boats:** | Several pontoon rafts; 12 passengers |
| **Trips:** | Four 2-hour trips daily at 7:30 a.m., 9:30 a.m., 11:30 a.m., and 1:30 p.m. Sometimes a 3:30 p.m. trip is added. |
| **Fare:** | Adults, $39; children, $29. Early-bird fare for 7:30 trip is $29 for everyone. Reservations advised. |
| **Departure:** | Trips leave from Lahaina Harbor. |
| **Naturalist:** | Naturalist from EarthTrust narrates. |

Maui Rafting Expeditions guarantees whale sightings.

## Ocean Riders

P.O. Box 967, Lahaina, Maui, HI 96767
(808) 661-3586

**Whales:**      Humpback

**Season:**      December through April

**Boats:**       Two rigid-hull inflatable rafts; 13 and 18 passengers

**Trips:**       Four 2-hour trips daily at 8:30 a.m., 10:45 a.m., 1 p.m., and 3:30 p.m.; one 3-hour trip daily at 7:30 a.m. that includes snorkeling.

**Fare:**        Adults, $45; children, $30. Add $10 for the snorkeling trip. Includes beverage, light snack, snorkeling equipment, and snorkeling instruction. Reservations required.

**Departure:**   Boats leave from Mala Wharf in Lahaina. Turn off Front Street near the Safeway, the cannery, and the "JESUS IS COMING" sign.

**Naturalist:**  Captains and crew are trained by researchers.

"We operate state-of-the-art rigid-hull inflatables that are the safest, fastest, and most fun boats in Pacific waters; the boat ride alone is worth the fare," says owner Sherrill Jeter. "We offer guaranteed whale sightings from January 5 through April 30, or your money back."

## Scotch Mist Sailing Charters

P.O. Box 831, Lahaina, Maui, HI 96767
(808) 661-0386

**Whales:**      Humpback

**Season:**    December to May

**Boats:**    One sailing yacht, the *Scotch Mist II*; 25 passengers

**Trips:**    Three 2-1/2-hour trips daily at 9:30 a.m., 1 p.m., and 4:30 p.m.

**Fare:**    Adults, $35; children under 12, $25. Beer, wine, and soft drinks included. Reservations required. Charters available.

**Departure:**    Boat leaves from Slip 9 in Lahaina Harbor, just off Front Street by the Pioneer Inn.

**Naturalist:**    None on board.

"Slip into whale country and see the humpbacks up close from the deck of a private yacht," says staff member Leslie Ferguson.

The *Scotch Mist II* was first to finish in the 1982 Victoria-to-Maui Yacht Race. It is available to visitors for sailing, snorkeling, champagne sunset cruises, moonlight sails, and whale watching.

# Windjammer Cruises

658 Front Street, # 101, Lahaina, Maui, HI 96761
(808) 661-8600

**Whales:**    Humpback

**Season:**    Mid-December through April

**Boats:**    One boat, the *Spirit of Windjammer*; 110 passengers

**Trips:**    Three 2-hour cruises daily at 9 a.m., 11:30 a.m., and 2 p.m.

**Fare:**    Adults, $36.50; children: ages 3 to 12, $18.25; under 3, free. Reservations required.

**Departure:**    Boat leaves from Slip 1 in Lahaina Harbor, just off Front Street, near the banyan tree.

**Naturalist:**    None on board.

"Help the whales by whale watching on a vessel that supports education and research on Hawaii's humpback whale," says a spokesman for Windjammer Cruises. The fare includes either a continental breakfast or an all-you-can-eat barbecue buffet prepared on board.

## MAALAEA AND LAHAINA

### Pacific Whale Foundation

101 North Kihei Road, Suite 25, Kihei, Maui, HI 96753
(800) WHALE-11 or (808) 879-8811; Fax (808) 879-2615

| | |
|---|---|
| **Whales:** | Humpback |
| **Season:** | Late November to May |
| **Boats:** | Two boats, the *Whale One*, a 53-foot motor yacht, and the *Whale II*, a 50-foot sailing yacht; 49 and 24 passengers respectively. From December to April, also a 65-foot catamaran that carries 109 passengers. |
| **Trips:** | Ten trips daily. Three 2-1/2-hour motor cruises at 11:30 a.m., 2, and 4:30 p.m. One 4-hour cruise at 7 a.m. that combines whale watching and snorkeling. Three sailing cruises, a 4-hour snorkel/whale watch at 8 a.m., and 2-1/2-hour cruises at 12:30 p.m. and 3:30 p.m. Three 2-hour catamaran cruises at 9:30 a.m., noon, and 3:30 p.m. |
| **Fare:** | Adults, $27.50 plus tax; children ages 4 to 12, $15 plus tax. Snorkel/whale watch trips cost $44.25 for adults and $34 for children. Reservations required. |
| **Departure:** | *Whale One* leaves from Slip 52 in Maalaea Harbor just off Highway 30. *Whale II* leaves from Slip 11 in Lahaina Harbor, just off Front Street. The catamaran check-in is at Slip 11 in Lahaina. |
| **Naturalist:** | Naturalists on board have marine field research experience. |

"We are a marine research, education, and conservation organization," says Dr. Paul Forestell, director of research and education. "Our interest in taking you out whale watching is to educate you experientially about the marine environment so you become more aware of what's at stake and more conscientious about the impact of both your own actions and those going on in your own backyard.

"The ocean is not a vast endless resource, and experiencing the wonder of these great mammals motivates people to change behaviors that are detrimental to them."

## Trilogy Excursions

P.O. Box 1121, Lahaina, Maui, HI 96761
(800) 874-2666 or (808) 661-4743

**Whales:**    Humpback

**Season:**    Mid-December to mid-April

**Boats:**    Four multi-hull sailing boats; 36, 36, 46, and 55 passengers respectively

**Trips:**    One 7-hour trip to Molokini Marine Preserve and one day-long trip to Hulopo'e Marine Sanctuary.

**Fare:**    The Molokini trip costs $75 plus tax for adults and $37.50 plus tax for children. The Hulopo'e trip costs $139 plus tax for adults and $69.50 plus tax for children. Reservations required.

**Departure:**    The Molokini trip leaves from Slip 99 at Maalaea Harbor. The Hulopo'e trip leaves from the Public Loading Dock at Lahaina Harbor.

**Naturalist:**    Yes

"Clear crystal waters at Molokini Marine Preserve provide some of the best snorkeling in the islands, and with several hundred calving and breeding humpback whales wintering off Maui's south shore, opportunities for excellent sightings are almost guaranteed," says a member of "the sailing Coon family," the owners.

"Or, cruise aboard the *Trilogy* to Lanai, where the world's best snorkeling and scuba diving at the famed Hulopo'e Marine Sanctuary can be part of the day-long adventure."

On either trip, passengers enjoy Mom's hot homemade cinnamon rolls and tasty barbecue or teriyaki chicken.

# MAUI, MOLOKAI, AND LANAI

## Oceanic Society Expeditions

Fort Mason Center, Building E, San Francisco, CA 94123
(800) 326-7491 or 415) 441-1106

| | |
|---|---|
| **Whales:** | Humpback, pilot, false killer whale |
| **Season:** | March |
| **Boats:** | One 50-foot sailboat, the *Maile*; 6 passengers |
| **Trips:** | Five-day trips, living on board and sailing the waters of Maui, Molokai, and Lanai, including Penguin Banks. |
| **Fare:** | Cost is $1,390 per person. Price includes meals, accommodations, guides. Reservations required. |
| **Departure:** | Trip begins upon arrival at Lahaina Harbor on Maui. |
| **Naturalist:** | Marine biologist. |

"With a marine biologist/naturalist, we sail the less-touristed waters off Maui, Molokai, and Lanai," says a spokeswoman. "We'll observe humpback whales in more secluded breeding areas, including Penguin Banks. Lying at anchor in sheltered coves, we snorkel in selected sites amid brilliant tropical fish and intricate corals. Under sail, we move to the rhythms of wind and sea, searching for false killer whales, pilot whales, and several species of dolphins."

Oceanic Society Expeditions has conducted natural history tours since 1972.

# OAHU

## HONOLULU

### Navatek I Whale Watching Adventure

P.O. Box 29816, Honolulu, Oahu, HI 96820
(808) 848-6360

| | |
|---|---|
| **Whales:** | Humpback |
| **Season:** | January through April |
| **Boats:** | One boat, the *Navatek* I; 130 passengers |
| **Trips:** | One 2-hour trip daily, at noon. |
| **Fare:** | Adults, $29; children 5 to 12, $19. For the deluxe luncheon cruise, adults, $45; children, $24.50. Reservations advised. |
| **Departure:** | Trips leave from Pier 6 in the Honolulu Harbor. |
| **Naturalist:** | Naturalist from EarthTrust narrates trips. |

"Some 600 humpback whales visit our islands from January through April," says a spokesman. "These 50-ton giants migrate to Hawaii's warm waters to calve and mate before returning to their summer home off Alaska."

# KANEOHE AND HONOLULU

## Honolulu Sailing Company

47-335 Lulani Street, Kaneohe, Oahu, HI 96744
(800) 829-0114 or (808) 239-3900; Fax (808) 836-0008

| | |
|---|---|
| **Whales:** | Humpback, pilot |
| **Season:** | January to May |
| **Boats:** | Two 50-foot sailing yachts; 8 passengers each |
| **Trips:** | Two half-day trips at 8 a.m. and 1 p.m. One all-day trip at 9 a.m. Overnight trips also available. Weekends are the busiest times. |
| **Fare:** | For half day, $50 per person; $90 for full day; $260 for overnight (two days). Reservations required. |
| **Departure:** | Boats leave from Kaneohe Bay or from Honolulu Harbor. Call for directions. |
| **Naturalist:** | None on board. |

"We have been observing humpback whales on our cruises longer than anyone," says Mike Mickelwait, one of the captains. "Quiet sailboats are much better for not disturbing whales."

# MUSEUMS

## HAWAII

### Whalers Village Museum

2435 Kaanapali Parkway, G-8, Lahaina, Maui, HI 96761
(808) 661-5992

The Museum's whale pavilion features the skeleton of a 40-foot sperm whale. The history of the whaling industry in Hawaii is portrayed through an extensive artifact and photo collection, along with a re-created ship's fo'castle and a model of a whaling bark.

New is "Hale Kohala" (House of the Whale), an educational exhibit featuring whale models, including a 16-foot baby humpback whale.

The Museum is in the Whalers Village Shopping Complex. Take the elevator or stairs to the third level of Building G. Hours are 9:30 a.m. to 10 p.m. daily. Admission is free.

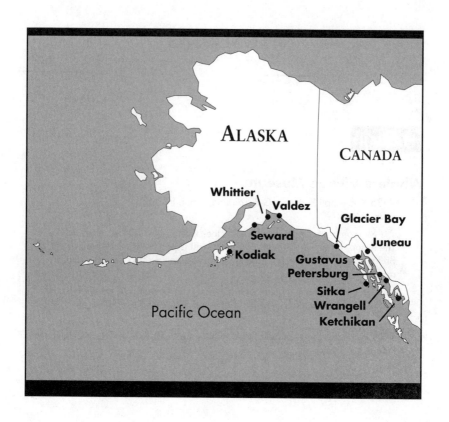

# ALASKA

Alaska, "The Great Land," has its share of great whales. Humpback, fin, gray whales, and orcas all swim off Alaskan shores. Still, the whale-watch industry is developing relatively slowly, although the many sportfishing charters and wilderness lodges have always considered sighting whales a normal occurrence.

The little town of Gustavus, just outside of the glorious Glacier Bay National Park and Preserve, probably offers the most whale-watch tours in Alaska. Trips also originate in Juneau, Ketchikan, Kodiak, Petersburg, Seward, Sitka, Valdez, and Wrangell. Extended tours visit several destinations in southeast and south-central Alaska, and most originate from points outside Alaska.

Some of the best serendipitous whale watching takes place aboard the Alaska state ferries that operate in southeast and south-central Alaska. The U.S. Forest Service provides forest interpreters on board to conduct programs on whales, marine mammals, and the special features of the Chugach and Tongass national forests. All programs are free to ferry passengers. Cruiseship passengers who keep a careful watch also may see whales. The scenery in Alaska is so magnificent that you're guaranteed a breathtaking backdrop for any whale sightings.

# TOURISM INFORMATION

## ALASKA

### Alaska Marine Highway
P.O. Box R, Juneau, AK 99811
(907) 789-7453 or (907) 465-3941 (in Canada)

### Alaska Tourism Marketing Council
P.O. Box E-501, Juneau, AK 9981
(907) 465-2010

# WHALE-WATCHING TRIPS

## ALASKA

### GLACIER BAY

### Alaska's Glacier Bay Tours and Cruises

520 Pike Street, Suite 1610, Seattle, WA 98101
(800) 451-5952 or (206) 623-7110; Fax (206) 623-7809

| | |
|---|---|
| **Whales:** | Humpback, orca, minke |
| **Season:** | Late May to mid-September |
| **Boats:** | Two boats; 300 and 60 passengers |
| **Trips:** | One 9-hour glacier cruise daily at 7 a.m.; two 3-1/2-hour whale-watch cruises at 9 a.m. and 1:30 p.m. |
| **Fare:** | For the glacier cruise, adults, $147; children 11 and younger, half fare. Lunch included. For the nature cruise, $89 per person. Reservations required. |
| **Departure:** | Trips leave from the lodge's dock in Bartlett Cove, Glacier Bay National Park, which is accessible by plane or ferry. Packages are available that include flight to Bartlett Cove, flight and lodging, or flight and multi-day cruise. |
| **Naturalist:** | National Park Service naturalist on board. |

Alaska's Glacier Bay Tours and Cruises is the concessionaire at Glacier Bay National Park in southeastern Alaska, about 60 miles northwest of Juneau. Bert Nordby, director of marketing, says that the park is famous for whale watching. "It is the dream trip for nature photographers and those who love to see wildlife, including whales."

Nordby adds, "Glacier Bay is also famous for its glaciers, with over 100 alpine glaciers and 16 tidewater glaciers calving icebergs into the picturesque fjords."

## GUSTAVUS

### Alaska Discovery Inc.

5449-4 Shaune Drive, Juneau, AK 99801
(907) 780-6226; Fax (907) 780-4220

| | |
|---|---|
| **Whales:** | Humpback, minke, orca |
| **Season:** | May through August |
| **Boats:** | Six kayaks; 2 people each |
| **Trips:** | Five 5-day trips kayaking and camping along Chichagof Island shoreline. |
| **Fare:** | $1,450 per person, which includes transfer to Gustavus dock, round-trip charter across Icy Strait, guides, tents, cooking gear, all meals in the field and user fees. Lodging and meals in Gustavus not included. |
| **Departure:** | Trips leave from and conclude in Gustavus, which is accessible only by boat or plane. |
| **Naturalist:** | Guides accompany trips. |

This Marine Mammal Discovery trip is a "must" for wildlife enthusiasts, says sales manager Kari Inga Espera. "Also, we are an environmentally sound company with a focus on a low-impact experience."

### Fairweather Fishing and Guide Service

P.O. Box 164, Gustavus, AK 99826 (June-August)
(907) 697-2335

P.O. Box 1335, Homer, AK 99603 (September-May)
(907) 235-5291 or (907) 235-3844

| | |
|---|---|
| **Whales:** | Humpback, minke, orca |
| **Season:** | May 30 to September 15 |
| **Boats:** | One boat, the *Tomten*; 6 passengers |
| **Trips:** | One trip per day on demand, 7 a.m. to 3:30 p.m. |

**Fare:** $90 per person for half day; $160 for full day, which includes lunch. Reservations required. For information on a package offer, contact Gustavus Inn, General Delivery, Gustavus, AK 99826.

**Departure:** Boat leaves from the dock in Gustavus, which is accessible by boat or air.

**Naturalist:** Yes

Says skipper Wayne Clark, "We have chartered trips with National Geographic, Audubon, National Wildlife, and International Wildlife organizations. The boat trip is a short 20-minute ride to an area that has had whale numbers consistent from May to September, anywhere from 6 to 12 humpbacks feeding right up against the shoreline. Eagles, seals, porpoises, and sea lions, also!"

Clark formerly worked as a rural bush teacher in the area.

# Glacier Bay Puffin Charters

P.O. Box 3, Gustavus, AK 99826
(907) 697-2260; Fax (907) 697-2258

**Whales:** Humpback

**Season:** May 15 to September 15

**Boats:** Two boats, the 42-foot *Gusto* and the 50-foot *Sea Breeze*; 6 passengers each. Other boats available.

**Trips:** One or two 4-hour trips per day at 7 a.m. and 1 p.m.; one 8-1/2-hour trip at 7 a.m. or by custom charter.

**Fare:** Adults, $160 for a full-day trip; $90 for half day. (Full-day trips preferred.) Children 12 and younger, free. Children 13 to 18, half price on most trips. Reservations advised. Packages available at Puffin's Bed and Breakfast, same address as above.

**Departure:** Boat leaves from Gustavus's dock. Gustavus is accessible only by plane or boat.

**Naturalist:** Naturalist or narrator aboard.

Owner Sandy Schroth says, "Glacier Bay Puffin Charters now serves as a central reservation service for all whale-watching charters in the area."

## Glacier Bay—Your Way!

Summer: P.O. Box 5, Gustavus, AK 99826
(907) 697-2288; Fax (907) 697-2289

Winter: P.O. Box 2557, St. George, UT 84771
(801) 673-8480; Fax (801) 673-8481

| | |
|---|---|
| **Whales:** | Orca, humpback |
| **Season:** | May 1 to September 15 |
| **Boats:** | Two boats, the *Pacific* and the *Frolic*; 6 passengers each |
| **Trips:** | Full- or half-day charters daily at 7:30 a.m. and noon. Overnight charters also available. Packages available at Glacier Bay Country Inn, at above address. |
| **Fare:** | $160 for full day (about 8 hours); $90 for half day (about 4 hours). Reservations advised. |
| **Departure:** | Boats leave from dock in Gustavus. Access to Gustavus is by boat or plane. |
| **Naturalist:** | Captain serves as naturalist. |

"Our area offers fantastic whale watching for humpbacks and orcas," says co-owner Annie Unrein. "We depart from the Gustavus dock and watch whales at nearby Point Adolphus, a rich feeding ground.

"We've put together a number of tour options, but guests are not limited to these exact tour options. We want them to experience Glacier Bay in a style that suits them! Owner-built and operated, we serve a maximum of 20 guests. Our small size and superior staff ensure warm, personal service to all."

## Glacier Guides Inc.

Summer: P.O. Box 66, Gustavus, AK 99826
(907) 697-2252 or (907) 463-1591

Winter: P.O. Box 460, Santa Clara, UT 84765
(801) 628-0973

| | |
|---|---|
| **Whales:** | Humpback, orca, minke |
| **Season:** | April to October |
| **Boats:** | The 72-foot yacht, *Alaskan Solitude*; 12 passengers |

**Trips:** One- to 6-day trips during which participants live on board; daily charters also.

**Fare:** Exclusive charter cost is $15,900 for 6-day trip for up to 6 passengers; $2,650 per additional person. Daily charter cost is $2,650 for up to 10 passengers; $200 for each additional person. Reservations required.

**Departure:** Boat leaves from the dock in Glacier Bay, which is accessible by ferry or plane.

**Naturalist:** Licensed Alaska Master Guide/Outfitter with 28 years experience in area serves as naturalist.

"Glacier Bay National Park's 16 glaciers calving into the sea is one of nature's major spectacles," says Jimmie C. Rosenbruch, a licensed Alaska Master Guide. "Less than 200 years ago, Glacier Bay was a great icefield. Today, ice has receded nearly 100 miles, leaving a magnificent bay full of all manner of wildlife and serving as summer feeding grounds for whales. We cruise the calm inside waters, so don't worry about motion sickness."

## Gustavus Inn at Glacier Bay

P.O. Box 60, Gustavus, AK 99826
(907) 697-2254 in summer; (913) 649-5220 in winter

**Whales:** Humpback, orca, minke, dolphin

**Season:** May 1 through September 15

**Boats:** Six boats that carry from 2 to 120 passengers

**Trips:** Short trips, half-day trips, full day, and overnight trips available throughout the season.

**Fare:** Short trips, $75. Chartered boat trips cost $100 per person for half days and $190 per person for full-day trips. Daily 8-hour trip to Glacier Bay on catamaran that carries 120 persons costs $157 for adults and $79 for children. 4-day kayak trips cost $500. Reservations advised.

**Departure:** Boats leave from Gustavus dock one mile from Gustavus Inn or from Bartlett Cove.

**Naturalist:** Naturalists from the National Park Service narrate the trips to Glacier Bay. Skippers narrate other trips.

"Since 1966, we have been hosting visitors to Glacier Bay in our unique home-stead," say owners JoAnn and David Lesh. "Humpback whales feed here in rich tidal currents at the mouth of Glacier Bay." The Leshes offer several packages that include whale-watch trips and a few days at their 14-room inn.

## Gustavus Marine Charters

P.O. Box 81W, Gustavus, AK 99826
(907) 697-2233

| | |
|---|---|
| **Whales:** | Humpback, orca, minke |
| **Season:** | May 15 to September 15 |
| **Boats:** | Two boats, 30 and 40 feet; 6 passengers each |
| **Trips:** | Single- or multi-day charters. |
| **Fare:** | For a party of 4, $1,200 a day, or $900 each for 3 days, 2 nights on board, with 4-person minimum. Reservations required. |
| **Departure:** | Boats leave from the dock in Gustavus. Access to Gustavus is by plane or boat. |
| **Naturalist:** | The captain, a former park ranger in Glacier Bay National Park, narrates. |

"Cruise the icy fjords in the comfort and privacy of your own diesel-powered yacht," owner Mike Nigro says. "Enjoy photography, birding, whale watching, and tidewater glaciers, plus the finest saltwater fishing Alaska has to offer. Spend three or four days getting to know this special part of the Great Land."

## Gusto Charters

P.O. Box 97, Gustavus, AK 99826
(907) 697-2290

| | |
|---|---|
| **Whales:** | Humpback, minke, orca |
| **Season:** | May 15 through September 15 |
| **Boat:** | One boat, the M V *Gusto*; 6 passengers |
| **Trips:** | Two 5-hour trips daily at 7 a.m. and noon. Full-day charters and custom overnight trips available. |
| **Fare:** | Adults, $160 for full day, $80 for half day. Children under 16 free. Reservations advised. |
| **Departure:** | Boats leave from Gustavus, which is accessible only by boat or plane. Pick-up available. |
| **Naturalist:** | None on board. |

Owner John "Rusty" Owen notes it's just a 30-minute trip from Gustavus to the whales, and there are no ocean swells. "We guarantee sightings of humpbacks, and we also see harbor seals, sea otters, eagles, puffins and more."

## Spirit Walker Expeditions

P.O. Box 240W, Gustavus, AK 99826
(800) KAYAKER or (907) 697-2266; Fax (907) 697-2211

| | |
|---|---|
| **Whales:** | Humpback, orca, minke, gray |
| **Season:** | May 1 to October 1 |
| **Boats:** | Twelve 2-person kayaks |
| **Trips:** | Two-, 5-, and 7-day trips kayaking in Icy Strait and camping on Chichago Island. |
| **Fare:** | From $550 to $1,488 per person, which includes charter transportation from Gustavus, all meals, and equipment. |
| **Departure:** | Trips leave from the dock in Gustavus, which is accessible by plane or limited tour boat access. |
| **Naturalist:** | Yes |

"Sea kayaking is probably the most exciting way to see whales," says Nathan Borson, president. "We have seen humpback whales on every 'WHALES! Trip' we have done. We get close, without chasing or disturbing whales. There is no engine noise, so we hear the whales breathing and slapping the water clearly. There is no prop noise to interfere with our hydrophone.

"Drifting right at the surface of the water, we see other life, too—sea lions, seals, birds, even plankton and kelp. We get a feeling of what it's like for a whale to live here. We camp on a beach that whales swim past at night, breathing noisily."

# JUNEAU, KETCHIKAN, AND PETERSBURG

## Outdoor Alaska

P.O. Box 7814, Ketchikan, AK 99901
(907) 225-6044; Fax (907) 225-8636

| | |
|---|---|
| **Whales:** | Humpback |
| **Season:** | June through September |
| **Boats:** | Three boats, the *Misty Fjord*, the *Emerald Fjord*, and the *Crystal Fjord*; up to 32 passengers each |
| **Trips:** | One-day or multi-day charters |
| **Fare:** | $118 to $200 per person per day depending on number of passengers. Reservations required. |
| **Departure:** | Trips leave from Juneau, Ketchikan, and Petersburg; all are accessible by air or boat. |
| **Naturalist:** | Skipper is a marine biologist. |

"Admiralty Island in southeast Alaska has surrounding it one of the largest populations of humpback whales in Alaska," says native Alaskan Captain Dale Pihlman. "These whales are concentrated for convenient viewing in the inland waters of Stephens Passage, Seymour Canal, and Frederick Sound."

## KODIAK

### Kodiak Nautical Discoveries

P.O. Box 95, Kodiak, AK 99615
(907) 486-5234

| | |
|---|---|
| **Whales:** | Gray, humpback, orca |
| **Season:** | May to November |
| **Boats:** | One boat, the *Sea Surgeon*; 6 passengers |
| **Trips:** | One trip daily at 8 a.m. |
| **Fare:** | $150 per person for 8-hour trip. |
| **Departure:** | Boat leaves from Slip 52 in the main boat harbor in Kodiak, on Marine Way at Shelikof Street. |
| **Naturalist:** | Skipper narrates trip. |

Ron Brockman, the skipper, was born and raised on Kodiak Island. He has operated a charter boat in Kodiak waters since 1970, has fished commercially, taught outdoor courses at Kodiak College, and holds a degree in biology from Alaska Methodist University.

Brockman is a semiretired orthopedic surgeon and a captain in the Naval Reserve. Brockman's partner, Tom Stick, is a former dentist who spent many months off the coasts of Alaska and Siberia in a U.S. Navy nuclear submarine. Off the boat, Stick guides hunts and has managed a fishing lodge.

### Kodiak Western Charters

P.O. Box 4123, Kodiak, AK 99615
(907) 486-2200; Fax (907) 486-2686

| | |
|---|---|
| **Whales:** | Fin, humpback, minke, orca, gray |
| **Season:** | April 1 through December |
| **Boats:** | One 50-foot boat, the *Ten Bears*; 6 passengers |
| **Trips:** | Single full-day trips or multi-day charters |
| **Fare:** | Fares vary according to use and season. Please write or call for rates. |

**Departure:**    Boat departs from St. Herman's Boat Harbor on Near Island, just across the bridge from Kodiak.

**Naturalist:**    Yes

Owner and operator Eric Stirrup has sailed Kodiak Island waters for 12 years. He has a degree in marine biology, and the oceans have been his interest and avocation since 1973.

"The rich shelf waters of the Gulf of Alaska are home to many resident and migrating whales. March brings the gray whales, and fin and humpbacks are common visitors during the summer. Minke and orcas are seen throughout the year."

## SEWARD

# Kenai Coastal Tours and Kenai Fjord Tours

P.O. Box 104783, Anchorage, AK 99510
(907) 277-2131 (Anchorage); (907) 224-7114 (Seward)

**Whales:**    Orca, humpback, gray

**Season:**    Mid-May to September

**Boats:**    Six boats, the 82-foot *Kenai Explorer* plus five others

**Trips:**    Three full-day trips daily at 8 a.m., 10 a.m., and 11:30 a.m. Two half-day trips daily at 8:30 a.m. and 1 p.m.

**Fare:**    For full day trips, $95 or $89, depending on the boat. For half-day trips, $58. Reservations required.

**Departure:**    Boats leave from Seward Boat Harbor; the office is on the boardwalk. Via highway, Seward is 125 miles south of Anchorage. You can also get there by train, bus, or plane.

**Naturalist:**    Yes

The Chiswell Islands, in Kenai Fjords National Park, are a designated marine wildlife refuge. "As the *Kenai Explorer* cruises the rugged coastline, you'll see large seabird rookeries and up to 1,000 vocal sea lions in one of the largest concentrations of marine wildlife anywhere," a spokeswoman says.

"Depending on the time of year, we see gray, humpback, or killer whales as well as playful porpoise and sea otters. Mountain goats and bald eagles are often sighted along the shoreline. At the 'Glacier of the Day,' look for harbor seals near the ice floes."

## Mariah Tours and Charters

3812 Katmai Circle, Anchorage, AK 99517
(907) 243-1238; Fax (907) 243-1238

| | |
|---|---|
| **Whales:** | Orca, humpback, gray, minke, fin |
| **Season:** | April 20 to September 30 |
| **Boats:** | Two boats; 22 passengers each |
| **Trips:** | Two 9-hour trips daily at 8 a.m. and 10 a.m. Saturday is the busiest day. Exclusive charters available. |
| **Fare:** | Adults, $80; children 12 and younger, $40. Reservations advised. |
| **Departure:** | Boats leave from Slip D6 and D10 in the Seward Boat Harbor. Via highway, Seward is 125 miles south of Anchorage. You can also get there by train, bus, or plane. |
| **Naturalist:** | Captains serve as naturalists. |

"Let us show you a unique natural setting in and around Kenai Fjords National Park and the Chiswell Islands National Wildlife Refuge," says owner/operator John Sheedy. "Both offer unsurpassed opportunities for close-up viewing of whales; a large sea lion colony; over 50 species of birds; huge concentrations of puffins, kittiwakes, and murres; and numerous bald eagles. We visit an active tidewater glacier up close and personal! And we limit the number of passengers so everyone has room, equal viewing opportunity, and more personalized service."

## Alaska Wyldewind Charters

617 Katlian, B-33, Sitka, AK 99835
(907) 747-5734

| | |
|---|---|
| **Whales:** | Humpback; occasionally gray, orca, minke |
| **Season:** | Late April to late September |
| **Boats:** | One boat, the *Wyldewind*; 6 passengers |
| **Trips:** | Numbers and times of trips depend on demand, accessibility of whales, and captain's availability |
| **Fare:** | Boat charter is $60 for half day; $85 for full day; $96 for 24 hours, sharing purchase and preparation of food; $140 for 24 hours, including meals. Minimum: 2 passengers. Reservations advised. Special room rate available at Westmark Shee Atika, P.O. Box 318, Sitka, AK 99835; (907) 747-6241. |
| **Departure:** | Boat leaves from Sitka, which is accessible by plane or ferry. |
| **Naturalist:** | Skipper serves as naturalist. |

Skipper Jerry Dzugan says, "We also combine other activities with whale watching, such as sailing, other wildlife viewing, hotsprings, hiking, and exploring. We have no set schedule of arrivals/departures but plan trips around our clients' schedules, interests, and budgets.

"Our whale-watching activities for the public emphasize nonintrusive observation techniques so as to cause the least amount of stress and disturbance to marine mammals' natural behavior. The ability to sail noiselessly along while observing the rich wildlife and spectacular scenery helps create a unique experience for those who appreciate unspoiled wilderness and rich wildlife viewing."

## Steller Charters

2810 Sawmill Creek Road, Sitka, AK 99835
(907) 747-6157 or (907) 747-6711

| | |
|---|---|
| **Whales:** | Humpback, gray, and occasionally minke |
| **Season:** | Year-round |
| **Boats:** | One boat, the *Steller J*; 6 passengers |
| **Trips:** | Two 3- to 4-hour trips per day; departure flexible. |
| **Fare:** | $50 per person, minimum 4 people. Special rates in December. Reservations advised. Package room rates available. |
| **Departure:** | Boat leaves from Crescent Harbor in downtown Sitka, accessible by plane or ferry. |
| **Naturalist:** | Captain is a naturalist. |

"I am a retired high school science teacher and live year-round in Sitka," says Captain William L. Foster. "Sitka is relatively mild at all seasons, and we are fortunate to have whale watching all the time. Humpbacks have been seen here every month of the year.

"Our most unique humpback watching is, however, in winter! Numbers vary, but at times there is a great gathering (up to 20 or more) from November through January while the whales feed on herring. They can be very vocal at that time."

Sitka is developing a whale-watching park near the best land viewing area.

## Alaskan Wilderness Sailing Safaris

P.O. Box 1313W, Valdez, AK 99686
(907) 835-5175; Fax (907) 835-5679

| | |
|---|---|
| **Whales:** | Orca, humpback, minke, fin |
| **Season:** | June 1 to September 1 |
| **Boats:** | Three boats; two with 4-passenger capacity; one carries 6 passengers |

| | |
|---|---|
| **Trips:** | Four- to 12-day trips |
| **Fare:** | Prices vary according to length of trip; price includes meals and nightly lodging. Reservations required. |
| **Departure:** | Boats leave from Growler Island Wilderness Camp. Access by tour boat from Valdez or bush plane from Anchorage. |
| **Naturalist:** | Yes |

Owners Nancy and James Lethcoe say their trips afford an outstanding opportunity "to observe numerous species of whales and other marine mammals" and that the 12-day trip is a killer whale research trip. They also note that the area offers spectacular scenery.

# WRANGELL, KETCHIKAN, JUNEAU, AND SITKA

## Alaskan Star Charters

P.O. Box 2027, Wrangell, AK 99929
(907) 874-3084

| | |
|---|---|
| **Whales:** | Humpback, minke, orca |
| **Season:** | Mid-April to early November |
| **Boats:** | One boat, the *Star Queen*; 6 passengers |
| **Trips:** | Five- to 10-day trips, April through August. Charters until November. Longer trips available. |
| **Fare:** | $200 to $500 per day depending on service and season. Price includes double occupancy aboard, private bath, food, shore excursions. Reservations required. |
| **Departure:** | Boat leaves from Wrangell, Ketchikan, Juneau, and Sitka. |
| **Naturalist:** | Yes |

"These outings are designed to let guests experience the wildest areas while enjoying wine with dinner and other creature comforts," says Captain Ken Wyrick. "The day's activities can be planned to be rustic or rugged, but the boat and staff are available with comfort."

## VARIOUS DESTINATIONS

### Biological Journeys

1696 Ocean Drive, McKinleyville, CA 95521
(800) 548-7555 or (707) 839-0178; Fax (707) 839-4656

| | |
|---|---|
| **Whales:** | Orca, humpback, minke, gray, depending on trip |
| **Season:** | Late May to mid-October |
| **Boats:** | One boat, the 50-foot *Delphinius*; 8 passengers in three double staterooms and a 4-person berth. |
| **Trips:** | Seven- to 10-day cruises on various routes in southeastern Alaska, exploring areas such as Robson Bight, Misty Fjords National Monument, Frederick Sound, Glacier Bay, Icy Strait, and Kootznahoo (Admiralty) Island. Participants live on board. |
| **Fare:** | Range is from $2,495 for 7 days along the outer coast to $3,295 for 10 days on the Inside Passage. Price includes instruction, meals, accommodations, and transportation during the program. Reservations required. |
| **Departure:** | Boat departs from various ports in Alaska and British Columbia, depending on the trip. |
| **Naturalist:** | Yes |

"Are you inquisitive? Do you love nature? Do you dream of an unrivaled adventure?" ask Ronn Storro-Patterson and Ron LeValley. "Biological Journeys' natural history vacations are designed just for you. We provide a penetrating view of the world. Delight you with uncommon experiences. Enrich your understanding. Reawaken the sense of wonder and excitement you felt as a child!"

Ronn Storro-Patterson is one of the world's leading authorities on whales, and Ron LeValley is a world-renowned ornithological expert. "Our trips are so refreshingly different, we feel remiss in merely calling them wilderness cruises. We invite you to reach out and touch nature. You travel in safety aboard a comfortable cruise vessel, in harmony with nature and at nature's own pace."

# National Audubon Society

700 Broadway, New York, NY 10003
(212) 979-3066; Fax (212) 353-0190

| | |
|---|---|
| **Whales:** | Humpback |
| **Season:** | June |
| **Boats:** | One boat, the *Sea Bird*; 37 cabins for 70 passengers plus small inflatable landing craft for short expeditions. |
| **Trips:** | A 10-day cruise at least once a season to Misty Fjords, Le Conte Bay, Tracy Arm, Haines, Point Adolphus, Glacier Bay National Park, and the islands of southeast Alaska. |
| **Fare:** | $3,290 to $4,580 per person. Price includes cabin, meals, transfers, excursions, permits, tips, and taxes. Airfare not included. Reservations required. |
| **Departure:** | Group gathers in Seattle and flies to Ketchikan, where the cruise begins. |
| **Naturalist:** | Naturalist is Audubon research biologist. |

In June of 1989, the National Audubon Society sponsored its first excursion along the coast of southeast Alaska. A spokeswoman notes, "I wish I could share with you all the wonderful responses of those who sailed together. Even our seasoned, world-traveling Audubon staff guides come back with stories of unbelievable beauty and magnificent wildlife."

## Oceanic Society Expeditions

Fort Mason Center, Building E, San Francisco, CA 94123
(800) 326-7491 or (415) 441-1106; Fax (415) 474-3395

| | |
|---|---|
| **Whales:** | Humpback |
| **Season:** | July |
| **Boats:** | One boat, the 68-foot *Island Roamer*, which sleeps 12. Participants live aboard. A motorized inflatable raft is used for shore excursions. |
| **Trips:** | One 11-day cruise in Alaska's Inside Passage, from Prince Rupert to Petersburg. |
| **Fare:** | $2,950 per person, which includes accommodations, meals, guides, and a charter float plane trip back to Prince Rupert. Reservations required. |
| **Departure:** | Trip leaves from Prince Rupert, British Columbia |
| **Naturalist:** | Naturalist from Oceanic Society Expeditions. |

"Every summer, almost 100 humpback whales gather in Frederick Sound to feed on krill," says a spokeswoman. "It is one of the best places in the world to observe humpback whales feeding. It was here that 'bubble netting' was first observed, and the whales can be seen lunging into schools of fish with their mouths agape."

Other sights include bears at Anan Bay, the tidewater glacier at Le Conte Bay, plus porpoise, seals, dolphins, eagles, and seabirds.

## Sea Safaris

International Oceanographic Foundation
P.O. Box 4999000, Miami, FL 33149
(305) 361-4697

| | |
|---|---|
| **Whales:** | Humpback, orca |
| **Season:** | July |
| **Boats:** | One boat, the 152-foot *Sea Lion*; 70 passengers in 37 outside cabins |

**Trips:**    One annual 10-day trip to Southeast Alaska, which includes the Misty Fjords, Prince of Wales Island, Agate Beach, Petersburg, Admiralty Island, Muir Glacier, Glacier Bay National Park, and Point Adolphus. Participants live on the boat.

**Fare:**    $2,970 to $4,200 per person, depending on cabin size and location. Participants must be members of the International Oceanographic Foundation ($18 a year). Fare does not include airfare, alcoholic beverages, or tips. Reservations required.

**Departure:**    Trip leaves from Prince Rupert, British Columbia, and concludes in Seattle.

**Naturalist:**    Naturalists affiliated with the IOF are aboard.

"We immerse ourselves in the natural beauty of southeast Alaska," said a spokeswoman for the IOF Sea Safaris. "Staff members who have an in-depth knowledge of Alaska lead the travelers from forest to shoreline to witness bears, eagles, whales, and other wildlife, and a scientist is on hand to enhance the natural history experience."

The International Oceanographic Foundation publishes *Sea Frontiers* in collaboration with the University of Miami Rosenstiel School of Marine and Atmospheric Science.

# MUSEUMS

## ALASKA

### Pratt Museum

3779 Bartlett Street, Homer, AK 99603
(907) 235-8635; Fax (907) 235-2764

The Pratt Museum, run by the Homer Society of Natural History, collects, preserves, and interprets the history of the Kenai Peninsula. The whale exhibit includes a sperm whale skeleton, a beluga skeleton, a Bering beaked whale skeleton, a fin whale skull, and a Cuvier's beaked whale skull.

Hours are 10 a.m. to 6 p.m. daily in summer and noon to 5 p.m. Tuesday through Sunday in winter. The Museum is closed Thanksgiving, Christmas, and the month of January. Admission for nonmembers is $3 for adults, $2 for senior citizens, and free for children under 18.

### University of Alaska Museum

907 Yukon Drive, Fairbanks, AK 99775
(907) 474-7505; Fax (907) 474-5469

The mission of the Museum is to collect, interpret, and teach the natural and cultural history of the circumpolar area. Included in the exhibit on whales are the skull and lower jaw of a bowhead whale and paraphernalia related to the Eskimos' whale hunting. One such item is a twelve-person *umiak*, a boat made of split walrus hide with waterproof stitching.

From June through August, the Museum is open daily from 9 a.m. to 7 p.m.; in May and September, from 9 a.m. to 5 p.m.; from October through April, from noon to 5 p.m. Adults, $4; seniors, $3; children under 12, free. No admission is charged on Fridays during the winter.

# NATIONAL PARKS

**ALASKA**

## Glacier Bay National Park and Preserve

P.O. Box 140, Gustavus, AK 99826
(907) 697-2230

Glacier Bay National Park and Preserve was completely covered by ice just two hundred years ago. Today the Park has 16 tidewater glaciers, remnants of a general ice advance—the Little Ice Age—that began 4000 years ago. Wildlife in the Park and Preserve, which cover 3,328,000 acres, include humpback, minke, and orca whales. Write for a free brochure and map.

## Kenai Fjords National Park

National Park Service, P.O. Box 1727, Seward, AK 99664
(907) 224-3175

Glaciers, seabirds, marine mammals, and a rugged coast are the special features of the Kenai Fjords National Park, which covers 567,000 acres. Write for a free map and brochure.

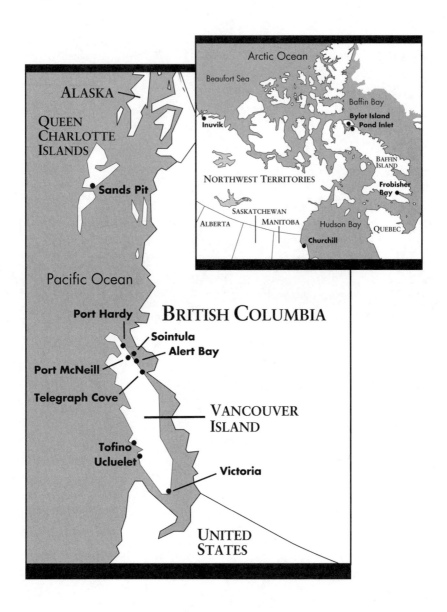

ALASKA

QUEEN
CHARLOTTE
ISLANDS

Sands Pit

Pacific Ocean

Port Hardy

Sointula
Alert Bay

Port McNeill

Telegraph Cove

BRITISH COLUMBIA

VANCOUVER
ISLAND

Tofino
Ucluelet

Victoria

UNITED
STATES

Arctic Ocean

Beaufort Sea

Baffin Bay

Inuvik

Bylot Island
Pond Inlet

BAFFIN
ISLAND

NORTHWEST TERRITORIES

Frobisher
Bay

SASKATCHEWAN

ALBERTA   MANITOBA   Hudson Bay   QUEBEC

Churchill

202

# WESTERN CANADA

When it comes to whales, Canada has something for everyone. The mighty blues, rare right whales, finbacks, humpbacks, almost-mythical bowheads, grays, tusked narwhals, pilot whales, orcas, and belugas swim in the seas off both coasts, inhabit arctic waters, and populate at least two rivers. Whales are also in Canada's gulfs, bays, and sounds, and at the right time of year, you can watch the whale of your choice from shore.

British Columbia can count on gray whales in March and April; orcas and minkes in July, August, and September; and maybe some finbacks and humpbacks later in the year. In response, tour operators sponsor trips from several cities on Vancouver Island and in the Queen Charlotte Islands. Some tour operators offer extended trips departing from various locations in British Columbia to better watch Canada's whales.

Every July and August, special expeditions leave Churchill, Manitoba, to see belugas in Hudson Bay and the Churchill River. The popular belugas can also be seen off Inuvik, in the Northwest Territories, in July and August. Trips to see the tusked narwhal and the seldom-observed bowhead originate from Baffin Island.

Basically, you can count on whales wherever there are whale-watch tour operators, but given the vast coastal exposures of Canada, don't be surprised if you encounter them elsewhere, too.

# TOURISM INFORMATION

## BRITISH COLUMBIA
### Tourism British Columbia
Parliament Buildings, Victoria, British Columbia, V8V 1X4 Canada
(800) 663-6000

## MANITOBA
### Travel Manitoba
Dept. 6020, Seventh Floor, 155 Carlton Avenue, Winnipeg,
Manitoba, R3C 3H8 Canada
800 (665-0040)

## NORTHWEST TERRITORIES
### TravelArctic
P.O. Box 1320, Yellowknife, Northwest Territories, XlA 2L9 Canada
(800) 661-0788

# WHALE-WATCHING TRIPS

## BRITISH COLUMBIA

### ALERT BAY AND ALDER BAY

### Sea Smoke/Sail with the Whales

P.O. Box 483, Alert Bay, British Columbia, V0N 1A0 Canada
(604) 974-5225; Fax (604) 974-2266

| | |
|---|---|
| **Whales:** | Orca, minke |
| **Season:** | May to October |
| **Boats:** | One 44-foot sailboat, the *Tuan*; 14 passengers |
| **Trips:** | One 5-1/2-hour trip daily to Robson Bight region from Alert Bay at 8:15 a.m. and Alder Bay at 8:45 a.m. |
| **Fare:** | Adults, $65 (Canadian); children: 5 to 12, $50; under 5, free. Reservations required. |
| **Departure:** | Boat leaves from Alert Bay and Alder Bay. |
| **Naturalist:** | Yes |

David and Maureen Towers say their trip is special because of their yacht—its interior is mahogany, teak, and brass—and their food: fresh fish at lunch and scones at tea time.

Also, they say, "We are quiet. There is no engine noise, only the sounds of the whales from our hydrophones as wind, water, whales, and yacht blend together in natural harmony."

## PORT HARDY

### American Cetacean Society Expeditions

P.O. Box 2639, San Pedro, CA 90731
(310) 548-6279; Fax (310) 548-6950

| | |
|---|---|
| **Whales:** | Orca |
| **Season:** | Late August to early September |
| **Boats:** | One 68-foot sailing yacht, the *Island Roamer*; 16 passengers |
| **Trips:** | One 7-day trip sailing and living on board. |
| **Fare:** | Members, $1,595 (U.S.) per person. Nonmembers, 10 percent more, or join ACS ($25 per family). Fare includes meals and accommodations. |
| **Departure:** | Trip starts in Port Hardy, on Vancouver Island. |
| **Naturalist:** | American Cetacean Society naturalist accompanies trip. |

The American Cetacean Society has been conducting specialized trips for small groups to see whales since 1973. "ACS trips are designed for people who are interested in the world about them and want adventure with whales and nature," says a spokeswoman.

"You will most likely encounter a resident population of 140 orcas. You also will visit several Indian villages and explore the beaches and tidepools."

### Oceanic Society Expeditions

Fort Mason Center, Building E, San Francisco, CA 94123
(800) 326-7491 or (415) 441-1106; Fax (415) 474-3395

| | |
|---|---|
| **Whales:** | Orca, minke |
| **Season:** | August |
| **Boats:** | One 68-foot ketch, the *Island Roamer*; 16 passengers |
| **Trips:** | Seven-day trip living on board and sailing off Vancouver Island. |
| **Fare:** | $1,540 (U.S.) per person. Price includes meals, accommodations, and guides. Reservations required. |

**Departure:**   Trip begins at Port Hardy, on north Vancouver Island.

**Naturalist:**   Yes

"Johnstone Strait is absolutely the best place in the world to see killer whales," says a spokeswoman for Oceanic Society Expeditions. "Nowhere else can you expect to experience such close encounters with these majestic mammals.

"Approximately 330 individual whales have been identified in the waters off British Columbia and Washington. Pods can contain up to 50 animals. Our expedition combines whale watching with sailing and exploring the shores of an island wilderness."

## PORT McNEILL

### Ecosummer Expeditions

1516 Duranleau Street, Vancouver, British Columbia, V6H 3S4 Canada
(800) 688-8605 or (604) 669-7741; Fax (604) 669-3244

**Whales:**   Orca, gray, minke

**Season:**   Late June to late September

**Boats:**   Six 2-person kayaks; 10 participants and two guides.

**Trips:**   Seven-day trips paddling and camping along the Inside Passage off Vancouver Island.

**Fare:**   $799 (U.S.) per person. Reservations required.

**Departure:**   Trips start at Port McNeill.

**Naturalist:**   Guides are naturalists.

"Although we have operated sea kayak adventures since the 1970s, the concept is still new to many people, who may have visions of paddling in the small unstable kayaks typically used for river trips," says a spokesman.

"However, in actuality we use very stable craft especially designed for ocean environments. These boats demand no previous experience, and all persons adapt very quickly to the paddling and sailing skill required."

Orca Watch, a land-based program, is also available. Write for information. Founded in 1976, Ecosummer Expeditions began as an adventure company that promoted environmental education, working primarily with high school students. Founder Jim Allan was soon deluged with requests from adults who wanted activity-oriented, natural history trips, and so Ecosummer Expeditions evolved.

## Northern Lights Expeditions

6141 Northeast Bothell Way, Suite 101, Seattle, WA 98155
(206) 483-6396

| | |
|---|---|
| **Whales:** | Orca, minke |
| **Season:** | June to September |
| **Boats:** | Six 2-person kayaks, plus two 1-person kayaks for guides |
| **Trips:** | Kayaking and camping for 6 days along the Inside Passage off Vancouver Island. |
| **Fare:** | $850 (U.S.) per person. Price includes food, kayak, and camping gear. Minimum age is 16. Reservations required. |
| **Departure:** | Trips leave from Port McNeill. |
| **Naturalist:** | Guides are naturalists. |

"Participants have a chance to live on the shores of the whale's environment for a week," says founder and head guide David Arcese. "You can hear the whales passing in the night, close to the beach. You can paddle within a few feet of the whales because the kayaks are silent and slow-moving, thereby not causing anxiety among the whales."

The trips are intended for people who have no experience kayaking, and the pace is relaxed, he says.

## Viking West Lodge & Charter

P.O. Box 113, Port McNeill, British Columbia, V0N 2R0 Canada
(604) 956-3431; Fax (604) 956-4633

| | |
|---|---|
| **Whales:** | Orca, minke, humpback |
| **Season:** | Mid-May through October |
| **Boats:** | Three boats; a rigid-hull inflatable Zodiac raft, a 24-foot cabin cruiser, and a 34-foot Beachcomber; 4, 5, and 9 passengers respectively |
| **Trips:** | One or two trips daily to Robson Bight area, leaving between 8 and 10 a.m. and returning by 5 or 7 p.m. |
| **Fare:** | Smaller boats rent for $40 (Canadian) an hour; larger boats, for $60 an hour. 4-hour minimum. Reservations advised. Multi-day packages available for lodging on board, in 3-bedroom floathouse, or in hotel. Write for details. |
| **Departure:** | From Port McNeill and Telegraph Cove |
| **Naturalist:** | Skipper serves as naturalist. |

The skipper, Dennis Richards, says, "Whale watching is the neatest thing in the water, except maybe swimming with them." All passengers receive a chart on which they may mark their route. They may also record the sounds of the whales. Richards is the area's first and only full-time professional guide, he says. "And I cook fresh-caught crab or fish on day charters—it's delicious!"

# SOINTULA

## WAYWARD WIND CHARTERS

P.O. Box 300, Sointula, British Columbia, V0N 3E0 Canada
(604) 973-6307

| | |
|---|---|
| **Whales:** | Orca, sometimes minke |
| **Season:** | Mid-June through early October |
| **Boats:** | One 28-foot sailboat; 8 to 10 passengers |

**Trips:** One 8-hour trip daily to Robson Bight area, a marine preserve set aside for orcas. Seafood luncheon and home-baked sweets served.

**Fare:** Adults, $65 (Canadian); seniors and children 5 to 12, $45. Reservations advised. Bed and breakfast available in the Wayward Wind Lodge.

**Departure:** Trips leave from Sointula, on Malcolm Island. Regular ferry service runs from Port McNeill to Sointula; the trip takes 30 minutes. Transportation from the ferry dock is provided, if necessary.

**Naturalist:** Skipper serves as naturalist on board.

John and Vilma Gamble say, "We feel our business is unique because of its personalized service. Depending on the group and time, a little fishing or sightseeing may be done." Wayward Wind's skipper has been sailing on the Pacific since the 1970s and gladly shares his extensive knowledge.

## TELEGRAPH COVE

## Raven Kayak Experiences

501 Harris, Bellingham, WA 98225
(206) 671-4528

**Whales:** Orca, minke, gray, harbor porpoise

**Season:** Mid-March through mid-October

**Boats:** Six 2-person kayaks

**Trips:** Several one- to eight-day trips, kayaking and camping in the San Juan Islands, Knight Inlet, or Barkley Sound. The Knight Inlet trip is the most popular.

**Fare:** Trips in the San Juan Islands range from $89 for one day to $449 for five days. Knight Inlet and Barkley Sound, both 8-day trips, cost $850. Meals prepared by a gourmet chef are part of the package. Reservations required.

**Departure:** Trips leave from Telegraph Cove. Transportation from Bellingham is provided.

**Naturalist:** Yes

"My guides and I are bridges to the natural world," says owner Jeff Albin. "We provide safe access to the wild places within and outside of us all. In these places, people learn much about themselves and their connection to the earth."

The trip storyteller tells traditional tales about the origin of whales, tales from indigenous cultures in the area of Vancouver, and the naturalist provides whale etiquette.

## Stubbs Island Charters Ltd.

P.O. Box 7, Telegraph Cove, British Columbia V0N 3J0 Canada
(604) 928-3185 or 928-3117

| | |
|---|---|
| **Whales**: | Orca |
| **Season:** | Late June to mid-October |
| **Boats:** | Two 60-foot motor vessels |
| **Trips:** | From late June to mid-July, one 4-to 5-hour trip daily to Johnstone Strait area. From mid-July to mid-October, two 4- to 5-hour trips a day. |
| **Fare:** | $60 (Canadian) per person, with discounts for senior citizens and children. Meals available for sale on board. Reservations advised. |
| **Departure:** | Trips leave from the end of the boardwalk in Telegraph Cove, south of Port McNeill. |
| **Naturalist:** | Skipper serves as naturalist. |

The Borrowman and Mackay families say that "After many seasons of whale watching, we are finding that it is an international 'sport' that has no language barrier!"

Their brochure advises: "Please remember to dress warmly and bring your camera with plenty of film."

## TOFINO

### Blue Moon Explorations

P.O. Box 2568WW, Bellingham, WA 98227
(206) 966-8805

| | |
|---|---|
| **Whales:** | Gray |
| **Season:** | March and April |
| **Boats:** | Eight 2-person kayaks |
| **Trips:** | Four 4-day trips to Vancouver Island, B.C., and Long Beach Peninsula. Accommodations are in bed and breakfast inns. Some trips are for women only. |
| **Fare:** | Fares range between $400 and $600, which includes kayaks, accommodations and meals, safety equipment, and guides. Reservations required. |
| **Departure:** | Trips begin at Tofino, B.C., or Olympia, WA. |
| **Naturalist:** | Yes |

Owner Kathleen Grimbly says, "Blue Moon Explorations are designed to expand our awareness of the many intricate relationships in the web of life. Traveling by kayak, we experience the whales more intimately and less intrusively. Our trips are designed for people of all ages and abilities."

### Clayoquot Sound Charters

P.O. Box 453, Tofino, British Columbia, V0R 2Z0 Canada
(604) 725-2888

| | |
|---|---|
| **Whales:** | Gray, orca |
| **Season:** | March 15 to October 15 |
| **Boats:** | One boat; 20 passengers |
| **Trips:** | Three 2-hour trips daily, at 10:30 a.m., 1 p.m., and 3:30 p.m. A 6 p.m. cruise is available in summer by request. Morning trips are busiest. |

**Fare:** Adults, $35 (Canadian); students and senior citizens, $30; children ages 6 to 12, $20; children under 6, free. Reservations advised. Cruiser suits provided.

**Departure:** Trips leave from Government Wharf in Tofino, just down the hill from the Maquinna Hotel. Check in at the office first, at 300 Main Street.

**Naturalist:** Yes

Owners Carl and Joe Martin, native Indians, also serve as skippers. "We have an incredible knowledge of local waters, and we designed our boat especially for whale watching. It is excellent for viewing and experiencing the Clayoquot Sound. Our guide is friendly, approachable, and knowledgeable, and our prices are low."

## Jamie's Whaling Station

P.O. Box 590, Tofino, British Columbia, V0R 2Z0 Canada
(604) 725-3919; Fax (604) 725-2138

**Whales:** Gray, orca, minke

**Season:** March 1 to October 30

**Boats:** Two rigid-hull inflatable Zodiacs, 12 passengers each; a 65-foot cabin cruiser, the *Lady Selkirk*, 56 passengers; and a 26-foot cabin cruiser, 12 passengers

**Trips:** Two to four 2-hour trips a day. Small boats go at 9:30 a.m., noon, 3 p.m., and 5:30 p.m. Large boats go at 10 or 11 a.m. and 1:30 p.m.

**Fare:** Zodiacs: adults, $40 (Canadian); youths, $25. Children under 6 not allowed on Zodiacs, which are also not recommended for senior citizens. Cruisers: adults, $50; senior citizens, $45; children: 6 to 16, $25; under 6, free. Family rates available. Reservations advised. Packages offered with Walrus Retreat Bed and Breakfast.

**Departure:** Boats depart from Tofino's Whaling Wharf, 606 Campbell in Tofino.

**Naturalist:** Yes

Watching whales off Vancouver Island's west coast in a rigid hull inflatable raft is "ideal for those who enjoy life in the fast wave," says president Jamie Bray.

"On our whale-watching cruises, you'll enjoy tall tales and local legends as we cruise past the islands and inlets that housed many a colorful character. Whale sightings guaranteed—whales you'll see or your next trip is free!

"Wild about wildlife? We've got more than whales to show you."

## Remote Passages

P.O. Box 624, Tofino, British Columbia, V0R 2Z0 Canada
(604) 725-3330; Fax (604) 725-3380

| | |
|---|---|
| **Whales:** | Gray, orca, minke |
| **Season:** | March 1 to October 31 |
| **Boats:** | Three rigid-hull inflatables; 12 passengers each; "cruiser suits," gloves, and rubber boots provided. |
| **Trips:** | Three 2-1/2-hour whale-watch trips daily at 9 a.m., noon, and 3 p.m. A 6-1/2-hour trip that leaves early in the afternoon includes a visit to Hot Springs Cove. Sunset tours in summer. |
| **Fare:** | For whale watch trips, adults, $40 (Canadian); students, $35; children under 12, $20. The Hot Springs Explorer costs $60 for adults, $55 for students and $40 for children. Reservations advised. Hotel package for $62.50 per person includes double occupancy ocean view accommodation, whale-watching tour, and whale information package. |
| **Departure:** | Trips leave from Meares Landing at Main and Wharf in Tofino. |
| **Naturalist:** | Naturalist is trained in marine biology. |

Owner Don Travers notes that the Hot Springs Explorer trips "give people another way to see the whales and appreciate the beauty of this area."

# UCLUELET

## Canadian Princess Resort

P.O. Box 939, Ucluelet, British Columbia, V0R 3A0 Canada
(800) 663-7090 or (604) 726-7771; Fax (604) 726-7121

| | |
|---|---|
| **Whales:** | Gray and occasionally orca |
| **Season:** | March 1 to September 31 |
| **Boats:** | Ten boats; 18 to 22 passengers each |
| **Trips:** | Two 3-hour trips daily at 9 a.m. and 1:30 p.m. |
| **Fare:** | Adults, $35 (Canadian); children 12 and under, $20. Family and group rates. Rates higher on weekends. Reservations advised on weekdays, required on weekends. Accommodations available at the resort's center, a 235-foot ship, the *Canadian Princess*, or on shore. |
| **Departure:** | Trips leave from Ucluelet Harbor. |
| **Naturalist:** | None on board. |

Lorena Kemps, service manager, says, "The mainstay of this resort and the reason we have so many return guests is our crew, who are the backbone of this operation. That is what makes us special. They really do care about the guests."

She adds, "The drive from Nanaimo to Ucluelet is very scenic, with lots of stops along the way. Traveling along the Pacific Rim Highway is breathtaking."

## Subtidal Adventures

P.O. Box 78, Ucluelet, British Columbia, V0R 3A0 Canada
(604) 726-7336 or 726-7061

| | |
|---|---|
| **Whales:** | Gray, humpback, orca |
| **Season:** | March 1 to October 31 |
| **Boats:** | One 36-foot ex-rescue boat, the *Dixie IV*, and a 24-foot rigid hull inflatable Zodiac; 24 passengers total |
| **Trips:** | Three or four trips daily of different durations to various destinations in Barkley Sound to see the gray whales and to the Big Banks to see humpbacks. |

215

| | |
|---|---|
| **Fare:** | Fares for gray whale trips in the spring are $35 (Canadian) for adults, $$20 for children 6 to 12, and $10 for children under 6. For humpback trips, $55, $35 and $25 respectively. Reservations advised. You can make them at the Gray Whale Deli in Ucluelet, (604) 726-7336. |
| **Departure:** | Boats depart from Ucluelet Boat Basin on Vancouver Island. |
| **Naturalist:** | Skipper serves as naturalist. |

"We are the oldest charter boat company here and have tailored our cruises to provide the best possible experience to our guests," says owner Brian Congdon. "Whichever cruise you choose, we know you will go home with memories to last a lifetime."

## Seacoast Expeditions Ltd.

1655 Ash Road, Victoria, British Columbia, V8N 2T2 Canada
(604) 383-2254; Fax (604) 383-4383

| | |
|---|---|
| **Whales:** | Orca, minke |
| **Season:** | May 1 to September 30; highest frequency of sightings is during June and July |
| **Boats:** | Three rigid-hull inflatable boats; each carries 12 passengers. Full-length cruiser suits provided. |
| **Trips:** | As many as six 3-hour trips daily at 9 a.m., 10:30 a.m., 1 p.m., 2:30 p.m., and 5 p.m. Some 2-hour trips also available most days during July and August. |
| **Fare:** | Adults, $70 (Canadian) plus tax; children under 14, $45. Guaranteed sightings, $75 and $50, respectively. Reservations advised. |
| **Departure:** | Boats depart from Ocean Pointe Resort, 45 Songhees Road at the west end of the Johnson Street Garage. |
| **Naturalist:** | Yes |

"Our naturalists have expertise on whales, dolphins, porpoises, birds, seals, and sea lions. Naturalists stimulate discussion, provide some commentary, and invite questions," says owner Alex Rhodes.

## VARIOUS DEPARTURE POINTS

### Bluewater Adventures

No. 202-1656 Duranleau Street
Vancouver, British Columbia, V6H 3S4 Canada
(604) 684-4575; Fax (604) 689-5926

| | |
|---|---|
| **Whales:** | Orca, gray, humpback, minke |
| **Season:** | April to October |
| **Boats:** | One 68-foot ketch, the *Island Roamer*; 16 passengers on multi-day live-aboard trips |
| **Trips:** | Three- to 11-day trips to the San Juan and Gulf Islands, the Queen Charlotte Islands, Johnstone Strait, or southeast Alaska. |
| **Fare:** | Sample fares: $395 (U.S.) per person for 3 days in the San Juan and Gulf Islands; $875 for 6 days in the San Juans; $1,325 for 8 days in the Inside Passage; $1,825 for 9 days in the Queen Charlotte Islands. Reservations required. |
| **Departure:** | Trips leave from Victoria, Vancouver, Port Hardy, or Sandspit, depending on the destination. |
| **Naturalist:** | Yes |

"*Island Roamer's* crew has 20 years' experience running quality sailing adventures," a spokesman says. "We have operated cruises for many well-known educational institutions and were privileged to be chosen by World Wildlife of Canada to run a whale-watching trip for His Royal Highness Prince Philip.

"You can rely on our experienced crew to offer you the finest sailing adventure possible. Their knowledge of marine biology, whales, native Indian culture, birds, and ecology will make your trip as interesting and as educational as you wish."

## Clavella Adventures

P.O. Box 866, Nanaimo, British Columbia, V9R 5N2 Canada
(604) 753-3751; Fax (604) 755-4014

**Whales:**       Minke, gray, humpback, orca

**Season:**       Year-round

**Boats:**        One boat, the 61-foot M V *Clavella*; 10 overnight guests or
                  30 day-trip passengers

**Trips:**        Several 3- to 7-day trips whale watching in the Gulf Islands,
                  Queen Charlotte Islands, or Johnstone Strait. Passengers live
                  aboard. Some day trips.

**Fare:**         $139 (U.S.) per day on weekdays and $159 per day on
                  weekends. Fare includes accommodations, meals, guided land
                  tours, cruising, and diving opportunities. Reservations required.

**Departure:**    Trips leave from Port Hardy and Port McNeill on Vancouver
                  Island.

**Naturalist:**   Veteran whale watcher and experienced captain narrates trips.

"The *Clavella* offers an overall experience," says Captain John deBoeck.
"Guests will be able to go to areas they would not normally reach on a land-
based excursion. Also, some of our trips offer a photo professional on board to
help with topside and underwater photo skills."

## Maple Leaf Adventures

19-2625 Muir Road, Courtenay, British Columbia, V9N 8S6 Canada
(604) 644-4343

**Whales:**       Orca, gray, humpback

**Season:**       April through September

**Boats:**        One boat, the 92-foot schooner *Maple Leaf*; 8 passengers

**Trips:**        Four-day to 2-week charters along the coast of British
                  Columbia, among the Queen Charlotte and Gulf Islands or
                  to southeast Alaska.

**Fare:**         Rates start at $600 (Canadian) per person for bed and board.
                  Reservations required.

**Departure:**   Departure from various ports, depending on destination.

**Naturalist:**   Yes

"While we see whales on just about all of our trips, the best time and area is Robson Bight in early September for orcas and June in Alaska for humpbacks. We often have prominent whale researchers on board and our own hydrophone," says owner and skipper Brian Falconer.

"*Maple Leaf's* accommodations are very comfortable. The spacious main cabin is open and airy by day and at night is divided by curtains into four double 'cabins' accommodating eight guests in extra-large bunks. Our experienced crew will help you to participate in the sailing of the ship, or you may wish just to relax and enjoy the experience."

# MANITOBA

## CHURCHILL

## Northern Expeditions

P.O. Box 614, Churchill, Manitoba, R0B 0E0 Canada
(204) 675-2121; Fax (204) 675-2647

**Whales:**   Beluga

**Season:**   July and August

**Boats:**   A 17-foot aluminum boat with outboard motor and a 36-foot cabin cruiser; 6 and 15 passengers respectively

**Trips:**   Two or three trips a day, depending on weather and tides in Hudson Bay. Trips cross the Churchill River for watching whales and visiting historic Fort Prince of Wales.

**Fare:**   $38 (Canadian) per person for a 2-1/2-hour tour. Reservations required 30 days in advance.

**Departure:**   Boats leave from the lower dock, behind the port of Churchill.

**Naturalist:**   Yes

"Northern Expeditions has designed special sightseeing tours," says a spokesman. Transportation by boat, van, all-terrain vehicle, or snowmobile ensures that vacationers see the highlights of each passing season. "Our tours are provided in both English and French. We have something for everyone, provided through an economical, courteous, and efficient tour company."

## Riding Mountain Nature Tours

P.O. Box 429, Erickson, Manitoba, R0J 0P0 Canada
(204) 636-2968; Fax (204) 636-2557

**Whales:**     Beluga

**Season:**     June 1 to August 30

**Boats:**      Aluminum boats or rigid-hull inflatable rafts; 10 to 30 passengers each

**Trips:**      Several multi-day tours of Manitoba each year include at least one day of whale watching on the Churchill River or in Hudson Bay. Tours also include birdwatching and viewing wildlife on the tundra.

**Fare:**       A 6-day tour of tundra, including whale watching, costs $1,475 (U.S.). Includes food, lodging, guides, equipment, and transportation from Winnipeg, where the tour originates. Reservations required.

**Departure:**  Participants fly to Churchill from Winnipeg.

**Naturalist:** Yes

"We are Manitoba's finest nature tour company and one of the only," says Daniel Weedon, owner and tour leader. "We have a complete package tour—deluxe design."

# Sea North Tours Ltd.

P.O. Box 222, Churchill, Manitoba, R0B 0E0 Canada
(204) 675-2195; Fax (204) 675-2198

| | |
|---|---|
| **Whales:** | Beluga |
| **Season:** | July 1 to mid-August |
| **Boats:** | Four Coast Guard-certified boats; capacity ranges from 10 to 30 passengers |
| **Trips:** | Daily trips on Churchill River and Hudson Bay, weather and tides permitting. Trips last 2-1/2 or 4 hours. |
| **Fare:** | Fares start at $40 (Canadian) for adults, $20 for children 12 and younger. Reservations advised. Most whale watching package tours to Churchill include Sea North's services. |
| **Departure:** | Trips leave from 39 Franklin Street in center of Churchill. |
| **Naturalist:** | Captain serves as naturalist. |

Mike and Doreen Macri say, "Our boats are frequently surrounded by hundreds of belugas during a tour. All boats are hydrophone-equipped to listen to their incredible vocalizations."

Captain Mike is also a professional wildlife photographer.

# NORTHWEST TERRITORIES

## BAFFIN ISLAND

### Atlantic Marine Wildlife Tours Ltd.

227 Wright Street, Fredericton, New Brunswick, E3B 2E3 Canada
(506) 459-7325; Fax (506) 453-3589

| | |
|---|---|
| **Whales:** | Narwhal, bowhead, beluga |
| **Season:** | May through August |
| **Boats:** | Glass-bottom Zodiac in August |
| **Trips:** | Two 10-day trips by plane, sled, and snowmobile to Baffin Island in the Arctic Circle, with stops at Frobisher Bay, Pond Inlet, and Bylot Island. Also, one 10-day trip in August to view narwhals from a boat. Food and lodging in hotels and tents. Trips conclude in Ottawa. |
| **Fare:** | $3,400 (U.S.) per person. Price includes airfare from Ottawa to Baffin Island, room, board, guides, tours, entertainment. Reservations required. |
| **Departure:** | Trips leave from Ottawa. |
| **Naturalist:** | Yes |

"The adjacent waters around Baffin Island and Bylot Island contain the richest profusion of marine mammals in the eastern Arctic, including concentrations of narwhal, bowhead, and beluga whales," says Dr. Eugene Lewis, president of Atlantic Marine Wildlife Tours.

"There are also many harp, bearded, and ring seals along with wandering polar bears, arctic foxes, and migratory birds en route to their summer nesting grounds."

The inlets and waterways are still frozen in May and June, but there are 24 hours of daylight, and the temperatures are above freezing. In July, the ice melts, and by August, navigation by boat is possible.

## INUVIK

### Arctic Tour Company

P.O. Box 2021, Inuvik, Northwest Territories, X0E 0T0 Canada
(403) 979-4100; Fax (403) 873-3488

| | |
|---|---|
| **Whales:** | Beluga |
| **Season:** | July and August |
| **Boats:** | One boat; 6 passengers and a guide |
| **Trips:** | Several 2-day trips down the Mackenzie River to Kendall Island. Trips conclude in Inuvik. |
| **Fare:** | $295 (Canadian) per person, which includes boat and land tours, tent accommodations, meals, and guide. Reservations required. |
| **Departure:** | Boat leaves from Inuvik. |
| **Naturalist:** | Guide is native Inuit. |

"The Arctic Tour Company is located in Inuvik, 150 miles north of the Arctic Circle," notes manager Kimberly Staples. "We offer a variety of tours and services within the Western Arctic year-round."

The whale-watching tour includes visiting an Inuit family's subsistence whaling campground and viewing the beluga whales and scenery. The Inuit guide will share the history and stories of the area.

## SOMERSET ISLAND

### Biological Journeys

1696 Ocean Drive, McKinleyville, CA 95521
(800) 548-7555 or (707) 839-0178; Fax (707) 839-4656

| | |
|---|---|
| **Whales:** | Beluga, narwhal |
| **Season:** | July |

**Boats:**        No boats

**Trips:**        Several 10-day trips to Somerset Island in the High Arctic, north of the Arctic Circle. Participants stay in high-tech dome tents at the Arctic Watch Lodge on the banks of the Cunningham River. Whale watching is all land-based.

**Fare:**         $4,795 (U.S.) per person, which includes accommodations in Edmonton two nights, all meals, all air transportation on the trip, services of guide staff and lodge staff.

**Departure:**    Trips begin and end in Edmonton, Alberta.

**Naturalist:**   Naturalists from Biological Journeys.

"One of the last remote and unexplored areas of the globe is that of the far north: the land of the polar bear, musk ox, caribou, and Arctic fox," says owner Ron LeValley. "The ocean waters—home to belugas, narwhals, walrus, many seals, and countless seabirds—are characterized by icebergs and incredible plankton blooms during the short but intense summer season."

# MUSEUMS, AQUARIUMS, AND SCIENCE CENTERS

## BRITISH COLUMBIA

### Vancouver Aquarium

P.O. Box 3232, Vancouver, British Columbia, V6B 3X8 Canada
(604) 685-3364 or 682-1118 (recording); Fax (604) 631-2529

Situated downtown in Stanley Park, the Aquarium showcases aquatic life from the Arctic Ocean to the Amazon jungle, the tropical Pacific Ocean to British Columbia's own waters. Two orcas inhabit a four-million-litre re-creation of a west coast Gulf Islands habitat. Five belugas live in a similarly-sized re-creation of Lancaster Sound, in the Canadian high Arctic. Training, research, and feeding sessions with the whales occur throughout the day. Both exhibits have above- and underwater viewing and interpretive galleries with hands-on exhibits.

The Aquarium is open 365 days a year, 9:30 a.m. to 8 p.m. in July and August and 10 a.m. to 5:30 p.m. the remainder of the year. Admission is $9.50 (Canadian) for adults; $8.25 for seniors and youths 13 to 18; $6.25 for children 5 to 12; and free to children 4 and younger. Group rates are available.

### Whale Center

411 Campbell Street, P.O. Box 393, Tofino, British Columbia V0R 2Z0 Canada
(604) 725-2132

The Maritime Museum displays artifacts from early native cultures, the first European explorers, traders, settlers, fishermen, and shipwrecks. The Whale Center, situated on the main floor, exhibits information, research developments, and artwork about living whales as well as whale bones, artifacts, and historical accounts from the early whaling era. The center offers guided tours, films, and lectures for groups; a marine charter reservation service; and a gift shop.

Hours are 9 a.m. to 5:30 p.m. daily from early March to mid-October. Admission is free.

## Wickaninnish Centre

Pacific Rim National Park
P.O. Box 280, Ucluelet, British Columbia, V0R 3A0 Canada
(604) 726-7721

The Centre is situated at the surf line on the bay for which it was named.
A window on the ocean side allows a view of whales, seals, and sea lions.
Telescopes are available outside. Within the Centre are exhibits, displays,
and films presented by heritage communicators.

Open daily 11 a.m. to 5 p.m. from mid-March to mid-September. Admission is
free. During March and April, the communities along the west coast of Vancouver
Island celebrate the spring migration of the gray whale with the Pacific Rim
Whale Festival. Among the activities in the park are guided hikes, slide shows,
movies, and lectures. For specific dates and more information, write Box 280,
Ucluelet, British Columbia, V0R 3A0 Canada or phone (604) 726-7721.

## MANITOBA

## Manitoba Museum of Man & Nature

190 Rupert Avenue, Winnipeg, Manitoba, R3B ON2 Canada
(204) 956-2830 or 943-3139 (recording)

This is an interpretive museum of the natural and human history of the province
of Manitoba. Visitors walk through three-dimensional exhibits that depict the various areas of the province from the north to the south. The whale exhibit features
the history of the beluga in Hudson Bay.

Victoria Day through Labor Day, open 10 a.m. to 6 p.m. The remainder of the
year, closed Monday; open 10 a.m. to 4 p.m. Tuesday through Friday, 10 a.m.
to 5 p.m. Saturday, Sunday, and holidays. Admission is $4 (Canadian) for
adults, $3 for senior citizens 65 and older and youths 4 to 17. Free to children
under 3. Group rates are available.

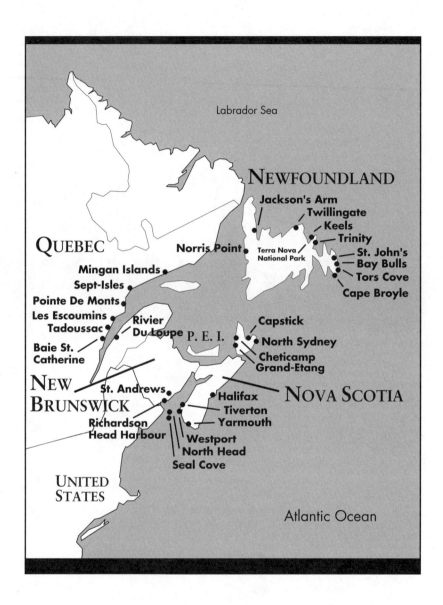

Labrador Sea

**NEWFOUNDLAND**

**Jackson's Arm**
**Twillingate**
**Keels**
**Trinity**

**QUEBEC**

**Norris Point** • Terra Nova National Park

**St. John's**
**Bay Bulls**
**Tors Cove**
**Cape Broyle**

**Mingan Islands** •
**Sept-Isles** •
**Pointe De Monts** •
**Les Escoumins** •
**Tadoussac** •
**Rivier Du Loupe** • **P. E. I.**

**Capstick**
**North Sydney**
**Cheticamp**
**Grand-Etang**

**Baie St. Catherine**

**NEW BRUNSWICK**

**St. Andrews**

**Halifax**
**Tiverton**
**Yarmouth**

**NOVA SCOTIA**

**Richardson Head Harbour**

**Westport**
**North Head**
**Seal Cove**

**UNITED STATES**

Atlantic Ocean

# EASTERN CANADA

Visitors to Western Canada expect to see orcas and gray whales, but whale watchers who travel to the coastal areas of Eastern Canada may see blue whales, rare right whales, humpbacks, and belugas.

In Newfoundland, tour operators take people to see humpbacks, finbacks, minkes, and pilot whales from May through September. Those same species, plus right whales and the occasional sperm whale, can be seen off Nova Scotia and New Brunswick from June through September. Blue whales, along with finback, minke, and belugas, are found near the junction of the St. Lawrence Seaway and the Saguenay River, just off Quebec, from June through September.

As in Western Canada, whales may often be sighted from shore or encountered in the wild well beyond the reaches of the whale-watch tour operators.

# TOURISM INFORMATION

## MARITIME PROVINCES TOURISM INFORMATION
(800) 565-2627

## NEW BRUNSWICK
### Tourism New Brunswick
P.O. Box 12345, Fredericton, New Brunswick, E3B 5C3 Canada
(800) 561-0123

## NEWFOUNDLAND
### Tourism Newfoundland
P.O. Box 8730, St. John's, Newfoundland, A1B 4J6 Canada
(800) 563-6353

## NOVA SCOTIA
### Nova Scotia Tourism
P.O. Box 130, Halifax, Nova Scotia B3J 2R5 Canada
(800) 341-6096

## QUEBEC
### Tourisme Quebec
C.P. 979, Montreal, Quebec H3C 2W3 Canada
(800) 363-7777

# WHALE-WATCHING TRIPS

## NEW BRUNSWICK

### NORTH HEAD

#### Ocean Search Ltd.

P.O. Box 129, North Head
Grand Manan Island, New Brunswick; E0G 2MO Canada
(506) 662-8144

| | |
|---|---|
| **Whales:** | North Atlantic right, fin, humpback |
| **Season:** | Early July to mid-September |
| **Boats:** | One schooner, the *D'Sonoqua*; 20 passengers |
| **Trips:** | One 6-½-hour trip daily at 9:30 a.m. |
| **Fare:** | Adults, $69; children under 12 accompanied by a parent, $25. Lunch, evening lecture included. Group rates offered. Reservations advised. Guests on a package tour receive a discount. |
| **Departure:** | Boat leaves from North Head Wharf on Grand Manan Island, close to the ferry terminal. |
| **Naturalist:** | Naturalist on board is a marine biologist. |

"Ocean Search tours offer more than a search," owner James Leslie says. "They offer an exciting sailing adventure aboard a traditionally rigged oceangoing schooner, expertly manned and equipped for your safety and comfort.

"Grand Manan is a special place: an island set aside in time and beauty. The magic of an island, the romance of sailing, and the thrill of marine life are all part of your holiday."

## ST. ANDREWS, RICHARDSON, HEAD HARBOUR

### Cline Marine

Leonardville, Deer Island, New Brunswick, E0G 2G0 Canada
(506) 529-4188 (in season) or (506) 747-2287 (off season)
Fax (506) 747-2287

**Whales:** Fin, minke, humpback, right

**Season:** May through October; scheduled tours July 1 through Labor Day

**Boats:** One boat; 60 passengers

**Trips:** Scenic whale-watch trips from three locations. Two 5-hour trips daily from St. Andrews, at 8:30 a.m. and 2 p.m.; two 3-hour trips daily from Richardson at 9:30 a.m. and 3 p.m.; two 2-hour trips from Campobello at 10 a.m. and 3:30 p.m. Charter rates available.

**Fare:** For the 5-hour trip, $50 (Canadian) for adults, $45 with coupon (coupon available in brochure), and $25 for children ages 5 to 15. For the 3-hour trip, $40, $35, and $20 respectively; for the 2-hour trip, $30, $25, and $15. Reservations advised.

**Departure:** Boat picks up at the St. Andrews town wharf, the Deer Island Wharf at Richardson, and Campobello Wharf at Head Harbour.

**Naturalist:** Captain serves as narrator, and the ship's purser is a historian specializing in the area.

Captain R. C. Cline says, "You'll travel through the proposed national marine park en route to the morning whale search, and you'll discover its secrets on the afternoon Inner Islands Adventure Tour." He promises bald eagles, sea birds, osprey, seals, porpoise, dolphins, and whales, and he says one of the world's largest tidal whirlpools could be on the agenda.

## SEAL COVE

### Sea Watch Tours

Seal Cove, Grand Manan Island, New Brunswick, E0G 3B0 Canada
(506) 662-8296

| | |
|---|---|
| **Whales:** | Minke, fin, humpback, right |
| **Season:** | August 1 to September 30 |
| **Boats:** | One boat, the *Sea Watcher*; 30 passengers |
| **Trips:** | At least one 5-hour trip daily at 9 a.m. Monday through Saturday. Bring your own lunch. Shorter evening trip added if demand justifies. |
| **Fare:** | Cost: $40 (Canadian) per person. Reservations required. |
| **Departure:** | Boat leaves from Fishermens Wharf in Seal Cove on Grand Manan Island. Upon arriving in Seal Cove, turn down the road across from the two churches. Follow this road as it takes a sharp right, over to the last pier. |
| **Naturalist:** | Yes |

Peter Wilcox, son of owner Preston Wilcox, says, "There are very few North Atlantic right whales left, perhaps as few as 250. The Grand Manan Basin has become one of the most concentrated areas of right whales during the months of August and September, perhaps with 50 or 60 different animals.

"Their location is so predictable that it is almost certain that we will see them. In 10 years of whale watching, we have had only one day that we have not seen a whale."

233

# NEWFOUNDLAND

## BAY BULLS

### Bird Island Charters

150 Old Topsail Road, St. John's, Newfoundland, A1E 2B1 Canada
(709) 753-4850 or 334-2355; Fax (707) 753-3140

| | |
|---|---|
| **Whales:** | Humpback, minke, fin |
| **Season:** | June, July, and August |
| **Boats:** | Two boats; 48 passengers each |
| **Trips:** | At least four 2-1/2 hour trips daily at 9:30 a.m., 11 a.m., 2 p.m., and 5 p.m. |
| **Fare:** | Adults, $25 (Canadian) in June; $30 in July and August. Children 6 to 15, $15; 1 to 5, $10. Reservations required. |
| **Departure:** | Boats leave from Bay Bulls, Lower Road, south of St. John's. A daily shuttle runs from major hotels in St. John's; reservations required. |
| **Naturalist:** | Captain serves as naturalist. |

"We are working on photographing whales that come to our area," says Captain Loyola O'Brien, president. Researchers identify the flukes of individual whales "so that we can put names on those that travel along the coast."

On board, the captain will sing for you and dance with you as part of the entire cultural experience.

### Gatherall's Sanctuary Boat Charters

Bay Bulls, Newfoundland, A0A 1C0 Canada
(709) 334-2887

| | |
|---|---|
| **Whales:** | Humpback, minke, fin |

| | |
|---|---|
| **Season:** | May to October |
| **Boats:** | Two boats; 30 and 40 passengers respectively |
| **Trips:** | At least three 2-hour trips in Witless Bay daily at 10 a.m., 1 p.m., and 4 p.m. Additional trips scheduled according to demand. |
| **Fare:** | Adults, $25 (Canadian); children: 14 and under, $12.50; children 5 and younger, $5. Reservations advised. |
| **Departure:** | Departure from North Side Road in Bay Bulls on Route 10, about 30 minutes south of St. John's and 10 minutes from Route 1. |
| **Naturalist:** | Guide serves as naturalist. |

"This is a guided boat tour; the guide is a well-qualified 'amateur' naturalist," says owner Rosemary Gatherall. "Our interpretive program will enrich and enhance the traveler's appreciation of nature, conservation, and the Newfoundland cultural heritage."

Gatherall's has been singled out for its whale watching, its sensitivity to the marine environment, and its wildlife, she notes. The Canadian government has named the Gatherall family "Canadian Tourism Ambassadors" for "outstanding hospitality to international visitors."

## CAPE BROYLE

## Great Island Tours

P.O. Box 21, Cape Broyle, Newfoundland, A0A 1P0 Canada
(709) 432-2272 or 432-2781

| | |
|---|---|
| **Whales:** | Humpback, minke, fin |
| **Season:** | May 15 to October 31 |
| **Boats:** | One boat, the *Historic Venture*; 18 passengers |
| **Trips:** | Private charter trips on demand |
| **Fare:** | Cost is $60 per hour. Reservations required. |
| **Departure:** | Boat leaves from Cape Broyle Harbor. From St. John's, take scenic Route 10. |

**Naturalist:**    Yes

"We offer unique outdoor, scenic, life-style, and cultural experiences of historic Newfoundland," says owner Sylvester Hawkins.

The tour to Great Island, which has the largest Atlantic puffin colony in North American, is a must for birdwatchers as well as whale watchers, he says. The tour of Cape Broyle harbor offers passengers beautiful scenery as well as the opportunity to try their luck at jigging a cod, sculpin, squid, or flounder.

# JACKSON'S ARM

## Pelley Inn

P.O. Box 428, Springdale, Newfoundland, A0J 1T0 Canada
(709) 673-3931; Fax (709) 673-3934

| | |
|---|---|
| **Whales:** | Humpback, pilot |
| **Season:** | May 1 to September 30 |
| **Boats:** | One boat; 6 to 10 passengers |
| **Trips:** | Whale watching included in week-long visit that starts at Pelley Inn in Springdale and moves to Little Harbour Deep Wilderness Lodge on White Bay. On shorter visits, whales may be seen during the two-hour cruise to the lodge. |
| **Fare:** | Cost is $140 (Canadian) a day for single accommodations; $220 a day for double; $810 for single for 7 days, 6 nights; $1,620 for double. Reservations required. |
| **Departure:** | Boat leaves from Jackson's Arm, a one-hour drive from Springdale. |
| **Naturalist:** | Naturalist available upon request. |

Cyril R. Pelley says, "We own and operate the Pelley Inn, a 22-room inn at Springdale, on the northeast coast of our island province. Our customers usually drive or fly via Deer Lake or Gander airport, where they are picked up by our limousine service and returned to the inn.

"However, our emphasis is on our new wilderness lodge in the great White Bay, just north of Springdale. A one-hour drive and a two-hour cruise get visitors to the lodge, where they may hike, fish, relax, or go on whale-watching or bird-watching excursions," Pelley says.

# KEELS

## Harbour Tours

Keels, Bonavista Bay, Newfoundland, A0C 1R0 Canada
(709) 447-3131; Fax (709) 447-3140

| | |
|---|---|
| **Whales:** | Humpback, minke |
| **Season:** | Mid-June to early September |
| **Boats:** | Two boats; a 20-foot wooden hulled vessel and a 14-foot inflatable Zodiac; 6 passengers and 3 passengers, respectively |
| **Trips:** | Three trips daily Monday through Saturday, usually at 10 a.m., 2 p.m., and 7 p.m. One trip Sunday afternoon. Length of trips varies according to passengers' wishes. |
| **Fare:** | For the Zodiac, rates are $50 (Canadian) per hour for 1-3 hours; $42.50 for 4-6 hours; and $37.50 for more than 6 hours. For the wooden boat, rates are $65 for 1-3 hours; $55.25 for 4-6 hours; and $48.75 for more than 6 hours. Reservations advised. |
| **Departure:** | Trips leave from the Community Wharf in Keels. Please register at the Hubert and James Mesh General Store on the main road. |
| **Naturalist:** | None on board. |

"Our relatively small size means we can be quite flexible in terms of the itinerary and duration of our trips," says co-owner John Hofstetter. "We're in the center of a region with some of the most interesting and varied coastal scenery to be found. Although we can't guarantee whale sightings, they are not an uncommon feature of many of our outings."

## NORRIS POINT

### Bontours

Norris Point, Newfoundland, A0K 3V0 Canada
(709) 458-2256; Fax (709) 458-2841

| | |
|---|---|
| **Whales:** | Humpback |
| **Season:** | June 1 to September 30 |
| **Boats:** | One motor cruiser; 46 passengers |
| **Trips:** | One 2-hour trip daily at 1 p.m. |
| **Fare:** | Adults, $20 (Canadian); children 12 or younger, $6. Group rates available. Reservations advised. |
| **Departure:** | Boat leaves from the government wharf at Norris Point on Newfoundland's west coast, on the Gulf of St. Lawrence. |
| **Naturalist:** | None on board. |

Owner Reg Williams says, "Cruise the spectacularly beautiful Bonne Bay. This two-hour cruise along the eastern and western arms of Bonne Bay affords vistas of Gros Morne, Killdevil, the Tablelands, and the Long Range Mountains. We pass over the deepest water in the area—756 feet deep—which gives opportunity for cod jigging and mackerel fishing. Photographic opportunities abound."

## ST. JOHN'S

### Adventure Tours of Newfoundland

P.O. Box 5395, St. John's, Newfoundland, A1C 5W2 Canada
(709) 726-5000; Fax (709) 722-3999

| | |
|---|---|
| **Whales:** | Humpback, fin, minke |
| **Season:** | May 1 to October 1 |
| **Boats:** | Several boats in prime whale-watching areas |
| **Trips:** | Four 2-hour trips daily at 10 a.m., noon, 2 p.m., and 4 p.m. A moonlight harbor cruise is also available. The busiest day is Saturday. |

**Fare:**        Cost is $22.50 (Canadian) per person. Reservations advised.

**Departure:**   Departure from Pier No. 7 in St. John's downtown harbor.

**Naturalist:**  None on board.

Owner Charles Anonsen has provided whale-watching tours since 1976. He says that in addition to whale watching, his tours offer "listening to Newfoundland traditional music; meeting Bosun, our Newfoundland dog; sailing around North America's most easterly point; and enjoying the hospitality of the people from one of the oldest cities in North America, St. John's."

# Wildland Tours

124 Water Street, P.O. Box 383, Station C
St. John's, Newfoundland, A1C 5J9 Canada
(709) 722-3335; Fax (same)

**Whales:**      Humpback, minke, fin

**Season:**      Early May to mid-August

**Boats:**       The best boats available to go where the whales are.

**Trips:**       Tours of 7 days or longer to watch whales and view other wildlife in Newfoundland. June and July are the best months.

**Fare:**        Prices depend on package but start at $1,750 (Canadian). Packages include accommodations, boats, ground transportation, and some meals. Reservations required.

**Departure:**   All tours start in St. John's.

**Naturalist:**  Biologist accompanies each trip.

David Snow, president, says, "Whales are a very special part of our product, but we do not ignore North America's largest puffin colony, the world's largest murre colonies, the world's largest storm petrel colonies, and huge collections of seabirds numbering in the millions visiting from the Arctic and Antarctic."

His company offers "probably the best marine wildlife-watching opportunities in the world, combined with small group travel. We are Canada's best-kept secret," Snow says. The Snows run a nature-oriented gallery in St. John's called Wild Things, where they sell their tapes of whale songs.

239

## ST. JOHN'S, TORS COVE, AND CAPE BROYLE

### Eastern Edge Outfitters Ltd.

P.O. Box 17, Site 14, RR #2
Paradise, Newfoundland, A1L 1C2 Canada
(709) 782-1465

| | |
|---|---|
| **Whales:** | Humpback, minke, pilot, and the possibility of twenty other species |
| **Season:** | June 2 to September 30 |
| **Boats:** | Eleven sea kayaks, singles and doubles |
| **Trips:** | One-day trips on weekdays during June and July, 9 a.m. to 5 p.m. Four- and 11-day trips kayaking and camping along the coasts of Newfoundland and Labrador. |
| **Fare:** | One day, $100 (Canadian), lunch included. 4 days, $500; 11 days, $1,200. Reservations required. |
| **Departure:** | Departures from St. John's, Tors Cove, or Cape Broyle, depending on trip. |
| **Naturalist:** | Guides serve as naturalists. |

"We are the only company in Newfoundland offering bird- and whale-watching tours by sea kayak," says co-owner Jim Price. "On all our tours we give initial instruction so guests will be able to paddle their kayaks on their own. We will paddle alongside whales and near towering icebergs and will view thundering waterfalls crashing into the sea. All this while learning the skills of ocean kayak travel and breathing the clear zesty ocean air."

## TERRA NOVA NATIONAL PARK

### Ocean Watch Tours

Doryman Marine, Squid Tickle, Burnside, Newfoundland, A0G 1K0 Canada
(709) 533-2801 in season; (709) 677-2327 off season

| | |
|---|---|
| **Whales:** | Humpback, minke |
| **Season:** | Late June to Labor Day |
| **Boats:** | One boat, the *Northern Fulmar*; 30 passengers |
| **Trips:** | Four 3-hour trips daily at 9 a.m., 12:30 p.m., 3:30 p.m., and 7:30 p.m. |
| **Fare:** | Adults, $22 to $26 (Canadian), depending on the season; children under 12, half price. Reservations advised. |
| **Departure:** | Boat leaves from Newman Sound in Terra Nova National Park. |
| **Naturalist:** | Internationally experienced naturalists. |

"Terra Nova, Canada's most easterly national park, is famous for whales, icebergs, and bald eagles. You'll travel the ice-scoured fjords through a maze of sheltered coves, looming cliffs, and narrow tickles," says Fraser Carpenter of Ocean Watch.

"Our special scientific permit issued by the Canadian government allows passengers to take part in a fascinating program of ocean exploration and research, and every trip is different in this world ruled by wind and tide."

## TRINITY

### Ocean Contact Ltd.

P.O. Box 10, Trinity, Newfoundland, A0C 2S0 Canada
(709) 464-3269; Fax (709) 464-3700

| | |
|---|---|
| **Whales:** | Humpback, fin, minke, pilot |
| **Season:** | May to October |
| **Boats:** | One 26-foot rigid-hull inflatable; 6 to 12 passengers. Other power boats chartered as needed. Full-length flotation suits provided on the inflatable. |

| **Trips:** | Half-day or whole-day excursions and multi-day expeditions offered. |
| **Fare:** | For excursions, rates start at $39 (Canadian) for adults; $27 for youths 13 to 15; $19.50 for children 4 to 12. Multi-day expedition rates start (for 3 days) at $465, $339, and $254, respectively by age. Reservations advised. Hotel packages are available at the Village Inn. Write for details. |
| **Departure:** | Boats leave from Trinity, on Trinity Bay on the east coast. |
| **Naturalist:** | Yes |

Dr. Peter Beamish of Ocean Contact says, "Whale watching is free in Newfoundland! You can sit on a cliff near Trinity all day and watch whales. We, on the other hand, guide people into our spectacular marine environment so that the whales can watch us!"

Beamish, who has decades of experience at this, offers passengers the opportunity to make contact with whales by means of computer-driven acoustic signals. "The ensuing communications," he says, "may involve full breaches, tail or flipper slaps, exhalations, etc., and these are then easily predictable in time, allowing for spectacular photographs."

Beamish has written a book called *Dancing With Whales*. Write for information.

# TWILLINGATE

## Twillingate Island Boat Tours Ltd.

P.O. Box 127, Twillingate, Newfoundland, A0G 4M0 Canada
(709) 884-2317

| **Whales:** | Humpback, fin, pilot, minke |
| **Season:** | Late May to late September |
| **Boats:** | One boat; up to 10 passengers |
| **Trips:** | Two 2-hour trips a day at 9:30 a.m. and 2 p.m. into Notre Dame Bay, on the "iceberg alley" route. |
| **Fare:** | Adults, $25 (Canadian); children, $15. Reservations advised. |
| **Departure:** | Boat leaves from Twillingate dock. |
| **Naturalist:** | None on board. |

Owner Cecil G. Stockley says, "Whales swim around this island all year-round on their migratory routes. Any place on this 15-mile-diameter island, whales can be seen a stone's throw away from the island's shore."

He adds that icebergs in all sizes and shapes "from peaked to pancake flat" usually appear in May. They take two to three years to travel from Greenland, where the great ice packs break up and unleash their frozen landscape piece by piece into the southbound Labrador Current.

"As they pass by, the icebergs growl, rumble, and crackle like thunder. Sometimes they split in half or roll over. But mostly they just sail off into the sun to meet their fate a final meltdown in the warmer waters off the Grand Banks."

# NOVA SCOTIA

## CAPSTICK

### Whale Works Enterprises Ltd.

Capstick, Nova Scotia, B0E 1E0 Canada
(902) 383-2981

| | |
|---|---|
| **Whales:** | Finback, minke, pilot; rarely blue and beluga |
| **Season:** | June through October |
| **Boats:** | One boat; 25 passengers |
| **Trips:** | Three 2-1/2-hour trips daily in July and August at 10:15 a.m., 1:30 p.m., and 4:30 p.m.; fewer trips off season, according to demand. |
| **Fare:** | Adults, $25 (Canadian); senior citizens over 65, $22; children under 12, $12.50; children under 5, free. Reservations advised. |

**Departure:**    Trips leave from the Bay St. Lawrence Wharf, 2 kilometers past the Co-op Store on the left.

**Naturalist:**    Sometimes.

Captain Dennis Cox and his wife, Lori Cox, operate out of Bay St. Lawrence on the northernmost tip of Cape Breton Island. At one time, they were involved in lobster fishing and other inshore fishing, Lori Cox says, and then they started taking friends out to see the whales. Now, whale watching is their primary focus.

"It's so incredibly beautiful! The coast is uninhabited, and the whales we see are so close to shore that sometimes, it is overwhelming."

## CHETICAMP

# Whale Cruisers (Cheticamp) Ltd.

P.O. Box 183, Cheticamp, Nova Scotia, B0E 1H0 Canada
(902) 224-3376; Fax (902) 224-1166

**Whales:**    Fin, minke, pilot

**Season:**    Mid-May to mid-October

**Boats:**    Two boats; 30 passengers each

**Trips:**    One trip daily at 5 p.m. in May and June; three trips from July to early September, usually at 9 a.m., 1 p.m., and 6 p.m.; one trip at 4 p.m. after September 15. All trips last about 3 hours. Weekday afternoons are busiest.

**Fare:**    Cost: $25 (Canadian) per person. Reservations advised.

**Departure:**    Boats leave from Government Wharf at Cheticamp Harbour, opposite the large stone church.

**Naturalist:**    Experienced narrators aboard.

"We were the first whale-watch tour operation in Nova Scotia," says owner Poirier Calixte. "We never guarantee whales, but our success rate is between 75 and 80 percent. Also, the coastline is breathtakingly beautiful. From the water, we see Cabot Trail and the coastline of Cape Breton Highlands National Park."

## TIVERTON

### Ocean Explorations

Box 719, Tiverton, Long Island, Nova Scotia, B0V 1G0 Canada
(902) 839-2417

| | |
|---|---|
| **Whales:** | Humpback, minke, right, finback |
| **Season:** | July through October |
| **Boats:** | Two Zodiac inflatable rafts; 6 to 8 passengers each |
| **Trips:** | Usually 2 half-day trips, at 8:30 a.m. and 1:30 p.m.; sometimes a third trip at 5:30 p.m. |
| **Fare:** | Adults, $85 for two; $35 for each additional person for 3 or 4 people; $30 each if 5 or more. children half price. Reservations advised. |
| **Departure:** | Trips leave from Gallery-by-the-Sea, an art and gift shop owned by the tour operator, at the main wharf in Tiverton, just 100 yards from the ferry wharf. |
| **Naturalist:** | Narration by owner Tom Goodwin, a marine biologist. |

"We're the only tour in the Maritimes owned and operated by a fully qualified marine biologist," says Tom Goodwin. "We emphasize education, and our passengers are invited to participate in various research efforts." Goodwin also operates a bed and breakfast, and he has a travel video for sale. Write for information.

### Pirate's Cove Whale Cruises

Tiverton, Long Island, Nova Scotia, B0V 1G0 Canada
(902) 839-2242; Fax (902) 829-2271

| | |
|---|---|
| **Whales:** | Humpback, fin, minke, right, dolphins |
| **Season:** | June through September |
| **Boats:** | One boat, the 34-foot M V *Todd and Cherida*; 20 passengers |
| **Trips:** | Two 3-hour cruises daily, at 8 a.m. and 1 p.m. Occasional sunset cruise at 5:30 p.m. |

**Fare:**        Adults, $33 (Canadian); children 6 through 14, $16; children 5 and under, free; 10 percent discount for senior citizens and groups. Reservations required.

**Departure:**    Trips leave from Tiverton, on the tip of Long Island.

**Naturalist:**    Crew narrates trips.

The Sollows family owns and operates Pirate's Cove Whale Cruises. "Sighting success on our cruises is very high. In addition to whales, you will see seals and various seabirds, and we'll give you a raincheck if for some reason no whales are found."

# WESTPORT

## Brier Island Whale and Seabird Cruises, Ltd.

Westport, Brier Island, Nova Scotia, B0V 1H0 Canada
(902) 839-2995

**Whales:**    Humpback, fin, minke, pilot, right

**Season:**    June to October

**Boats:**    Two boats, the 45-foot *Cetacean Adventure* and the 52-foot *Cetacean Quest*; up to 50 passengers each

**Trips:**    Two 4-hour trips a day at 8:30 a.m. and 1:30 p.m. Sunset trips sometimes available. Weekends are busiest.

**Fare:**    Cost: $33 (Canadian) per person. Charter, group, and family rates available. Reservations required.

**Departure:**    Departure from Westport, on Brier Island, at the southwestern end of Nova Scotia.

**Naturalist:**    Field researcher or scientist from the Brier Island Ocean Study accompanies each trip.

Carl Haycock and Harold Graham, co-owners/operators, say their whale-watching trips are unusual in that the whales are normally close to the island, and the four-hour trips are especially convenient.

"Brier Island is located at the southwestern tip of Nova Scotia. Highly saline marine water flows into the Bay of Fundy along the Nova Scotia coast, bringing large numbers of zooplankton. Plankton and fish productivity is enhanced by the nutrients brought to the surface by the strong tidal currents, which average 25 feet or more. Local tide rips and eddies concentrate plankton; these, in turn, attract large schools of herring and mackerel that the whales, dolphins, and seabirds feed on."

# QUEBEC

## LES ESCOUMINS

### Club Vacances Sault-au-Mouton Inc.

81, rue Principale, Sault-au-Mouton, Quebec, G0T 1Z0 Canada
(800) 463-1298 or (418) 231-2214

| | |
|---|---|
| **Whales:** | Blue |
| **Season:** | April 15 to October 15 |
| **Boats:** | One motor boat; 10 passengers |
| **Trips:** | Two 3-hour trips on the St. Lawrence River scheduled daily according to tides. Passengers are outfitted in full-length isothermic suits. |
| **Fare:** | Adults, $30 (Canadian); children 6 to 14, $25. Reservations required. Package including seafood supper, bed, breakfast, and whale watching available at the Club Vacances Sault-au-Mouton lodge. Week-long packages are available. |
| **Departure:** | Boat leaves from Petits Escoumins, about 10 miles east of Les Escoumins. |

**Naturalist:**     Yes

Club Vacances Sault-au-Mouton is a former youth hostel on the St. Lawrence River that has been renovated as a resort for families and groups.

# Tan Incorporated

29, rue des Pilotes, Les Escoumins, Quebec, G0T 1K0 Canada
(418) 233-3488; Fax (418) 233-2593

| | |
|---|---|
| **Whales:** | Blue, humpback, beluga, minke, fin |
| **Season:** | May to November |
| **Boats:** | An 8-passenger 20-foot Zodiac; two 12-passenger 23-foot hard-bottom inflatable Zeppelin rafts, and a 12-passenger 27-foot cruiser |
| **Trips:** | Nine trips per day, with three options to choose from: a 1- to 3-hour whale-watch cruise, a 4-hour trip to watch blue whales, and a 1-day whale-watch cruise up the Saguenay Fjord. The 3-hour trips on Sundays are the most popular. |
| **Fare:** | Prices vary depending on the boat. For the three shorter trips: adults, $15 to $25 (Canadian); children over 6, $15; children under 6, free. For the day-long trip: adults, $95 (Canadian); children 14 and younger, $85; children 6 or younger, $15. Group rates. Survival suits, boots, gloves, and hats provided. Reservations advised. Accommodations in dorms and rooms at reasonable rates. |
| **Departure:** | Trips depart from L'Auberge de la Mer, a resort just west of Les Escoumins, 250 kilometers downriver from Quebec City. |
| **Naturalist:** | A guide provides commentary on all trips. |

"The natural beauty and abundance of the marine life in the St. Lawrence River makes the harbor of Les Escoumins one of the most sought-after sites in North America," a representative from Tan Inc. says. "And we love whales!"

## MINGAN

### Mingan Island Cetacean Study

*Summer:* 124 Bord de la Mer, Longue-Pointe-de-Mingan,
Quebec, G0G 1V0 Canada
(418) 949-2845; Fax is same number

*Winter:* 285 rue Green, St. Lambert, Quebec, J4P lT3 Canada
(514) 465-9176; Fax is same number

| | |
|---|---|
| **Whales:** | Blue, humpback, fin, minke, orca |
| **Season:** | June to October |
| **Boats:** | Four 24-foot and two 16-foot rigid-hull inflatables |
| **Trips:** | Several 5-, 7- and 10-day sessions with the Mingan Island Cetacean Study, a nonprofit research group in the Gulf of St. Lawrence. Participants live among and observe the work of research scientists in a coastal village or camp. Day trips on the St. Lawrence River for 35 to 40 passengers from late June to late October. |
| **Fare:** | Cost is $160 (U.S.) per person per day for multi-day trips. Day trip: adults, $65; students, $55; groups of 4 or more, $55 a person. Reservations required. |
| **Departure:** | Trips depart from Longue Pointe, the gateway to the Mingan Islands, east of Sept-Iles. Representatives of MICS will meet participants who arrive by air at Sept-Iles. |
| **Naturalist:** | Naturalists are scientists with the research group. |

MICS is the first organization in the world to have carried out long-term studies of the blue whale. Through photo-identification techniques developed by MICS, a catalog of more than 325 blue whales now exists for the northwest Atlantic.

Director Richard Sears says, "Our research sessions offer the public the opportunity to get away to the solitude of the sea and immerse themselves in an educational adventure."

MICS has a new research building that includes a small museum on marine mammals, with illustrations, skeletons, and interactive displays.

# POINTE DES MONTS

## Le Gite du Phare de Pointe des Monts

1684 Joliet Boulevard, Baie Comeau, Quebec, G5C 1P8 Canada
(418) 589-8408 or (418) 939-2332

**Whales:** Blue, humpback

**Season:** June 1 to September 30

**Boats:** Three boats; 3 to 12 passengers each

**Trips:** Two trips on the St. Lawrence River on weekdays; 3 trips each Saturday and Sunday; times depend on tides.

**Fare:** Cost is $36 (Canadian) for 4-hour trip, $18 for 2-hour trip. Half price for children. Reservations required. Lodge and chalets available at the same address.

**Departure:** Boats leave from Pointe des Monts on Trinity Bay.

**Naturalist:** Guide serves as naturalist.

Owner Jean Louis Frenette says, "For monolingual English customers, Pointe des Monts might be a difficult place to visit. Everything is in French, and the guides on the sea are less bilingual than I am myself.

"In the future, I will try to make a better place for the English tourists because Pointe des Monts is a very splendid place. The sea is rich, pure, and wild. It is very deep next to the shoreline, so you see and hear the whales from your bedroom."

Frenette's lodge is a restored 1830 lighthouse that he rents from the government.

## TADOUSSAC

### Famille DuFour Hotel Tadoussac

*Summer:* 165 Bord-de-l'Eau, Tadoussac, Quebec, G0T 2A0 Canada
(800) 463-5250 or (418) 235-4421; Fax (418) 235-4607

*Winter:* C.P. 490, Beaupre, Quebec, G0A 1E0 Canada

| | |
|---|---|
| **Whales:** | Beluga, blue, humpback |
| **Season:** | May 13 to October 16 |
| **Boats:** | Two boats, the historic 130-foot schooner *Marie Clarisse* and the *Famille DuFour*; 100 and 450 passengers respectively |
| **Trips:** | Three 3-hour trips on the St. Lawrence River daily at 9 a.m., 1 p.m., and 4 p.m.; plus 2 trips on the Saguenay River at 9:30 a.m. and 4 p.m. |
| **Fare:** | Adults, $30 (Canadian); children, $15. Group rates available. Reservations required. Packages available at Hotel Tadoussac. |
| **Departure:** | Departure from Hotel Tadoussac. |
| **Naturalist:** | Yes |

Tadoussac is situated at the confluence of the freshwater Saguenay River and the saltwater St. Lawrence River. For this "whale sightseeing safari," owner Alain DuFour says, "Bring along your cameras, and experience the thrill of a fascinating encounter with these giant nomads.

"Every summer, the whales return to the very rich and fertile waters of the St. Lawrence. After having given birth to their young in the waters of warmer climes during the winter, they find here the great quantities of food they must have."

# TADOUSSAC AND BAIE ST. CATHERINE

## Compagnie de la Baie de Tadoussac

9145 Bord-de-l'eau, Tadoussac, Quebec, G0T 2A0 Canada
(418) 235-4548

| | |
|---|---|
| **Whales:** | Fin, minke, beluga, some blue |
| **Season:** | May 1 to October 15 (August and September are the best months) |
| **Boats:** | Three rigid-hull inflatable rafts; 10 or 12 passengers each; cruise suits provided. |
| **Trips:** | Three 3-hour trips a day on the St. Lawrence River at 8:30 a.m., 12:30 p.m., and 4 p.m. Special trips at 5 a.m. |
| **Fare:** | Cost is $32 (Canadian) per person. Ten percent discount for groups and students with ID. No children under 12. Reservations advised. |
| **Departure:** | Boats leave from Tadoussac and Baie St. Catherine. |
| **Naturalist:** | Yes |

"We use inflatable boats, a smaller boat, closer to the marine environment and with smaller groups aboard. We offer a more intimate experience," says a staff member.

## Croisieres Navimex Inc.

25 Place Marche Champlain, Suite 101
Quebec City, Quebec, G1K 4H2 Canada
(418) 692-4643; Fax (418) 694-1533

| | |
|---|---|
| **Whales:** | Beluga, minke, fin, occasionally blue |
| **Season:** | End of May to October 15 |
| **Boats:** | Three boats; 300, 400, and 600 passengers |
| **Trips:** | Three 3-hour trips on the St. Lawrence River daily at 10 a.m., 1:15 p.m., and 4:30 p.m. Additional trip at 2:30 p.m. during peak season. |

**Fare:**       Adults, $30 (Canadian); children 14 and under, $15. Group discounts. Reservations advised.

**Departure:**   Trips leave from the village wharves in Tadoussac and Baie St. Catherine and Riviere-du-Loup.

**Naturalist:**   Yes

"A discovery cruise will allow you to explore a major whale refuge, the mouth of the Saguenay River," says vice president Guy Gagnon. "You will be able to observe first-hand several species of whales, such as the beluga, minkes, and finbacks."

# MUSEUMS, AQUARIUMS, AND SCIENCE CENTERS

## NEWFOUNDLAND

### Ocean Sciences Centre

Memorial University of Newfoundland
St. John's, Newfoundland, A1C 5S7 Canada
(709) 737-3706; Fax (709) 737-3220

Situated in a building designed to resemble the internal anatomy of a sea anemone, the Centre is a research unit of the Science Faculty of Memorial University. The focus of study is cold oceans. Guides offer hour-long tours of the research facility.

Visitors meet a wide variety of fish, crabs, lobsters, sea stars, anemones, and other sea creatures in the aquaria and touch tank in the Discovery Room. You will also meet the Centre's family of harbour seals. Other sights include special videos and exhibits, a display of diving gear, and an energy recompression chamber.

Tours are available every half hour from 10 a.m. to 5 p.m., seven days a week from mid-June to early September. Admission is $2.50 (Canadian) for adults, $1.50 for children, and free to senior citizens and children under 6. Group rates available if booked in advance.

## NOVA SCOTIA

### Nova Scotia Museum of Natural History

1747 Summer Street, Halifax, Nova Scotia, B3H 3A6 Canada
(902) 424-7353 or 424-6099 (recording); Fax (902) 424-0560

An Aquatic Environments gallery features freshwater and saltwater exhibits with specimens or models of Nova Scotia seaweeds, invertebrates, amphibians, reptiles, fish, and mammals. Among these are the skeleton of a pilot whale and life-sized models of sharks and a 48-foot sei whale.

From June 1 to October 15, the Museum is open 9:30 a.m. to 5:30 p.m. daily except Wednesday, when it is open 9:30 a.m. to 8 p.m., and Sunday, when the hours are 1 p.m. to 5:30 p.m. From October 16 to May 31, the museum is closed on Monday and closes at 5 p.m. Sunday, Tuesday, Thursday, Friday, and Saturday. Admission is free.

## QUEBEC

## The Interpretative Center of Marine Mammals

108 rue de la Cale-seche, Tadoussac, Quebec, G0T 2A0 Canada
(418) 235-4701

Using exhibits, an aquarium, marine mammal skeletons, a model of a 32-foot fin whale, posters, videos, and slide shows, the center teaches about whales and their marine environment. A movie features the endangered beluga whales of the St. Lawrence River.

The Center is associated with the Group of Research and Education on the Marine Environment, a nonprofit organization dedicated to preserving the marine environment and educating the public.

The Center is situated near the marina in Tadoussac. Hours are 10 a.m. to 6 p.m. from June through mid-October. Admission is $4.50 (Canadian) for adults, $1.50 per child, and $2.65 per group member.

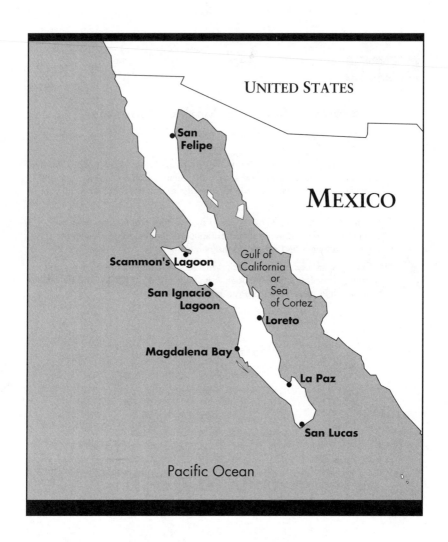

UNITED STATES

San
Felipe

MEXICO

Scammon's Lagoon

Gulf of
California
or
Sea
of Cortez

San Ignacio
Lagoon

Loreto

Magdalena Bay

La Paz

San Lucas

Pacific Ocean

# MEXICO

Those photographs that you've seen of exhilarated whale watchers leaning out of tiny boats to pet gray whales were taken in the lagoons off Baja California, in Mexico. Every year the grays migrate south from the Bering and Chukchi seas, supporting a flourishing whale-watch industry along the entire Pacific Coast of the United States. Once in the calm, warm waters of Mexico, the whales mate and give birth, and people watch.

Aluminum skiffs, Zodiac rafts, and sea kayaks now dot Scammon's Lagoon, San Ignacio Lagoon, and Magdalena Bay in February, March, and part of April. On the other side of the peninsula, in the Sea of Cortez, boats go forth in March and April to see blue, humpback, fin, and pilot whales.

As it's unlikely that anyone would go to Baja California by chance—it's difficult to reach, although well worth the trouble—most whale-watch trips to the area are a week long. Among the groups sponsoring the trips are commercial tour operators; research organizations and scientific institutions, most of which travel by boat; and adventure outfitters, who offer kayaking and camping.

The sponsoring organizations are primarily based in the United States and Canada. Therefore, the listings in this chapter are organized by destination rather than by departure point. Separate index listings are given for destinations and departure points. Should you find yourself in Baja under other circumstances, you will be able to find a fisherman who will happily take you out in a boat for the afternoon to see the whales. By all means, go.

# WHALE-WATCHING TRIPS

## MEXICO

## BAJA PENINSULA, EAST AND WEST COASTS

### Baja Expeditions

2625 Garnet Avenue, San Diego, CA 9210
(800) 843-6967 or (619) 581-3311; Fax (619) 581-6542

| | |
|---|---|
| **Whales:** | Gray, blue, humpback, finback |
| **Season:** | Mid-January through mid-March |
| **Boats:** | Two boats: the 80-foot *Don José* carries 14 passengers in 7 staterooms; the 88-foot *Copper Sky*, a sailboat, sleeps 12 in 6 cabins. Participants live aboard. Whale watching from boats and skiffs. |
| **Trips:** | Eight 8-day trips that combine a visit to Magdalena Bay with a trip around Cabo San Lucas to the Sea of Cortez, with a stop at Cabo Pulmo and Espiritu Santo Island. Trips conclude in either La Paz or Magdalena Bay. |
| **Fare:** | $1,895 per person. Price includes land arrangements, accommodations, meals, beverages, and most related trip equipment. Airfare, tips, and airport taxes are not included. |
| **Departure:** | Trips leave from La Paz and Magdalena Bay, with bus transportation to the boat. |
| **Naturalist:** | Yes |

This itinerary combines two days in Magdalena Bay with a trip around the tip of Baja to view humpback whales and others migrating south or to the Sea of Cortez.

Baja Expeditions made its first trip in 1974, inspired by John Steinbeck's *Log from the Sea of Cortez*. Founder Tim Means notes that the company is the largest and oldest outfitter of natural history and adventure travel in Mexico.

## Biological Journeys

1696 Ocean Drive, McKinleyville, CA 95521
(800) 548-7555 or (707) 839-0178; Fax (707) 839-4656

**Whales:** Gray, humpback, blue, fin, minke

**Season:** Mid-February to early March

**Boats:** One boat, the 80-foot *Don José*; 7 staterooms for 2-4 people each. Participants live aboard, except for the last night, which is spent in a hotel. Whale watching from aluminum skiffs and from the boats.

**Trips:** One 8-day trip, with stops in Magdalena Bay, Cabo San Lucas, Gorda Bank, Bahia Los Frailes, Cerralvo or Los Islotes Islands, and Espiritu Santo Island. Trips conclude in La Paz.

**Fare:** $2,295 per person. Price includes accommodations, meals and transportation while aboard the vessel, and a Mexican fishing license. Rate does not include transportation to La Paz, airport departure taxes, meals, tips, or lodging en route. Travel arrangements can be made through the trip operator's agent, Eureka Travel Agency.

**Departure:** Trip leaves from La Paz, with transportation to the boat.

**Naturalist:** Yes

"This cruise offers the potential of encountering more whale species than any comparable trip in the world," says Biological Journeys. "You'll witness sights and sounds that create one of the most exciting spectacles on the face of the earth!"

Ronn Storro-Patterson and Ron LeValley head up Biological Journeys, which has sponsored Baja California trips since 1970.

## Oceanic Society Expeditions

Fort Mason Center, Building E, San Francisco, CA 94123
(800) 326-7491 or (415) 441-1106; Fax (415) 474-3395

**Whales:** Blue, fin, gray, humpback, sperm, minke, orca, several species of dolphin

**Season:** Mid-February through early April

**Boats:** One boat, the 86-foot *Spirit of Adventure*; 14 cabins for 28 passengers and staff. Participants live on board. Whale watching from small skiffs.

**Trips:** A 12-day trip with stops at San Benito Islands, San Ignacio Lagoon, Magdalena Bay, Cabo San Lucas, Los Islotes Island, Santa Catalina Island, and San Jose Island. Trip concludes in La Paz.

**Fare:** $2,210 per person. Price does not include airfare or transfers.

**Departure:** Trips leave from San Diego.

**Naturalist:** Experienced naturalists affiliated with Oceanic Society Expeditions accompany all trips.

"Our movement from temperate to tropical waters makes this one of the richest and most varied expeditions possible," notes Oceanic Society Expeditions. Slide shows and informal lectures are held each evening on board, and assorted optional activities are available each day. Oceanic Society Expeditions has conducted nature study tours since 1972.

# MAGDALENA BAY

## Baja Expeditions

2625 Garnet Avenue, San Diego, CA 92109
(800) 843-6967 or (619) 581-3311; Fax (619) 581-6542

**Whales:** Gray

**Season:** January, February, and March

**Boats:** Two boats: The 80-foot *Don José* accommodates 14 passengers in 7 staterooms; or the 88-foot *Copper Sky*, a sailboat, sleeps 12 in 6 cabins. Participants live aboard on all trips. Whale watching from boat and from small skiffs.

**Trips:** Several 4- and 7-day trips to Magdalena Bay. Trips conclude in La Paz.

**Fare:** From $995 to $1,895 per person. Price includes land arrangements, accommodations, meals, beverages, and most related trip equipment. Airfare, tips, and airport taxes are not included.

**Departure:** Trips leave from La Paz, with bus transportation to the boat.

**Naturalist:** Yes

"Magdalena Bay is formed by a long, low barrier island barely half a mile wide but 40 miles long," notes a spokesman for Baja Expeditions. "The Pacific shore is wild and windswept, the remains of boats and whales, large and small, can be found buried in the beach or half covered by a dune. On the eastern shore, mangrove-lined estuaries are the winter home of thousands of migratory birds."

Baja Expeditions made its first trip in 1974 in a rented fishing boat with a well-thumbed copy of John Steinbeck's *Log from the Sea of Cortez* aboard. Tim Means, founder, notes that today the company is the largest and oldest outfitter of natural history and adventure travel in Mexico. (Note: For information on Baja Expeditions' kayaking and sailing trips, see next listings.)

## Baja Expeditions

2625 Garnet Avenue, San Diego, CA 92109
(800) 843-6967 or (619) 581-3311; Fax (619) 581-6542

| | |
|---|---|
| **Whales:** | Gray |
| **Season:** | January through March |
| **Boats:** | Sea kayaks. Participants camp, except for the first and last nights, which are spent in a hotel. Skiffs carry the camping supplies throughout the trip. |
| **Trips:** | Weekly departures for 5- and 8-day trips to Magdalena Bay. Novice paddlers welcome. Trips conclude in La Paz. |
| **Fare:** | From $695 to $1,150 per person. Price includes land arrangements, accommodations, meals, beverages, hotels scheduled in itinerary, and all specialized equipment, including tents, kayaking gear, cookware, and utensils. Sleeping bags may be rented. Airfare, gratuities, and airport taxes are not included. |
| **Departure:** | Trips leave from La Paz, with bus transportation to Magdalena Bay. |
| **Naturalist:** | Yes |

"Kayaks allow us to observe at close quarters the fascinating behaviors of the gray whale as we explore the lagoon and mangrove estuaries," says a spokesman at Baja Expeditions. Skiffs are used to carry camping equipment and to view whales.

# Baja Expeditions

2625 Garnet Avenue, San Diego, CA 92109
(800) 843-6967 or (619) 581-3311; Fax (619) 581-6542

| | |
|---|---|
| **Whales:** | Gray |
| **Season:** | January through March |
| **Boats:** | Three twin-masted 22-foot sailing boats; 5 passengers each |
| **Trips:** | Several 8-day wilderness sailing trips in Magdalena Bay and around the island. Participants camp at night and learn to sail during the day. |
| **Fare:** | $1,150 per person, which includes equipment, meals, two nights in hotels, and guides. |
| **Departure:** | Trips begin and end in La Paz. |
| **Naturalist:** | Yes |

"On our wilderness sailing trip to see the whales, you'll also learn basic seamanship and emergency procedures, and how to snorkel, fish and camp safely and gently in the delicate desert environment," says Kristin Kirk, public relations coordinator.

# Natural Habitat Adventures

One Sussex Station, Suite #110, Sussex, NJ 07461
(800) 543-8917 or (201) 702-1525; Fax (201)702-1335

| | |
|---|---|
| **Whales:** | Gray, common and bottlenose dolphin |
| **Season:** | January |
| **Boats:** | One boat, the 80-foot *Don José*, sleeps 14. Participants live aboard. Whale watching from skiffs. |
| **Trips:** | Three 8-day trips to Magdalena Bay. One trip includes time in the Sea of Cortez, with visits at Espiritu Santo Island and Cabo San Lucas. |
| **Fare:** | $2,175 per person, which includes roundtrip airfare from Tucson or Los Angeles, guide services, hotel in La Paz on the last night, all meals and all transfers. |
| **Departure:** | All trips begin and end in La Paz, Mexico. |
| **Naturalist:** | Yes |

Ben Bressler, director of Natural Habitat, says, "We take adventurers, photographers, and animal enthusiasts of all ages to visit some of the most incredible animals on the face of the earth. We are committed to the idea that it is far better to see the animals as they live, wild and free, in their own natural environment."

## Oceanic Society Expeditions

Fort Mason Center, Building E, San Francisco, CA 94123
(800) 326-7491 or (415) 441-1106; Fax (415) 474-3395

| | |
|---|---|
| **Whales:** | Gray |
| **Season:** | January and February |
| **Boats:** | Several 21-foot Drascombe sailboats. Participants camp and sail. |
| **Trips:** | Two 8-day camping trips in Magdalena Bay, limited to 12 people per trip. |
| **Fare:** | $1,090 per person, which includes camping, meals, sailing instruction, and guides. |
| **Departure:** | Trips begin and end in Loreto, Mexico. |
| **Naturalist:** | Naturalist from Oceanic Society Expeditions. |

"In Magdalena Bay, a gray whale calving lagoon, our days are spent under sail, exploring spectacular, pristine coastal beaches inaccessible from land," says a spokeswoman. "We spend two full days observing and learning about the mighty gray whales, and this is a unique way to closely and unobtrusively approach them."

# SAN IGNACIO LAGOON

## Baja Discovery

P.O. Box 152527, San Diego, CA 92115
(800) 829-BAJA or (619) 262-0700

| | |
|---|---|
| **Whales:** | Gray |
| **Season:** | January through March |
| **Boats:** | Whale watching from 22-foot fiberglass skiffs |
| **Trips:** | Several 5-, 6-, and 8-day trips to Baja Discovery's "safari style" camp on an island in San Ignacio Lagoon. Participants go out in skiffs twice a day. Full meal service provided in the dining tent. Trips restricted to 18 participants. |
| **Fare:** | $1,450 to $1,750 per person, which includes round-trip charter flight to San Ignacio, meals, accommodations, equipment, guides, and one night in a hotel. Custom itineraries available. |
| **Departure:** | Trips begin and end in San Diego. |
| **Naturalist:** | Knowledgeable hosts and guides at campsite. |

"The Baja Discovery adventure focuses on one of the most spectacular wildlife phenomena in the world—the annual gathering of thousands of gray whales in the shallow, warm waters of the Baja lagoons," says owner Karen Ivey. "Our land-based shore camp on an inner lagoon lies adjacent to the largest concentration of whales in Laguna San Ignacio." Baja Discovery has operated the environmentally conscious camp since 1966.

## Baja Expeditions

2625 Garnet Avenue, San Diego, CA 92109
(800) 843-6967 or (619) 581-3311; Fax (619) 581 6542

| | |
|---|---|
| **Whales:** | Gray |
| **Season:** | January through March |
| **Boats:** | Whale watching from skiffs |

**Trips:** Several 5-day trips to Baja Expeditions' "safari style" camp on an island in San Ignacio Lagoon. Participants go out in skiffs twice a day. Full meal service provided in the kitchen tent.

**Fare:** $1,395 per person, which includes charter flight to San Ignacio, meals, accommodations, equipment, and guides.

**Departure:** Trips begin and end in San Diego.

**Naturalist:** Yes

Kristin Kirk, public relations coordinator, says it is not unusual for San Ignacio's "friendly" whales to approach the boats and allow themselves to be touched. Baja Expeditions made its first trip in 1974. Founder Tim Means notes that the company is the largest and oldest outfitter of natural history and adventure in Mexico.

# Biological Journeys

1696 Ocean Drive, McKinleyville, CA 95521
(800) 548-7555 or (707) 839-0178; Fax (707) 839-4656

**Whales:** Gray

**Season:** Late January through mid-March

**Boats:** One boat, the 105-foot sportfishing vessel *Searcher*; up to 26 passengers in 13 cabins. Participants live aboard throughout the trip. Whale watching from aluminum skiffs.

**Trips:** Eight 12-day trips to San Ignacio Lagoon, with stops at Todos Santos Island, San Benito Islands, Cedros Island, and San Martin Island. Some trips continue on to the Sea of Cortez. Trips conclude in San Diego.

**Fare:** Trips range from $1,700 to $2,993 per person. Price includes instructions, accommodations, meals and transportation while aboard the vessels, and a Mexican fishing license. Rate does not include transportation to San Diego, airport departure taxes, meals or lodging en route, or tips. Travel arrangements can be made through the trip operator's agent, Eureka Travel Agency.

**Departure:** Trips leave from San Diego, California.

**Naturalist:** Yes

Biological Journeys has visited San Ignacio lagoon and its gray whales every winter since 1970. Ronn Storro-Patterson, a leading authority on whales, and Ron LeValley, an ornithological expert, head up Biological Journeys, which sponsors these natural history trips to Baja California.

## Ecosummer Expeditions International, Inc.

P.O. Box 8014-240, 936 Peace Portal Drive, Blaine, WA 98230
(800) 688-8605 (in the U.S.); Fax (604) 669-3244

In Canada: 1516 Duranleau Street, Granville Island, Vancouver,
British Columbia, V6H 3S4 Canada
(800) 465-8884 or (604) 669-7741; Fax (604) 669-3244

| | |
|---|---|
| **Whales:** | Gray |
| **Season:** | January through March |
| **Boats:** | Sea kayaks |
| **Trips:** | Five 7-day trips to the Pacific lagoons with gray whales. The trips are specifically geared to whale watching. Participants camp except for the first and last nights spent in a hotel in La Paz. |
| **Fare:** | $995 for the 7-day trip, which includes guides, group equipment, ground transportation, meals, and hotel accommodations. |
| **Departure:** | Trips begin and conclude in La Paz. |
| **Naturalist:** | Guides familiar with Baja's flora and fauna accompany each trip. |

"Sharing the waters with the magnificent gray whales will provide you with an understanding of the absolute necessity of preserving their breeding habitat— . intact—for the success of their future generations," says Ecosummer operations manager Jean Barbeau.

Founded in 1976, Ecosummer Expeditions began as an adventure company that promoted environmental education, working primarily with high school students. Founder Jim Allan was soon deluged with requests from adults who wanted activity-oriented natural history wilderness trips and so Ecosummer Expeditions evolved.

## Oceanic Society Expeditions

Fort Mason Center, Building E, San Francisco, CA 94123
(800) 326-7491 or (415) 441-1106; Fax (415) 474-3395

| | |
|---|---|
| **Whales:** | Gray |
| **Season:** | Mid-February to late March |
| **Boats:** | The 86-foot *Spirit of Adventure*; 14 cabins accommodate 28 passengers and staff. Participants live aboard. Whale watching from small skiffs. |
| **Trips:** | Nine-day trips to San Ignacio Lagoon, with stops at San Benito Islands, Cedros Island, and Todos Santos Island. Trips conclude in San Diego. |
| **Fare:** | $1,635 per person. Price does not include airfare or airport transfers. |
| **Departure:** | Trips leave from San Diego, California. |
| **Naturalist:** | Two naturalists from Oceanic Society Expeditions accompany each trip. |

Oceanic Society Expeditions is a national nonprofit environmental organization that has conducted nature study trips since 1972. "On this expedition, we will enjoy close encounters with some of the hundreds of whales that frequent this lagoon," a spokeswoman said. Trips include slide shows and informal lectures each evening and a choice of optional activities each day.

## Pacific Queen/Biological Adventures

Fisherman's Landing, 2838 Garrison, San Diego, CA 92106
(619) 222-0391

| | |
|---|---|
| **Whales:** | Gray, blue, fin, minke, orca, humpback |
| **Season:** | January through April |
| **Boats:** | One boat, the 88-foot sportfishing vessel *Pacific Queen*; with double and quadruple compartments; participation limited to 30. Participants live aboard. |
| **Trips:** | Six 9- and 10-day trips to San Ignacio Lagoon. Itineraries vary slightly, but most trips include stops at West San Benito Islands, Cedros Island, San Martin Island, and Todos Santos Island. Trips conclude in San Diego. |

**Fare:**      $1,425 per person. Price includes food and lodging and natural history programs on board each evening.

**Departure:**      Trips leave from San Diego, California.

**Naturalist:**      A staff of biologists accompanies each trip.

Captain Ed McEwen, owner of the *Pacific Queen*, leads each cruise, accompanied by a crew of six and a staff of biologists who are experts in the biology and oceanography of Baja California. Expedition biologist and director Margie Stinson has made more than 100 such trips, leading expeditions since the late 1960s. "Our philosophy is that each guest is treated as you would wish your parents to be treated by strangers," Margie Stinson notes. "Consequently, friendships are lifelong."

## Pacific Sea Fari Tours

2803 Emerson Street, San Diego, CA 92106
(619) 226-8224

**Whales:**      Gray

**Season:**      Late January to late March

**Boats:**      One boat, the 88-foot *Big Game*, holds 30 passengers in 14 cabins. Participants live aboard. Whale watching from skiffs.

**Trips:**      Seven-, 8-, and 9-day trips to San Ignacio Lagoon, with stops at San Martin Island, San Benito Islands, Cedros Island, Todos Santos Island, and Ensenada. Trip concludes in San Diego.

**Fare:**      $1,340 to $1,895 per person. Price includes meals and snacks, accommodations, related equipment, and services of a naturalist staff. Tips aboard, airfare, and transfers not included.

**Departure:**      Trips leave from San Diego, California.

**Naturalist:**      Yes

Pacific Sea Fari Tours' natural history program has been developed under the leadership of Dr. Theodore J. Walker, a noted author, lecturer, and researcher. Considered one of the world's foremost experts on gray whales, Dr. Walker wrote *Whale Primer*, the first authoritative work of its kind, and founded the whale observatory at the Cabrillo National Monument. Dr. Walker accompanies about one-third of the trips himself. No two trips are exactly alike.

## SAN IGNACIO LAGOON AND SEA OF CORTEZ

### American Cetacean Society Expeditions

P.O. Box 2639, San Pedro, CA 90731
(310) 548-6279; Fax (310) 548-6950

| | |
|---|---|
| **Whales:** | Gray |
| **Season:** | February and March |
| **Boats:** | One boat, the 95-foot sportfishing vessel *Searcher*; 16 cabins accommodate up to 31 passengers. Participants live aboard. Whale watching from small skiffs. |
| **Trips:** | Three trips: one 8-day trip in mid-February, a 9-day trip in late February, and an 11-day trip late in March. Trips focus on San Ignacio Lagoon with stops at Scammon's Lagoon, San Martin Island, San Benito Islands, Cedros Island, and Todos Santos Island. Trips conclude in San Diego, Cabo San Lucas, or La Paz. |
| **Fare:** | For ACS members: the 8-day trip is $1,725; the 9-day trip is $2,050 plus $250 back to San Diego; the 11-day trip is $2,350 plus $215 back to San Diego. Add 10 percent for non-members. Fares do not include tips, personal items, or alcohol. |
| **Departure:** | Trips leave from San Diego, California. |
| **Naturalist:** | Naturalists from American Cetacean Society accompany all trips. |

The American Cetacean Society has conducted specialized trips for small groups to see whales since 1973. "Our trips take place in some of the great wilderness areas and are led by experienced naturalists. All our trips are really spectacular!" says a spokeswoman.

"San Ignacio Lagoon is the home of the friendly gray whales; you will enjoy close-encounter whale watching from small skiffs."

## Special Expeditions

720 Fifth Avenue, New York, NY 10019
(212) 765-7740; Fax, (212) 265-3770

**Whales:** Gray, humpback, blue

**Season:** January through April

**Boats:** Two boats, the M V *Sea Lion* and the M V *Sea Bird*. Each carries 70 passengers. Participants live aboard. Whale watching from small skiffs.

**Trips:** Numerous 8-day trips to San Ignacio Lagoon and among the islands in the Sea of Cortez, including Islas Los Islotes, Espiritu Santo, and Isla Santa Catalinas. Trips conclude in Tucson, Arizona.

**Fare:** From $2,750 to $3,950, depending on accommodations. Fares do not include air transportation or tips.

**Departure:** Trips leave from La Paz.

**Naturalist:** Yes

Special Expeditions' voyages travel with top naturalists who know the region intimately and are experts on its flora and fauna, says marketing director Ralph Hammelbacher. "Three days are spent whale watching, using Zodiac landing craft for close-up views. Hiking on islands in the Sea of Cortez and snorkeling on coral reefs complete the experience."

# SEA OF CORTEZ

## Baja Expeditions

2625 Garnet Avenue, San Diego, CA 92109
(800) 843-6967 or (619) 581-3311; Fax (619) 581-6542

**Whales:** Blue, finback

**Season:** April, May, and June

| | |
|---|---|
| **Boats:** | Two boats: the 80-foot *Don José* has 7 cabins that accommodate 2 people each; the *Copper Sky*, an 88-foot sailboat, sleeps 12 in 6 cabins. Participants live aboard. |
| **Trips:** | Ten-day trips in the Sea of Cortez, with stops at Espiritu Santo Island, San Jose Island, Santa Catalina Island, Ildefonso Island, and Raza Island. Trips disembark in San Felipe and passengers board a bus back to San Diego. |
| **Fare:** | $2,195 per person. Price includes land arrangements, accommodations, meals, beverages, and most related trip equipment. Airfare, gratuities, and airport taxes are not included. |
| **Departure:** | Trips leave from La Paz, with bus transportation to the boat. |
| **Naturalist:** | Yes |

Baja Expeditions made its first trip in 1974 in a rented fishing boat with a well-thumbed copy of John Steinbeck's *Log from the Sea of Cortez* aboard. The company's offerings to the Sea of Cortez recapture the sights, sounds, and experiences of Steinbeck's trip.

Tim Means, founder, notes that today the company is the largest and oldest outfitter of natural history and adventure travel in Mexico.

# Biological Journeys

1696 Ocean Drive, McKinleyville, CA 95521
(800) 548-7555 or (707) 839-0178; Fax (707) 839-4656

| | |
|---|---|
| **Whales:** | Blue |
| **Season:** | Mid-March |
| **Boats:** | One boat, the 80-foot *Don José*; 7 staterooms accommodate 2-4 passengers each. Participants live aboard. |
| **Trips:** | One 8-day trip to the Sea of Cortez, with stops at Espiritu Santo Island, Santa Catalina Island, Los Islotes, and La Paz. |
| **Fare:** | $2,195 per person. Price includes accommodations, meals and transportation while aboard the vessel, and a Mexican fishing license. Rate does not include transportation to San Diego or La Paz, airport departure taxes, meals or lodging en route, or tips. Travel arrangements can be made through the trip operator's agent, Eureka Travel Agency. |

**Departure:**    Trip leaves from La Paz, with transportation to the boat.

**Naturalist:**    Yes

"We proudly feature a cruise that combines the color and charm of Baja with all the might and majesty of the world's largest animals. You will be awed by their size and astonished by their gentle behavior."

Ronn Storro-Patterson, an authority on whales, and Ron LeValley, an ornithologist, head up Biological Journeys, which has sponsored natural history trips to Baja California since 1970. (Note: For other Biological Journeys trips to the Sea of Cortez, see next two entries.)

# Biological Journeys

1696 Ocean Drive, McKinleyville, CA 95521
(800) 548-7555 or (707) 839-0178; Fax (707) 839-4656

**Whales:**    Gray, humpback, blue

**Season:**    January through April

**Boats:**    One boat, the 92-foot *Royal Star*; 24 passengers in 12 cabins. Participants live aboard. Whale watching from aluminum skiffs.

**Trips:**    Two 12-day trips to the Sea of Cortez, with stops at Todos Santos Island, Scammon's Lagoon, San Ignacio Lagoon, Magdalena Bay, Cabo San Lucas, Gorda Bank, Bahia Los Frailes, Cerralvo Island, Espiritu Santo Island, San Francisco Island, and La Paz.

**Fare:**    $2,995 per person. Price includes accommodations, meals and transportation while aboard the vessel and transportation back to San Diego. Rate does not include airport departure taxes, meals or lodging en route, or tips. Travel arrangements can be made through the trip operator's agent, Eureka Travel Agency.

**Departure:**    Trip leaves from San Diego, California.

**Naturalist:**    Yes

"You will cruise from San Diego to La Paz, basking in the great variety of natural history experiences offered by this wilderness area. You may see as many as ten species of whales!" says Biological Journeys.

Ronn Storro-Patterson and Ron LeValley head up Biological Journeys, which has sponsored Baja California trips since 1970.

# Ecosummer Expeditions International Inc.

P.O. Box 8014-240, 936 Peace Portal Drive, Blaine, WA 98230
(800) 688-8605 (in the U.S.); Fax (604) 669-3244

In Canada: 1516 Duranleau Street, Granville Island Vancouver,
British Columbia, V6H 3S4 Canada
(800) 465-8884; Fax (604) 669-3244

| | |
|---|---|
| **Whales:** | Humpback, blue, gray |
| **Season:** | January through March |
| **Boats:** | Sea kayaks |
| **Trips:** | Two 14-day trips among the islands of the Sea of Cortez. Participants camp except for the first and last nights spent in a hotel in La Paz. |
| **Fare:** | $1,795 per person. Price includes guides, group equipment, ground transportation, meals, and hotel accommodations. |
| **Departure:** | Trips begin and conclude in La Paz. |
| **Naturalist:** | Guides familiar with Baja's flora and fauna accompany each trip. |

"This exciting itinerary follows the most breathtaking coastline Baja has to offer between the historic mission town of Loreto and the pleasant capital of Baja del Sur, La Paz," says Ecosummer operations manager Jean Barbeau.

Founded in 1976, Ecosummer Expeditions began as an adventure company that promoted environmental education, working primarily with high school students. Founder Jim Allan was soon deluged with requests from adults who wanted activity-oriented natural history wilderness trips and so Ecosummer Expeditions evolved.

## Elakah! Kayak Tours

P.O. Box 4092, Bellingham, WA 98227
(206) 734-7270

| | |
|---|---|
| **Whales:** | Fin, dolphin |
| **Season:** | February through April |
| **Boats:** | Six kayaks; each holds two |
| **Trips:** | Several 10-day kayak, camping and overland desert tours in and around Bahia de Los Angeles in the Sea of Cortez. |
| **Fare:** | $895, which includes experienced guides, complete kayaking instruction, South-of-the-Border cuisine, camping gear, and round-trip shuttle service. |
| **Departure:** | Trips leave from San Diego Airport. |
| **Naturalist:** | Guides knowledgeable about the natural and cultural history of the area accompany each trip. |

"Elakah! Kayak Tours has the capability of bringing nature and people together and producing a very special form of magic," says owner Jennifer Hahn. "On our Baja trips, we visit an unusual place, an island-spangled coast like no other in Baja."

## Mingan Island Cetacean Study

Summer: 124 Bord de la Mer, Longue-Pointe-de-Mingan
Quebec, G0G 1V0 Canada
(418) 949-2845

Winter: 285, rue Green, St. Lambert, Quebec, J4P lT3 Canada
(514) 465-9176

| | |
|---|---|
| **Whales:** | Blue, finback, orca, humpback, gray, several species of dolphin |
| **Season:** | March |
| **Boats:** | Two 22-foot fiberglass boats |
| **Trips:** | Several 7-day trips in March, with a Loreto hotel as the base of operations. |
| **Fare:** | $165 per day per person. Airfare to Mexico not included. |
| **Departure:** | All trips start in Loreto, Mexico. |
| **Naturalist:** | Yes |

The Mingan Island Cetacean Study operates a research station in the Mingan Island region of the Quebec North Shore from May to November, studying local populations of blue, humpback, finback, and minke whales. Since 1983, founder Richard Sears has also offered educational research programs in the Sea of Cortez.

"Guests are invited to the coastal community of Loreto on the Sea of Cortez, Mexico, to participate in our winter/spring research season," Sears says. "The striking blue waters of this area offer a rich environment in which to observe a great variety of marine mammals, birds, and fishes."

## National Audubon Society Travel

700 Broadway, New York, NY 10003
(212) 979-3000; Fax (212) 979-3188

**Whales:**    Gray, humpback, blue

**Season:**    February

**Boats:**    One boat, the 152-foot *Sea Bird*; 70 passengers in 37 outside cabins. Participants live aboard. Whale watching from motorized inflatable rafts.

**Trips:**    One 10-day trip to the Sea of Cortez, with stops in Magdalena Bay, Cabo San Lucas, Islas Los Islotes, Espiritu Santo, Isla Santa Catalina, Isla San Marcos, and Isla San Esteban. Trips conclude in Tucson, Arizona.

**Fare:**    For Audubon Society members, $2,750 to $3,950, depending on the location of the stateroom. Fare includes all meals, accommodations on board, and transfers. Airfare and tips not included.

**Departure:**    Trips leave from La Paz.

**Naturalist:**    Natural history staff from the Audubon Society and guest lecturers accompany trips.

"The M V *Sea Bird* is ideal for exploring the region. Built to glide effortlessly, it will get you as close as possible to the whales and other sea life," says an Audubon spokeswoman. "Where the *Sea Bird* can't go, the ship's fleet of rubber landing craft will be launched, ready to land you almost anywhere at will."

The National Audubon Society will also offer a kayak trip in 1995.

# Pacific Sea Fari Tours

2803 Emerson Street, San Diego, CA 92106
(619) 226-8224

| | |
|---|---|
| **Whales:** | Gray |
| **Season:** | Late February to mid-April |
| **Boats:** | One boat, the 88-foot *Big Game*; holds 30 passengers in 14 cabins. Participants live aboard the boat. Whale watching from skiffs. |
| **Trips:** | Eight- and 11-day trips to the Sea of Cortez, with stops at San Benito Islands, San Ignacio Lagoon, Magdalena Bay, Cabo San Lucas, Espiritu Santo Island, San Jose Island, Santa Catalina Island, Ildefonso Island, and La Paz. Trip concludes in La Paz. |
| **Fare:** | $1,400 to $2,210 per person includes meals and snacks, accommodations, related equipment, and services of a naturalist staff. Tips aboard, airfare, and transfers not included. |
| **Departure:** | Trips leave from San Diego, California. |
| **Naturalist:** | Yes |

Pacific Sea Fari Tours' natural history program has been developed under the leadership of Dr. Theodore J. Walker, a noted author, lecturer, and researcher. Considered one of the world's foremost experts on gray whales, Dr. Walker wrote *Whale Primer*, the first authoritative work of its kind, and founded the whale observatory at the Cabrillo National Monument. Dr. Walker accompanies about one-third of the trips himself, and no two trips are alike.

# Sea Quest Expeditions

Zoetic Research, P.O. Box 2424R, Friday Harbor, WA 98250
(206) 378-5767

| | |
|---|---|
| **Whales:** | Fin, minke, blue; occasional humpback, gray, orca |
| **Season:** | February through April |
| **Boats:** | Sea kayak |
| **Trips:** | Several trips with varied 5- or 7-day itineraries in the Sea of Cortez. Participants camp overnight on uninhabited nature preserve islands. |

**Fare:**    $599 to $849 per person. Price includes everything except air-fare to Mexico.

**Departure:**    Trips originate in Loreto, Mexico.

**Naturalist:**    Biologist with field research and teaching experience accompanies trips.

Executive director Mark Lewis notes that whale and dolphin watching is excellent from February through April in what he calls the "Blue Triangle." So far, nearly 300 individual blue whales have been identified in the area, including cows with calves. The desert seascapes and snorkeling with tropical fish are added attractions.

Sea Quest also offers research trips that qualify for college credit, and they will design custom trips.

# Smithsonian National Associates Travel Program

Smithsonian Institution, 1100 Jefferson Drive S.W., Washington, D.C. 20560
(202) 357-4700

**Whales:**    Finback, blue

**Season:**    February

**Boats:**    One boat, the M V *Sea Bird*; private baths, outside cabins with lower berths and air conditioning, with accommodations for up to 65 people. Participants live aboard.

**Trips:**    One 8-day trip in the Sea of Cortez, with stops at Loreto, Santa Catalina Island, San Marcos Island, Raza Island, San Esteban Island, and the Midriff Islands. Trip concludes in Los Angeles.

**Fare:**    $2,750 to $3,950, depending on cabin location. Price includes meals, accommodations, transfers, and services of study guide and naturalists.

**Departure:**    Trips leave from Los Angeles, California.

**Naturalists:**    Experienced naturalists affiliated with the Smithsonian National Associates Travel Program accompany the trip.

The Smithsonian Institution sponsors numerous study tours. The Sea of Cortez trip features whale watching, bird watching, walks on the beaches, and lectures on the islands, the flora and fauna.

## Thompson Voyages and Research

P.O. Box 217, Laguna Beach, CA 92652
(714) 497-1055; Fax (714) 497-9320

| | |
|---|---|
| **Whales:** | Gray, humpback, finback, blue |
| **Season:** | March through May |
| **Boats:** | One boat, the 72-foot catamaran *The Serendy*; 6 staterooms for 12 people. Whale watching from skiffs. |
| **Trips:** | Six 7-day trips in the Sea of Cortez, with a stop in Magdalena Bay. |
| **Fare:** | $1,695 per person, which includes meals, accommodations aboard, guides, and land transfers. Airfare to and from Cabo San Lucas or La Paz is not included, but Thompson Voyages will help make reservations from Los Angeles. |
| **Departure:** | Trips begin and end in Cabo San Lucas or La Paz. |
| **Naturalist:** | Naturalist and biologist accompany trips. |

"We will be exploring many of the incredible uninhabited islands and beautiful coves of the Sea of Cortez," says owner Doug Thompson. "In Magdalena Bay, it is common to see grown gray whales and their babies within arms' reach of our skiffs, an experience you will never forget."

Thompson has been making trips to Baja California since 1971 and says, "I'm still just as excited as I was the first time."

# WHERE WHALES ARE WHEN

This chapter is a calendar that tells where and when you can find whales. The time span shown encompasses the early weeks when a few whales are present; the height of the season; and the end of season, when just a few laggers may still be around. Dolphins' migratory patterns are not as well known as those of the great whales, so the listings here emphasize the whereabouts of the larger animals.

This calendar has not been reviewed or approved by whales and may not correspond exactly with their comings and goings. Also, keep in mind that whales do not observe our territorial boundaries and may spill over into neighboring states and even countries other than those listed here.

## JANUARY

**Gray whales:** Off the coasts of California and Oregon

**Humpback whales:** In Hawaiian waters

## FEBRUARY

**Gray whales:** Off the coasts of California and Oregon and in the lagoons off the west coast of Baja California, Mexico

**Humpback whales:** In Hawaiian waters

## MARCH

**Blue whales, fin whales, and pilot whales:** In the Sea of Cortez, off the east coast of Baja California, Mexico

**Gray whales:** Off the coasts of California, Oregon, and Washington; in Alaskan waters; in the lagoons off the west coast of Baja California, Mexico; and off British Columbia

**Humpback whales:** In Hawaiian waters and in the Sea of Cortez, off the east coast of Baja California, Mexico

## APRIL

**Blue whales:** In the Sea of Cortez, off the east coast of Baja California, Mexico

**Fin whales:** Off the northeast U.S. coast

**Gray whales:** Off the coasts of northern California, Oregon, and Washington; in the lagoons off the west coast of Baja California, Mexico; and off British Columbia

**Humpback whales:** In Hawaiian waters; in the Sea of Cortez, off the east coast of Baja California, Mexico; and off the northeast U.S. coast

**Minke whales:** Off the northeast U.S. coast

**Right whales:** Off the northeast U.S. coast

## MAY

**Beluga whales:** Off the Northwest Territories in Canada

**Bowhead whales:** Off the Northwest Territories in Canada

**Fin whales:** Off the northeast U.S. coast

**Gray whales:** Off the coasts of Oregon and Washington

**Humpback whales:** In Alaskan waters and off the northeast U.S. coast

**Minke whales:** In Alaskan waters and off the northeast U.S. coast

**Narwhals:** Off the Northwest Territories in Canada

**Orcas:** In Alaskan waters

**Right whales:** Off the northeast U.S. coast

## JUNE

**Beluga whales:** Off the Northwest Territories and in the St. Lawrence River in Quebec, Canada

**Blue whales:** In the St. Lawrence River in Quebec, Canada

**Bowhead whales:** Off the Northwest Territories in Canada

**Fin whales:** Off the northeast U.S. coast, in Alaskan waters, off Nova Scotia and Newfoundland, and in the St. Lawrence River in Quebec, Canada

**Humpback whales:** In Alaskan waters, off the northeast U.S. coast, off Newfoundland and Nova Scotia in Canada, and off the Oregon coast

**Minke whales:** In Alaskan waters, off the northeast U.S. coast, off Nova Scotia and Newfoundland, and in the St. Lawrence River in Quebec, Canada

**Narwhals:** Off the Northwest Territories in Canada

**Orcas:** In Alaskan waters, off British Columbia, in the San Juan Islands, and off the Oregon coast

**Right whales:** Off the northeast U.S. coast and Nova Scotia, Canada

## JULY

**Beluga whales:** Off the Northwest Territories, in the St. Lawrence River in Quebec, and in Manitoba, Canada

**Orcas:** In Alaskan waters, off British Columbia, in the San Juan Islands, and off the Oregon coast

**Right whales:** Off the northeast U.S. coast and Nova Scotia, Canada

**Sperm whales:** Off the coast of California

## AUGUST

**Beluga whales:** Off the Northwest Territories, in the St. Lawrence River in Quebec, and in Manitoba, Canada

**Blue whales:** In the St. Lawrence River in Quebec, Canada, and off the coast of California

**Fin whales:** Off the northeast U.S. coast; off Nova Scotia, Newfoundland, and New Brunswick; and in the St. Lawrence River in Quebec, Canada

**Humpback whales:** In Alaskan waters; off the northeast U.S. coast; off Newfoundland, New Brunswick, and Nova Scotia in Canada; and off the California and Oregon coasts

**Minke whales:** In Alaskan waters, off the northeast U.S. coast, off Nova Scotia and Newfoundland, and in the St. Lawrence River in Quebec, Canada

**Orcas:** In Alaskan waters, off British Columbia, in the San Juan Islands, and off the Oregon coast

**Right whales:** Off the northeast U.S. coast and Nova Scotia, Canada

**Sperm whales:** Off the coast of California

## SEPTEMBER

**Beluga whales:** In the St. Lawrence River in Quebec, Canada

**Blue whales:** In the St. Lawrence River in Quebec, Canada, and off the coast of California

**Fin whales:** Off the northeast U.S. coast, off Nova Scotia and Newfoundland, and in the St. Lawrence River in Quebec, Canada

**Humpback whales:** In Alaskan waters, off the northeast U.S. coast, off Newfoundland and Nova Scotia in Canada, and off the California and Oregon coasts

**Minke whales:** In Alaskan waters, off the northeast U.S. coast, off Nova Scotia and Newfoundland, and in the St. Lawrence River in Quebec, Canada

**Orcas:** In Alaskan waters and off British Columbia

**Right whales:** Off the northeast U.S. coast and Nova Scotia, Canada

## OCTOBER

**Beluga whales:** In the St. Lawrence River in Quebec, Canada

**Blue whales:** In the St. Lawrence River in Quebec, Canada

**Fin whales:** Off the northeast U.S. coast and in the St. Lawrence River in Quebec, Canada

**Humpback whales:** Off the northeast U.S. coast

**Minke whales:** Off the northeast U.S. coast and in the St. Lawrence River in Quebec, Canada

**Right whales:** Off the northeast U.S. coast

## NOVEMBER

This is a great month to plan whale-watch trips!

## DECEMBER

**Gray whales:** Off the coast of Oregon

**Humpback whales:** In Hawaiian waters

# ADDITIONAL TRIPS

Some tour operators sponsor whale-watch (and other nature study) trips to destinations other than those included in this book. Here is a list of those tour operators and brief information about their varied offerings. Write for more information.

## Biological Journeys

1696 Ocean Drive, McKinleyville, CA 95521

(800) 548-7555 or (707) 839-0178

In addition to the many destinations listed in this book, Biological Journeys sponsors trips to the Galapagos Islands, the Amazon, the Great Barrier Reef, New Zealand, and Costa Rica.

## Bluewater Adventures

#202-1656 Duranleau Street
Vancouver, British Columbia, V6H 3S4 Canada

(604) 684 4575

Bluewater Adventures offers trips to Costa Rica in addition to numerous nature study trips off the western coast of Canada.

## Canadian Nature Tours

Federation of Ontario Naturalists
355 Lesmill Road, Don Mills, Ontario, M3B 2W8 Canada

(416) 444 8419

More than 50 trips are available, including canoe and backpacking trips, to such destinations as Cuba, Costa Rica, the Galapagos Islands, and throughout Canada.

## Dirigo Cruises

39 Waterside Lane, Clinton, CT 06413

(203) 669-7068

Scheduled and custom-tailored trips are available on twelve sailing ships cruising New England, the Caribbean, and the South Pacific. Teacher-training courses and educational expeditions for teenagers are also available.

## Earthwatch

680 Mt. Auburn Street, Box 403N, Watertown, MA 02272

(617) 926-8200

This nonprofit organization sponsors scholarly field research trips that allow volunteers to help scientists. Since its founding in 1971, Earthwatch has overseen hundreds of projects, many of them marine studies, in 87 countries and 36 states.

## Ecosummer Expeditions

1516 Duranleau Street
Vancouver, British Columbia, V6H 354 Canada

(604) 669-7741

In addition to trips off the west coast of Canada, Ecosummer Expeditions offers trips to the North Pole; in the Northwest Territories; off the coast of Greenland; and to Iceland, Belize, Patagonia, Africa, and Antarctica.

## Island Institute

4004 58th Place S.W., Seattle, WA 98116

(206) 938-0345

Island Institute offers marine science camps for children and adults with one day, overnight and week-long programs available at a private facility on Spieden Island in the San Juan Islands. Participants study orcas, learning from scientists and researchers such as Richard Osborne (author of *Marine Mammals of Greater Puget Sound*) and Ken McCann (*Whale Song*).

## Nature Expeditions International

474 Willamette, P.O. Box 11496, Eugene, OR 97440

(503) 484-6529

Something on the order of 99 trips are offered each year to such destinations as Australia, the West Indies, Africa, the Galapagos, Easter Island, Nepal, Peru, Oregon, the Amazon, New Guinea, and Costa Rica.

## Northwest Outdoor Center

2100 Westlake Avenue North, Seattle, WA 98109

(206) 281-9694

Founded in October, 1980, Northwest Outdoor Center specializes in kayak and canoe classes and nature trips. Day trips and extended vacations are offered throughout the San Juan Islands, in New Zealand, and on area lakes and rivers.

## Oceanic Society Expeditions

Fort Mason Center, Building E, San Francisco, CA 94123

(800) 326-7491 or (415) 441-1106; Fax (415) 474-3395

Trips are available year-round to such destinations as Antarctica, the Virgin Islands, Dominica, the Galapagos Islands, Costa Rica, the Bahamas, Patagonia, and Australia.

## Sea Quest Expeditions

Zoetic Research, P.O. Box 2424R, Friday Harbor, WA 98250

(206) 378-5767

Sea Quest Expeditions sponsors sailing and kayak trips to the Dry Tortugas, the Florida Keys, and the Everglades in addition to the trips in the San Juan Islands and off the coast of Baja California that are listed in this book.

## Sea Safaris

International Oceanographic Foundation, P.O. Box 499900, Miami, FL 33149

(305) 361-4697

The Sea Safaris program offered by the IOF includes European adventures as well as trips in the San Juan Islands, Canada, and Alaska.

## Smithsonian National Associates Travel Program

Smithsonian Institution/Department 0049
Washington, D.C. 20073

(202) 357-4700

Domestic and foreign study tours are offered to Alaska, the Grand Canyon, Europe, the West Indies, Africa, Japan, and Jamaica.

## Thompson Voyages and Research

P.O. Box 217, Laguna Beach, CA 92652

(714) 497-1055; Fax (714) 497-9320

In addition to trips to San Ignacio Lagoon in Baja California, Thompson Voyages conducts wildlife expeditions to the Galapagos Islands, the Catalina Islands, and the Bahamas.

# WHALE CONSERVATION AND RESEARCH ORGANIZATIONS

L ike-minded people have come together all over the United States and Canada to work for the conservation of whales and other endangered species. Some of the organizations listed here concentrate on research, some on direct aid to the animals, some on political activism, and some on education; some ably combine all four missions. A few of the organizations sponsor occasional whale-watch trips for members, and others even recruit people to assist in research projects. For details, write to those organizations that interest you.

### Alaska Geographic Society
Box 4-EEE, Anchorage, AK 99509
(907) 274-0521

### Allied Whale
College of the Atlantic, 105 Eden Street, Bar Harbor, ME 04609
(207) 288-5644

### American Association of Zoological Parks and Aquariums
Oglebay Park, Wheeling, WV 26003
(304) 242-2160

### American Cetacean Society
P.O. Box 2639, San Pedro, CA 90731
(213) 548-6279

### American Oceans Campaign
725 Arizona Avenue, Suite 102, Santa Monica, CA 90401
(800) 862-3260 or (310) 576-6162

## Animal Protection Institute of America

P.O. Box 22505, 6130 Freemont Boulevard, Sacramento, CA 95822
(916) 422-1921

## Animal Welfare Institute

P.O. Box 3650, Washington, D.C. 20007
(202) 337-2333

## Brier Island Ocean Study

Westport, Digby County, Nova Scotia, BOV lH0 Canada
(902) 839-2960

## British Columbia Wildlife Federation

102-6070 200th Street, Langley, British Columbia, V3A 1N4 Canada
(604) 576-8288

## Canadian Nature Federation

453 Sussex Drive, Ottawa, Ontario, KlN 6Z4 Canada
(613) 238-6154

## Canadian Wildlife Federation

1673 Carling Avenue, Ottawa, Ontario, K2A 3Z1 Canada
(613) 725-2191

## Center for Coastal Studies

59 Commercial Street, Box 1036, Provincetown, MA 02657
(508) 487-3622

## Center for Marine Conservation

1725 DeSales Street NW, Suite 500, Washington, D.C. 20036
(202) 429-5609

## Center for Whale Research

1359 Smuggler's Cove, Friday Harbor, WA 98250
(206) 378-5835

## Cetacean Research Unit
P.O. Box 159, Gloucester, MA 01930
(508) 281-6351

## Cetacean Society International
P.O. Box 290145, Wethersfield, CT 06109
(203) 793-8400

## Cousteau Society
930 West 21st Street, Norfolk, VA 23517
(804) 627-1144

## Defenders of Wildlife
1244 19th Street NW, Washington, D.C. 20036
(202) 659-9510

## Delta Society
P.O. Box 1080, 321 Burnett Avenue South, Renton, WA 98057
(206) 226-7357

## Dolphin Research Center
P.O. Box 2875, Marathon Shores, FL 33052
(305) 289-0002

## Earth Island Institute
300 Broadway, Suite 28, San Francisco, CA 94133
(415) 788-3666

## Earthtrust Wildlife Society
P.O. Box 5361, Lahaina, Maui, HI 96761
(808) 667-0437

## Earthwatch
680 Mt. Auburn Street, Box 403N, Watertown, MA 02272
(617) 926-8200

## Elsa Wild Animal Appeal

P.O. Box 4572, North Hollywood, CA 91617
(818) 761-8387

## Environmental Defense Fund

257 Park Avenue South, New York, NY 10010
(212) 505-2100

## Friends of the Animals

11 West 60th Street, New York, NY 10023
(212) 247-8120

## Friends of the Earth

218 D Street SE, Washington, D.C. 20003
(202) 544-2600

## Fund for Animals

200 W. 57th Street, New York, NY 10019
(212) 246-2096

## Greenpeace USA

1436 U Street NW, Washington, D.C. 20009
(202) 462-1177

## Humane Society of the United States

2100 L Street NW, Washington, D.C. 20037
(202) 452-1100

## International Fund for Animal Welfare

P.O. Box 193, Yarmouthport, MA 02675
(508) 362-4944

## International Oceanographic Foundation

4600 Rickenbacker Causeway, P.O. Box 499900, Miami, FL 33149
(305) 361-4888

## International Wildlife Coalition

634 North Falmouth Highway, P.O. Box 388, North Falmouth, MA 02556
(508) 548-8328

## Manitoba Wildlife Federation

1770 Notre Dame Avenue, Winnipeg, Manitoba, R3E 3K2 Canada
(204) 633-5967

## Marine Mammal Fund

Fort Mason Center, Building E, San Francisco, CA 94123
(415) 775-4636

## Marine Mammal Research Group

Box 6244, Victoria, British Columbia, V8P 5L5 Canada
(800) 665-5939

## Marine Mammal Stranding Center

P.O. Box 773, 3625 Brigantine Boulevard, Brigantine, NJ 08203
(609) 266-0538

## Mingan Island Cetacean Study

Summer: 124 Bord de la Mer, Longue-Pointe-de-Mingan, Quebec, G0G 1V0 Canada
(418) 949-2845
Winter: 285, rue Green, St. Lambert, Quebec, J4P IT3 Canada
(514) 465-9176

## Monitor

1506 19th Street NW, Washington, D.C. 20036
(202) 234-6576

## National Audubon Society

950 Third Avenue, New York, NY 10022
(212) 832-3200

## National Wildlife Federation

1400 16th Street NW, Washington, D.C. 20036
(202) 797-6800

## Nature Conservancy

1815 North Lynn Street, Arlington, VA 22209
(703) 841-5300

## New Brunswick Wildlife Federation

190 Cameron Street, Moncton, New Brunswick, EIC 5Z2 Canada
(506) 857-2056

## Newfoundland/Labrador Wildlife Federation

c/o P.O. Box 1041, Corner Brook, Newfoundland, A2H 6C6 Canada
(709) 364-8415

## New York Zoological Society

The Zoological Park, Bronx, NY 10460
(212) 220-5100

## Northwest Territories Wildlife Federation

Box 495, Hay River, Northwest Territories, XOE ORO Canada
(403) 874-3746

## Nova Scotia Wildlife Federation

P.O. Box 654, Halifax, Nova Scotia, B3J 2T3 Canada
(902) 423-6793

## Okeanos Ocean Research Foundation

Box 776, Hampton Bays, NY 11946
(516) 728-4522

## Oregon Natural Resources Council

1050 Yeon Building, 522 Southwest Fifth Avenue, Portland, OR 97204
(503) 223-9001

## Pacific Whale Foundation

101 North Kihei Road, Kihei, Maui, HI 96753
(800) 942-5311 or (808) 879-8811

## Quebec Wildlife Federation

319 Est, rue St. Zotique, Montreal, Quebec, H2S IL5 Canada
(514) 217-2487

## St. Lawrence National Institute of Ecotoxicology

310, avenue des Ursulines, Rimouski, Quebec, G5L 3A1 Canada
(418) 724-1746

## Save the Whales

P.O. Box 3650, Washington, D.C. 20007
(202) 337-2332

## Sea Shepherd Conservation Society

1314 2nd Street, Santa Monica, CA 90410
(213) 394-3198

## Sierra Club

730 Polk Street, San Francisco, CA 94109
(415) 776-2211

## Society for Animal Protective Legislation

P.O. Box 3719, Georgetown Station, Washington, D.C. 20007
(202) 337-2334

## Whale Conservation Institute

191 Weston Road, Lincoln, MA 01773
(617) 259-0423

## Whale Center

411 Campbell Street, Tofino, British Columbia, VOR 2Z0 Canada
(604) 725-2132

## The Wilderness Society

900 17th Street NW, Washington, D.C. 20006

(202) 833-2300

## Wildlife Conservation International

New York Zoological Society

185th Street and South Boulevard, Building A, Bronx, NY 10460

(212) 220-5155

## Wildlife Preservation Trust

34th Street and Girard, Philadelphia, PA 19104

(215) 222-3636

## Wildlife Society

5410 Grosvenor Lane, Betheseda, MD 20814

(301) 897-9770

## Worldwatch Institute

1776 Massachusetts Avenue NW, Washington, D.C. 20036

(202) 452-1999

## World Wildlife Fund

1250 24th Street NW, Washington, D.C. 20037

(202) 293-4800

# ADOPT-A-WHALE PROGRAMS

If whales have captured your heart or your imagination, you may want to "adopt" a whale for yourself or as a gift for a friend or family member. The sponsoring organizations (most of them research or conservation programs) typically provide adoptive parents with a photo of the adoptee, an official certificate, news about sightings of your whale, a one-year membership in the organization, a newsletter subscription, and other materials related to whale research and conservation.

When you adopt a whale, you aren't signing up to help save a nameless, faceless whale. Research scientists who study annual whale migrations recognize individual animals year after year, based on cross-referenced photo-identification files. Whales can be distinguished from one another by specific markings, coloring, scars from boat propellers, and—for humpbacks—the unique patterns on the underside of their tails. If you go whale watching at the right time in the right place, you may very well meet your adopted whale.

Write or call the organizations listed here for more information.

## BELUGA WHALES

### Adopt A Beluga

St. Lawrence National Institute of Ecotoxicology
310 Avenue des Ursulines, Rimouski, Quebec, G5L 3A1 Canada
(418) 724-1746

Nearly 80 individuals of the 400 to 500 belugas in the St. Lawrence River have been identified. The minimum donation to adopt a beluga is $5,000.

## BLUE WHALES

### Adopt A Giant

Mingan Island Cetacean Study
Summer: 124 Bord de la Mer, Longue-Pointe-de-Mingan, Quebec,
    G0G 1V0 Canada
    (418) 949-2845

Winter: 285 rue Green, St. Lambert, Quebec, J4P IT3 Canada
    (514) 465-9176

The Adopt A Giant program offers 325 blue whales that live in the Gulf of St. Lawrence and 285 in the Sea of Cortez. Each whale costs $100 per person, $1,000 for a corporate adoption, and a minimum of $50 for school children. Blue whales are the largest creatures ever to live on earth.

## FINBACK WHALES

### Adopt-A-Finback-Whale Program

Allied Whale, College of the Atlantic, 105 Eden Street, Bar Harbor, ME 04609
(207) 288-5644; Fax (207) 288-5395

About 35 individual finback whales are available for $30; a mother and calf cost $50. The finback is the second largest animal ever to live on earth.

## HUMPBACK WHALES

### Adopt A Fundy Whale

Brier Island Ocean Study, Westport, Digby County, Nova Scotia, B0V 1H0 Canada
(902) 839-2960

In its research, BIOS has identified more than 200 individual humpback whales known to be part of the Gulf of Maine-Scotian Shelf sub-stock of the Western North Atlantic population. Twelve of those whales are available for adoption for an annual fee of $25 each.

### Adopt-A-Whale Project

Pacific Whale Foundation, Kealia Beach Plaza, Suite 21, 101 North Kihei Road, Kihei, Maui, HI 96753
(800) 942-5311; Fax (808) 879-2615

Humpback whales from Hawaiian and Australian waters are available. There is a $25 fee for a nonexclusive adoption plus an annual support fee. An exclusive adoption costs $75—you get to name the whale—plus an annual support fee of $50.

### Humpback Whale Adoption/Project Megafam

The Whale Conservation Institute, 191 Weston Road, Lincoln, MA 01773
(617) 259-0423

Salt, a longtime favorite humpback on Stellwagen Bank, and her daughters are available for adoption. Salt costs $20; Salt and her offspring cost $25.

### Save the Whales International

Earthtrust, 25 Kaneohe Bay Drive, Kailua, HI 96734
(808) 254-2866; Fax (808) 254-6409

Save the Whales International, a project under the auspices of Earthtrust, calls its adoption program a "hanai" program, wherein interested people welcome a Hawaiian humpback whale into their family. Six named whales are available for $30 each. Earthtrust is a non-profit organization, and adoption profits go toward anti-whaling campaigns.

### Whale Adoption Project

International Wildlife Coalition
634 North Falmouth Highway, P.O. Box 388, North Falmouth, MA 02556
(508) 564-9980

More than 65 individual humpback whales that linger in the Gulf of Maine from April to October are available for $17 each.

## ORCAS

### Orca Adoption Program

The Whale Museum, P.O. Box 945, Friday Harbor, WA 98250
(206) 378-4710

More than 80 orcas (killer whales) that spend summers in the San Juan Islands are available for adoption. For $35, you receive a museum membership as well as an adoption; $25 covers just an adoption. A special classroom package for $55 gives each student a certificate inscribed with his or her name, and the teacher receives the museum membership.

### Whale Adoption Program

Vancouver Aquarium, P.O. Box 3232, Vancouver, British Columbia, V6B 3X8 Canada
(604) 685-2516; Fax (604) 631-2529

Northern residents and transient killer whales off British Columbia are available for adoption to help support the aquarium's field research on wild whales. The annual fee is $45 (Canadian) for individual or family adoption. Entire pods are available for $35 per whale. Annual renewal is $25.

## RIGHT WHALES

### Know Your Rights

The Whale Conservation Institute, 191 Weston Road, Lincoln, MA 01773
(617) 259-0423

Eight right whales regularly observed off Peninsula Valdes in Patagonia, Argentina, are available for adoption for $25 each. These endangered whales have been studied since 1970, and adoption fees support that research.

### Right Whale Adoption Program

New England Aquarium, Central Wharf, Boston, MA 02110
(617) 973-5294

A sponsorship package is available for $45 each; for $100, you get the complete package plus a "Right Whale Research Project" tee-shirt. The northern right whale is the rarest whale on earth, very close to extinction. Proceeds go to defray costs of field research and analysis.

## DOLPHINS

### Oceanic Project Dolphin

Oceanic Society Expeditions, Fort Mason Center, Building E,
San Francisco, CA 94123
(800) 326-7491 or (415) 441-1106; Fax (415) 474-3395

This program was created to photo-document individual spotted dolphins off the Bahamas so scientists may learn how dolphins feed, socialize, rest, and communicate, and to analyze the importance of their habitat. An adoption costs $35 a year. For a $250 tax-deductible donation, supporters may adopt and name a spotted dolphin.

# SUGGESTED READING

## NONFICTION

Audubon Society. *A Field Guide to North American Fishes, Whales and Dolphins*. Alfred A. Knopf, 1983.

Baker, Mary L. *Whales, Dolphins, and Porpoises of the World*. Doubleday, 1987.

Balcomb, Kenneth C., III. *The Whales of Hawaii*. Marine Mammal Fund, 1987.

Beamish, Peter. *Dancing With Whales*. Creative Publishers, 1993.

Bennett, Ben. *Oceanic Society Field Guide to the Gray Whale*. Legacy, 1983.

Bonner, Nigel. *Whales*. Blanford Press, 1980.

Bonner, Nigel. *Whales of the World*. Facts on File, 1989.

Brower, Kenneth. *Wake of the Whale*. Friends of the Earth/Dutton, 1979.

Burton, Robert. *The Life and Death of Whales*. 2d ed. Universe Books, 1980.

Caldwell, D.K. and M.C. *The World of the Bottlenosed Dolphin*. Lippincott, 1972.

Cousteau, Jacques. *The Whale: Mighty Monarch of the Sea*. Doubleday, 1972.

Cousteau, Jacques, and Yves Paccalet. *Whales*. Harry N. Abrams, 1988.

Daugherty, A.E. *Marine Mammals of California*. Rev. ed. California Department of Fish and Game, 1972.

Day, David. *The Whale War*. Sierra Club Books, 1987.

Dietz, Tim. *Tales of the Sea*. Guy Gannett, 1983.

Dietz, Tim. *Whales and Man*. Yankee Books, 1987.

Doak, Wade. *Encounters with Whales and Dolphins*. Sheridan House, 1989.

D'Vincent, Cynthia. *Voyaging with the Whales*. Oakwell Boulton, 1989.

Ellis, Richard. *Men and Whales*. Alfred A. Knopf, 1992.

Ellis, Richard. *Dolphins and Porpoises*. Alfred A. Knopf, 1982.

Ellis, Richard. *The Book of Whales*. Alfred A. Knopf, 1980.

Flaherty, Chuck. *Whales of the Northwest*. Cherry Lane Press, 1990.

Gatenby, Greg. *Whales: A Celebration*. Little, Brown & Company, 1983.

Gilmore, R.M. *The Story of the Gray Whale*. Gilmore, 1961, rev. 1972.

Gordon, David G., and Chuck Flaherty. *Field Guide to the Orca*. American Cetacean Society, 1990.

Gormley, Gerald. *Orcas of the Gulf: A Natural History*. Sierra Club Books, 1990.

Hand, Douglas. *Gone Whaling: A Search for Orcas in Northwest Waters*. Simon and Schuster, 1994.

Harrison, Richard, and Michael Bryden. *Whales, Dolphins, and Porpoises*. Intercontinental Publishing, 1988.

Hoyt, Erich. *Meeting the Whales*. Camden House, 1991.

Hoyt, Erich. *Seasons of the Whale*. Chelsea Green, 1990.

Hoyt, Erich. *Orca: The Whale Called Killer*. Rev. ed. E. P. Dutton, 1990.

Hoyt, Erich. *The Whale Watcher's Handbook*. Doubleday, 1984.

Jones, Mary Lou, Steven L. Swartz, and Stephen Leatherwood. *The Gray Whale*. Academic Press, 1984.

Katona, Steven K., Valerie Rough, and David T. Richardson. *A Field Guide to the Whales, Porpoises, and Seals of the Gulf of Maine and Eastern Canada*. 4th ed. Scribner's, 1983.

Kelly, John E., Scott Mercer, and Steve Wolf. *The Great Whale Book*. Center for Environmental Education, 1981.

Leatherwood, Stephen, and Randall R. Reeves. *The Bottlenose Dolphin*. Academic Press, 1989.

Leatherwood, Stephen, and Randall R. Reeves. *The Sierra Club Handbook of Whales and Dolphins*. Sierra Club Books, 1983.

Leatherwood, Stephen, Randall R. Reeves, William F. Perrin, and William E. Evans. *Whales, Dolphins, and Porpoises of the Eastern North Pacific and Adjacent Arctic Waters*. 2d ed. Dover, 1988.

Lien, Jon, and Steven Katona. *A Guide to the Photographic Identification of Individual Whales*. American Cetacean Society, 1990.

Lilly, John. *Man and Dolphin*. Doubleday and Company, 1961.

Matthews, L. H. *The Natural History of the Whale*. Columbia University Press, 1978.

Matthews, L. H. *The Whale*. Simon and Schuster, 1968.

May, John. *The Greenpeace Book of Dolphins*. Sterling Publications, 1990.

McIntyre, Joan. *Mind in the Waters*. Scribner's/Sierra Club, 1974.

McIntyre, Joan. *The Delicate Art of Whale Watching*. Sierra Club Books, 1982.

McNally, Robert. *So Remorseless a Havoc*. Little, Brown and Company, 1981.

Miller, Tom. *The World of the California Gray Whale*. Baja TraiPublications, 1975.

Minasian, Stanley M., Kenneth C. Balcomb III, and Larry Foster. *The World's Whales*. Smithsonian, 1984.

Mowat, Farley. *A Whale for the Killing*. Bantam Books, 1972.

Nakamura, Tsuneo. *Gentle Giant: At Sea With the Humpback Whale*. Chronicle Books, 1984.

Nickerson, Roy. *Brother Whale*. Chronicle Books, 1977.

Nickerson, Roy. *The Friendly Whales: A Whale Watcher's Guide to the Gray Whales of Baja Califomia*. Chronicle Books, 1987.

Nicklin, Flip. *With The Whales*. NorthWord Press, 1990.

Norris, K. *Whales, Dolphins and Porpoises*. University of California Press, 1966.

*Reeves, Randall R., and Stephen Leatherwood. The Sea World Book of Dolphins*. Harcourt Brace Jovanovich, 1987.

Scammon, Charles M. *The Marine Mammals of the Northwest Coast of North America*. Reprinted by Dover, 1968; originally published in 1874.

Scheffer, Victor. *A Natural History of Marine Mammals*. Scribner's & Sons, 1976.

Sears, Richard, Frederick Wenzel, and J. Michael Williamson. *The Blue Whale*. Mingan Island Cetacean Study, 1987.

Small, G.L. *The Blue Whale*. Columbia University Press, 1971.

Walker, Theodore J. *Whale Primer*. Cabrillo Historical Association, 1962 (since revised several times).

Watson, Lyall. *A Sea Guide to Whales of the World*. E. P. Dutton, 1982.

Watson, Paul. Sea Shepherd: *My Fight for Whales and Seals*. Norton, 1982.

Weyler, Rex. *Song of the Whale*. Anchor Press, 1986.

Whitehead, Hal. *Voyage to The Whales*. Stoddart Publishing, 1989.

Williams, Heathcote. *Falling for a Dolphin*. Harmony Books, 1989.

Williams, Heathcote. *Whale Nation*. Harmony Books, 1988.

Winn, Lois King, and Howard E. Winn. *Wings in the Sea: The Humpback Whale*. University Press of New England, 1985.

Yates, Steve. *Marine Life of Puget Sound, the San Juans, and the Strait of Georgia*. Globe Pequot Press, 1988.

## FICTION

Abbey, Lloyd. *The Last Whales*. Grove Weidenfeld, 1989.

Carrighar, Sally. *The Twilight Seas*. Dutton, 1989.

Lucas, Jeremy. *Whale*. Summit Books, 1981.

Melville, Herman. *Moby-Dick; or The Whale*. Numerous editions and publishers, 1851.

Scheffer, Victor. *The Year of the Whale*. Scribner's, 1969.

Searls, Hank. *Sounding*. Ballantine, 1982.

Siegel, Robert. *Whalesong*. Berkeley, 1981.

Spain, Stanley. *Rajac: A Story*. MacMillan, 1982.

# END NOTE

Ten percent of the author's income from this book will go to whale conservation and research organizations working to ensure that the world's whales do not become extinct.

In an effort to include every whale-watch tour operator serving customers in the geographical areas in this book, the author has checked, rechecked, and cross-checked with known tour operators, local chambers of commerce, state and local tourist bureaus, museums, aquariums, and conservation organizations and foundations.

If you were inadvertently left out or if you know someone who was, please make sure the omission will be remedied in revised editions by writing immediately to Patricia Corrigan in care of NorthWord Press, P.O. Box 1360, Minocqua, WI 54548.

# Index

# TOUR OPERATORS

## NORTHEAST U.S. COAST

### Maine

Acadian Whale Watcher
(Bar Harbor): 55

Frenchman Bay Company
(Bar Harbor): 56

Indian Whale Watch
(Kennebunkport): 56

Lubec Marine Services (Lubec): 58

Maine Whalewatch
(Northeast Harbor): 58

Nautilus Whale Watch
(Kennebunkport): 57

Odyssey Whale Watch
(Portland): 60

Richard M. Savage & Sons
(Northeast Harbor): 59

Ugly Anne (Ogunquit): 60

### Massachusetts

A.C. Cruise Line (Boston): 62

Boston Harbor Cruises (Boston): 63

Boston Harbor Whale Watch
(Boston): 63

Cape Ann Whale Watch
(Gloucester): 66

Cape Cod Cruises
(Provincetown): 73

Captain Bill & Sons Whale Watch
Cruises (Gloucester): 66

Captain John Boats (Plymouth): 71

Captain Tim Brady & Sons, Inc.
(Plymouth): 71

Dolphin Fleet of Provincetown
(Provincetown): 73

Hyannis Whale Watcher Cruises
(Barnstable): 61

Massachusetts Whale Watching
Center (Plymouth): 72

Nantucket Whale Watch
(Nantucket): 69

Newburyport Whale Watch
(Newburyport): 70

New England Aquarium
(Boston): 64

Oceanic Society Expeditions
(Boston): 65

Portuguese Princess Whale Watch
(Provincetown): 74

Provincetown Whale Watch Inc.
(Provincetown): 75

Seven Seas Whale Watch
(Gloucester): 67

Yankee Whalewatch
(Gloucester): 68

### New Hampshire

Al Gauron Deep Sea Fishing
(Hampton Beach): 76

Atlantic Fleet (Rye): 78

New Hampshire Seacoast
Cruises (Rye): 78

Oceanic Whale Watch
Expeditions (Portsmouth): 77

### New Jersey

Cape May Whale Watch and
Research Center (Cape May): 79

### New York

Okeanos Whale Watch
Cruises (Montauk): 80

## HAWAII

### Hawaii

## WESTERN CANADA

### British Columbia

American Cetacean Society
Expeditions (Port Hardy): 206

Blue Moon Explorations
(Tofino): 212

Bluewater Adventures
(various stops): 217

Canadian Princess Resort
(Ucluelet): 215

Clavella Adventures
(various stops): 218

Clayoquot Sound Charters
(Tofino): 212

Ecosummer Expeditions
(Port McNeill): 207

Jamie's Whaling Station
(Tofino): 213

Maple Leaf Adventures
(various stops): 218

Northern Lights Expeditions
(Port McNeill): 208

Oceanic Society Expeditions
(Port Hardy): 206

Raven Kayak Experiences
(Telegraph Cove): 210

Remote Passages (Tofino): 214

Seacoast Expeditions
(Victoria): 216

Sea Smoke/Sail With Whales
(Alert Bay, Alder Bay): 205

Stubbs Island Charters
(Telegraph Cove): 211

Subtidal Adventures (Ucluelet): 215

Viking West (Port McNeill,
Telegraph Cove): 209

Wayward Wind (Sointula): 209

### Manitoba

Northern Expeditions
(Churchill): 219

Riding Mountain Nature Tours
(Churchill): 220

Sea North Tours (Churchill): 221

### Northwest Territories

Atlantic Marine Wildlife Tours
(Baffin Island): 222

Arctic Tour Company
(Inuvik): 223

Biological Journeys
(Somerset Island): 223

## EASTERN CANADA

### New Brunswick

Cline Marine (Richardson, Head
Harbour, and St. Andrews): 232

Ocean Search Ltd.
(North Head): 231

Sea Watch Tours (Seal Cove): 233

### Newfoundland

Adventure Tours of Newfoundland
(St. John's): 238

Bird Island Charters
(Bay Bulls): 234

Bontours (Norris Point): 238

Eastern Edge Outfitters Ltd.
(Cape Broyle, St. John's, and
Tors Cove): 240

Gatherall's Sanctuary Boat
Charters (Bay Bulls): 234

Great Island Tours
(Cape Broyle): 235

Harbour Tours (Keels): 237

# MUSEUMS, AQUARIUMS, AND SCIENCE CENTERS

# NATIONAL PARKS, MARINE SANCTUARIES, AND MONUMENTS

# NOTES

_____

_____

_____

_____

_____

_____

_____

_____

_____

_____

# ABOUT THE AUTHOR

Patricia Corrigan, secretly a mermaid, lives in landlocked St. Louis, Missouri, with her teenage son and two orange cats that love water. As a mermaid who likes her dessert, she is the author of a heavenly cookbook, *Angels in the Kitchen*. Right now she is fulfilling a childhood dream working as a news reporter and columnist for the *St. Louis Post-Dispatch*. Eventually, she hopes to fulfill a more recent dream and move to the southern coast of Oregon. There she plans to watch whales from her living room window, when she isn't out on a boat in some equally whale-rich area of the world.

# ABOUT THE ILLUSTRATOR

David Peters is a commercial artist and author of *Giants of Land, Sea and Air—Past and Present, A Gallery of Dinosaurs and Other Prehistoric Reptiles, From the Beginning: The Story of Evolution*, and *The Strangest Animals of All Times*. He lives in St. Louis, Missouri, with his wife and two daughters.